Richard Cervin

D0035139

Second Language Writing

THE CAMBRIDGE APPLIED LINGUISTICS SERIES
Series editors: Michael H. Long and Jack C. Richards

This new series presents the findings of recent work in applied linguistics which are of direct relevance to language teaching and learning and of particular interest to applied linguists, researchers, language teachers, and teacher trainers.

In this series:

Second Language Writing

Research insights for the classroom

Edited by

Barbara Kroll

California State University, Northridge

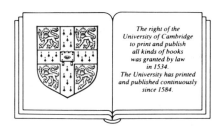

The right of the
University of Cambridge
to print and publish
all kinds of books
was granted by law
in 1534.
The University has printed
and published continuously
since 1584.

Cambridge University Press
Cambridge
New York   Port Chester
Melbourne   Sydney

Published by the Press Syndicate of the University of Cambridge
The Pitt Building, Trumpington Street, Cambridge CB2 1RP
40 West 20th Street, New York, NY 10011, USA
10 Stamford Road, Oakleigh, Melbourne 3166, Australia

© Cambridge University Press 1990

First published 1990
Second printing 1991

Printed in the United States of America

Library of Congress Cataloging-in-Publication Data

Second language writing: research insights for the classroom / edited
by Barbara Kroll.

p.   cm. – (Cambridge applied linguistics series)

Includes bibliographical references.

ISBN 0-521-38383-8 (hardcover)   ISBN 0-521-38778-7 (paperback)

1. English language – Study and teaching – Foreign speakers.
2. English language – Composition and exercises – Study and teaching.
I. Kroll, Barbara. II. Series.
PE1128.A2S33   1990
808′.042′07 – dc20   90–31067
                                                            CIP

British Library Cataloguing in Publication Data

Second language writing: research insights for the classroom. –

(Cambridge applied linguistics series)

1. Non-English speaking students. Curriculum subjects
I. Kroll, Barbara
808.04207

ISBN 0-521-38383-8 hardback
ISBN 0-521-38778-7 paperback

Contents

II CONSIDERATIONS FOR WRITING INSTRUCTION   103

Contributors

Cherry Campbell, Monterey Institute of International Studies, California
Marilda C. Cavalcanti, Universidade Estadual de Campinas, Brazil
Andrew D. Cohen, Hebrew University of Jerusalem, Israel
Ulla Connor, Indiana University, Indianapolis
Joan Carson Eisterhold, Georgia State University, Atlanta
Mary Farmer, Purdue University, West Lafayette, Indiana
Ann K. Fathman, College of Notre Dame, Belmont, California
Alexander Friedlander, Drexel University, Philadelphia, Pennsylvania
Liz Hamp-Lyons, University of Colorado, Denver
Ann M. Johns, San Diego State University, California
Alexandra Rowe Krapels, University of South Carolina, Columbia
Barbara Kroll, California State University, Northridge
Ilona Leki, University of Tennessee, Knoxville
Joy Reid, University of Wyoming, Laramie
Tony Silva, Auburn University, Alabama
Elizabeth Whalley, San Francisco State University, California

Series editors' preface

Since the early 1970s, the nature of written discourse as well as the writing process itself have attracted renewed interest from educational researchers, linguists, applied linguists, and teachers. In the United Kingdom, for example, researchers such as Britton observed young writers in the process of writing in order to identify the planning, decision making, and heuristics they employed. Complementary work in the United States by such researchers and educators as Emig, Murray, and Graves led to the emergence of the "process" school in writing theory and practice. This view emphasizes that writing is a recursive rather than a linear process, that writers rarely write to a preconceived plan or model, that the process of writing creates its own form and meaning, and that there is a significant degree of individual variation in the composing behaviors of both first and second language writers.

While the enthusiasm that this view of writing generated has led some of its advocates to propose yet another pedagogical orthodoxy – the process approach – much remains to be discovered about how second language writers write and learn to write, and about the kinds of writing instruction they are most likely to benefit from. It was this need that prompted the present book.

The contributors explore the major issues that have emerged from the past twenty years of research and practice, particularly in North America. These include the relationship between reading first language and second language writing, the relationship between reading and writing, approaches to feedback, the role of revision, assessment, and the role of the writing teacher. Original empirical studies are presented, and assumptions behind current practices in the teaching of writing are explored. At the same time the contributors present examples of both quantitative and qualitative approaches to the study of second language writing and writing instruction. This important book will provide a valuable source of information for teachers, for researchers, and for those who need an informed assessment of the current status of research and practice in second language writing.

Michael H. Long
Jack C. Richards

Preface

In 1979, while teaching at the University of Hawaii, I had my first opportunity to teach a graduate course designed to prepare future second language writing teachers. There was no question of using a text, since none were available at the time, and it was relatively easy to put together a packet of readings, as there was little published scholarship in the field to choose from. It might be fair to say that the seeds for this book project were planted then; they continued to grow as I subsequently continued to offer teacher training courses at successive institutions where I taught, always looking for and never finding the text that would provide what I hope this book now offers.

I wish to thank the contributors for working with me to create a book that reflects the vitality of second language writing research and teaching, expertly revising their chapters time and again to answer my never-ending stream of questions. I am also particularly grateful to Martha Pennington for urging me to turn my desire to see such a book into reality. I appreciate the Affirmative Action Faculty Development program at California State University, Northridge, for granting me a reduced teaching load one semester to allow for more focused attention to this project. Holly Jacobs offered invaluable advice and insightful suggestions in reading earlier drafts of the manuscript, helping me to focus on the objectives of the whole project. Joan Carson Eisterhold and Joy Reid offered graceful editorial feedback on my own contributions to this book, guiding me to eliminate both purple prose and excessive obfuscation. The able series editors, Jack C. Richards and Michael H. Long, provided welcome support and encouragement. Last, and anything but least, I thank Ruth Spielman, whose patience with my impatience merits boundless praise.

Barbara Kroll

Introduction

Barbara Kroll

Becoming a writer is a complex and ongoing process, and becoming a writing teacher is no less complex. A teacher's journey toward understanding the complexity of both writing and teaching often begins with a look to the past, for scholarship originates from the ability to synthesize past insights and apply them in the pursuit of continued inquiry. It is, therefore, encouraging to realize that a great deal about writing has been learned from studying how native speakers of English acquire skill in writing, knowledge gleaned from a field of study almost unknown in its modern sense a quarter of a century ago. A vigorous developing tradition of scholarship in composition and rhetoric has recently produced excellent bibliographical resource guides (e.g., Moran and Lunsford 1984; Lindemann 1987, 1988; Tate 1987) as well as in-depth reviews of scholarship (e.g., Hillocks 1986), guides to conducting research in the field (e.g., Myers 1985; Lauer and Asher 1988; Daiker and Morenberg 1990), and attempts to define the field of study itself (e.g., McClelland and Donovan 1985; North 1987).

The emergence of composition studies in the past quarter century as an area of professional emphasis within academic communities has also spurred on a tremendous metamorphosis in the teaching of writing, for composition teachers are now being schooled in ways unheard of before the late 1960s. As the eminent rhetorician Edward Corbett noted:

When I contrast the knowledge and competence commanded by my own graduate students and by the young teachers I hear talk at our conferences and conventions with the folklore and trial-by-error that I relied on when I was their age, I am duly humbled but simultaneously inspirited. The enhanced professionalism of the young composition teachers is due, for the most part, to the formal training they have received in rhetoric and composition. (Corbett 1987: 445)

One result of such formal training has been a recognition of the dynamic nature of the teaching process itself and a fuller understanding on the part of writing teachers of how they must acquire the knowledge and skills that form the basis of many typical teacher training programs (Freeman 1989). Bartholomae (1986) sums up how best to

1

view those who teach writing: "What characterizes writing teachers, I think, is not that they have a set of 'methods' for the teaching of writing, but they have a commitment to writing as an intellectual activity and to what that activity can produce in the classroom" (p. 5).

For those engaged in teaching second language learners, what is needed is both a firm grounding in the theoretical issues of first and second language writing and an understanding of a broad range of pedagogical issues that shape classroom writing instruction. As teachers, we must realize that for those engaged in learning to write in a second language, the complexity of mastering writing skills is compounded both by the difficulties inherent in learning a second language and by the way in which first language literacy skills may transfer to or detract from the acquisition of second language skills.

In fact, while a background in first language writing may help inform the explorations of second language writing teachers and researchers, it should not be presumed that the act of writing in one's first language is the same as the act of writing in one's second language. For example, first and second language learners may not approach a writing task in the same way nor attend to feedback in the same way. What teachers need is an understanding of all facets of this complex field of writing, and then to filter that understanding through a prism that can reflect how the factor of using a nonnative code affects second language performance. Indeed, much work in second language research has replicated research conducted with native speakers, and the result is that the ways in which second language writing lessons are now often conducted derive in part from the attempt "to incorporate into our work much that is being discovered about language acquisition" itself (Raimes 1983: 543), as well as from a shifting paradigm within the field itself.

In English as a second language (ESL), an increased professional concern in the teaching of writing has perhaps most manifested itself at the annual TESOL (Teachers of English to Speakers of Other Languages) convention. At the TESOL conventions of the late 1970s, for example, there were less than half a dozen presentations on writing listed on the program each year, whereas the annual conventions starting in the mid-1980s and continuing to the present offer a multitude of workshops, demonstrations, papers, and colloquia on issues related to the teaching of writing and to research findings on the writing of nonnative speakers. Further evidence of increased professional concern is found in the proliferation of dissertations in the field of second language writing, while more articles are becoming available in professional journals. The authors of the chapters in this volume hereby join in the rich dialogue of inquiry we are engaged in today as we move forward to improve our students' abilities and our teaching powers.

Rationale and plan of the book

This book is addressed to those about to embark on the teaching of second language writing as well as to those already engaged in the field. Teachers are dedicated to fostering growth in writing by providing a sequence of lessons and courses designed to move students beyond their entering skill level, and by enabling students to acquire skills and strategies that are not only geared toward promoting success in an academic environment but are operable across a range of potential writing situations. Researchers want to investigate the questions that shed the greatest light on the problems of the field and contribute the most toward the development of a comprehensive theory of second language writing. The concerns of both these groups – teachers and researchers – are addressed in this book.

To accomplish their goals, teachers and researchers want to feel that they are functioning within a framework based on sound theoretical principles, and they also need to communicate clearly with each other. An awareness of the writer and the writing situation, and of the complex interactions between these two elements and with each emerging text, is essential as the writing teacher joins in the community of scholars conducting research in this field. So too, an awareness of classroom exigencies is essential for the researcher who explores the complex questions of writing performance. This book offers both a starting point for those seeking the training necessary for professional growth and a reference point for those already committed to the field.

This volume is divided into two sections. In the first section, six chapters present the current state of thinking on what the teaching of writing to nonnative speakers entails. Each of these chapters provides an overview perspective on one essential element in the total picture of second language writing instruction, providing insight into the evolution of second language writing instruction and the contributions to its understanding made by research in first language writing instruction. Rather than specifically addressing classroom materials or methods or even particular decisions made by writers or teachers, these chapters taken together will help teachers identify and understand what they must consider about the writing process and about the learner as they are designing programs, making curricular decisions, and planning individual lessons. These insights further help to identify the agenda for future classroom research, which can be conducted by the type of teacher-researcher Myers (1985) describes in his guidebook and which Zamel (1987) calls for in her review of writing instruction.

In the second section, seven chapters describe a variety of specific studies, each focused on a different aspect of writing and/or the writing classroom, representing some kind of option for either the student writer or the teacher. These options might be viewed as constraints on the writer or teacher, constraints that have an impact both on composing behavior and on course design. Through an awareness of insights derived from such research studies, teachers can work to shape curriculum design and to guide their teaching decisions in a more principled fashion.

All of the chapters have been specifically prepared for this volume, jointly covering a range of the most important issues confronting second language writing teachers today. This volume should prove especially useful in providing a coherent view of current thinking in the field, and can serve as a guide for teachers and researchers seeking to formulate a comprehensive philosophy of teaching.

References

Bartholomae, D. (1986). Words from afar. In A. R. Petrosky and D. Bartholomae (Eds.), *The teaching of writing*. Eighty-fifth Yearbook of the National Society for the Study of Education, Part II (pp. 1–7). Chicago, Ill.: National Society for the Study of Education.

Corbett, E.P.J. (1987). Teaching composition: Where we've been and where we're going. *College Composition and Communication, 38*, 444–452.

Daiker, D. A., and Morenberg, M. (Eds.) (1990). *The writing researcher as teacher: Essays in theory and practice of class-based research*. Portsmouth, N. H.: Boynton/Cook Heinemann.

Freeman, D. (1989). Teacher training, development, and decision making: A model of teaching and related strategies for language teacher education. *TESOL Quarterly, 23*, 27–45.

Hillocks, G., Jr. (1986). *Research on written composition: New directions for teaching*. Urbana, Ill.: National Conference on Research in English and ERIC Clearinghouse on Reading and Communication Skills.

Lauer, J. M., and Asher, J. W. (1988). *Composition research: Empirical designs*. New York: Oxford University Press.

Lindemann, E. (Ed.) (1987). *Longman bibliography of composition and rhetoric: 1984–1985*. New York: Longman.

(Ed.) (1988). *Longman bibliography of composition and rhetoric: 1986*. New York: Longman.

McClelland, B. W., and Donovan, T. R. (Eds.) (1985). *Perspectives on research and scholarship in composition*. New York: Modern Language Association.

Moran, M., and Lunsford, R. (Eds.) (1984). *Research in composition and rhetoric*. Westport, Conn.: Greenwood Press.

Myers, M. (1985). *The teacher-researcher: How to study writing in the classroom*. Urbana, Ill.: ERIC Clearinghouse on Reading and Communication Skills and National Council of Teachers of English.

North, S. M. (1987). *The making of knowledge in composition: Portrait of an emerging field*. Upper Montclair, N.J.: Boynton/Cook.

Raimes, A. (1983). Tradition and revolution in ESL teaching. *TESOL Quarterly, 17*, 535–552.

Tate, G. (Ed.) (1987). *Teaching composition: Twelve bibliographical essays*. Fort Worth: Texas Christian University Press.

Zamel, V. (1987). Recent research on writing pedagogy. *TESOL Quarterly, 21*, 697–715.

SECTION I:
PHILOSOPHICAL UNDERPINNINGS
OF SECOND LANGUAGE
WRITING INSTRUCTION

Section I presents several chapters which jointly address many of the paramount concerns of the second language writing teacher or researcher who must consider, among other issues, the classroom and the institutional setting of writing courses, the writer and the process of writing, the teacher and his or her responses to writing produced by students, and the written text as a meaning-making event that exists as a component of literacy skills in general. Among the questions the authors of these chapters address are some of the most important and yet complex in the field today.

How has the teaching of ESL writing evolved in the second half of the twentieth century?

Chapter 1, by Tony Silva, traces the history of second language writing instruction in terms of how writing has been viewed within the English as a second language (ESL) curriculum from the 1940s until the 1990s, focusing particularly on how the teaching of writing has changed during the same period. In reviewing the controlled composition model, current-traditional rhetoric, the process approach, and English for academic purposes, Silva provides a diachronic view of composition instruction that can additionally serve to help teachers evaluate curricula and materials in a larger historical framework. Silva's chapter also addresses theory building in the field, and he provides a proposed model within which to view the relationship between theory, research, and practice by focusing on several "givens" of many typical second language classrooms: the L2 writer, the L1 reader, the L2 text, and the L1 context.

What can we learn from work in the field of rhetoric and composition studies?

Chapter 2, by Ann M. Johns, also addresses theory development in ESL composition, but from a very different perspective. She describes the necessary components of any composition theory and how best to structure ESL writing classes in terms of three different approaches that dominate L1 literature and research: process approaches (discussed in the next paragraph), interactive views (focusing on the writer as one who interacts with an audience), and social constructionism (referring to the relationship between the writer, the text, and the social context in which that text comes into being). Johns reviews a number of insights from L1 theorists and explains that teachers invariably have a theoretical stance. She believes it crucial that they articulate and examine the assumptions that guide their choices in the classroom. Each of the three theories she discusses is presented in terms of how the theory views several of the "givens" that Silva also discusses: the writer, the reader (or audience), and the text and the context (as they embody reality and truth). Finally, Johns addresses how the function of language is addressed in each of the three theories.

What goes into the process of writing?

One of the perspectives discussed by both Silva and Johns is a concern with the processes by which writers produce text. Often viewed as evidence of a "paradigm shift" (Hairston 1982), the focus on the composing processes of student writers instead of on the written products they produce has had an enormous impact on research into first language writing. Applebee (1986) notes that the process approach "provided a way to think about writing in terms of what the writer does (planning, revising, and the like) instead of in terms of what the final product looks like (patterns of organization, spelling, grammar)" (p. 96). It is research into the composing process that forms the subject of Chapter 3, by Alexandra Rowe Krapels. She reviews the relationship between first language research and the growing body of research into second language, and particularly ESL, writing processes. She provides an extensive commentary on most of the major studies to date, allowing for both a comparative examination of specific research findings and for insights into potential pedagogical applications. (In Section II, several chapters focus on the effects of altering one specific feature of the composing process. Alexander Friedlander, Chapter 7, discusses how the use of one's native versus one's second language in the planning stage affects the final written product. Ulla Connor and Mary Farmer, Chapter 8, offer a specific teaching suggestion for dealing with revision. Barbara Kroll, Chapter 9, addresses how the amount of time allowed for the process affects the final product.)

How should we respond to writing that students produce?

Every writing class, regardless of its underlying philosophy and regardless of the varieties of composing processes activated by students, will invariably result in the production of student texts that teachers will need to respond to. A review of the issues involved in written commentary on student writing is provided in Chapter 4, by Ilona Leki. She presents both the advice of writing experts and the opinions of student writers on what kinds of teacher interventions help student writers improve their ability to compose and to revise, when these interventions best occur, and what form they take. Again, much of the research she reports on is based on work with native speakers of English, though the area of teacher response continues to be of major concern to second language teachers and researchers. (Two aspects of teacher feedback are explored in depth in Section II in chapters based on studies of specific teaching situations. Andrew D. Cohen and Marilda C. Cavalcanti, Chapter 10, report on the match between teachers' claimed agendas for providing feedback and the actual feedback they provide, as well as what students think about and do with the feedback. Ann Fathman and Elizabeth Whalley, Chapter 11, report on a study involving teacher feedback on content versus feedback on form.)

How can we assess writing for program and institutional purposes?

In Chapter 5, Liz Hamp-Lyons addresses the field of second language writing assessment, considering topic variables, human and contextual variables, and procedural variables, identified by Brossell (1986) as the factors which "create the conditions of assessment that approximate conditions under which good writing is known or is apt to occur" (p. 180). She presents an overview of the issues involved in both small-scale and large-scale assessment and key aspects of program development, focusing on the many concerns that must be addressed in the direct assessment of writing. After reviewing some of the issues in test reliability, Hamp-Lyons analyzes four kinds of validity: face validity, content validity, criterion validity, and construct validity. She points out that validity must be established for four components in testing – the task, the writer, the scoring procedure, and the reader – and discusses each of them at length. (The task component is addressed in Chapter 12, by Joy Reid, in terms of how variation in task can affect a student's score outcome.) All of these components form part of a complex network of interactions, and Hamp-Lyons argues that writing assessment works best and is most fair to the learner when it takes into account who the learner is, the parameters of the situation in which the learner produces writing, and the overall context in which educational success is to be achieved for that learner.

What are some ways to understand the connection between reading and writing?

Chapter 6, by Joan Carson Eisterhold, provides a discussion of the nature of the relationship between reading and writing skills. Classroom teachers are understandably concerned with how best to foster improvement in writing, and two important contributing factors are identifying input that would be appropriate for the acquisition of writing skills and identifying mental processes that promote progress. Eisterhold provides a framework for analyzing how reading may be said to supply that input as well as how particular cognitive processes may enhance the acquisition of writing skills. She reviews various hypotheses that focus on the ways in which processes may transfer across modalities (from reading to writing or from writing to reading) and the ways in which skills may transfer across languages for those already literate in their first language. She concludes by sketching a model designed to capture the various ways in which the transfer of literacy skills might be viewed. (The reading–writing connection is further explored in Chapter 13, by Cherry Campbell, who reports on an empirically based study analyzing how students used a background reading passage in the preparation of a writing assignment.)

References

Applebee, A. N. (1986). Problems in process approaches: Toward a reconceptualization of process instruction. In A. R. Petrosky and D. Bartholomae (Eds.), *The teaching of writing* (pp. 95–113). Chicago, Ill.: National Society for the Study of Education.

Brossell, G. (1986). Current research and unanswered questions in writing assessment. In K. L. Greenberg, H. S. Wiener, and R. A. Donovan (Eds.), *Writing assessment: Issues and strategies* (pp. 168–182). New York: Longman.

Hairston, M. (1982). The winds of change: Thomas Kuhn and the revolution in the teaching of writing. *College Composition and Communication, 33*, 76–88.

1 Second language composition instruction: developments, issues, and directions in ESL

Tony Silva

To be effective teachers of writing, English as a second language (ESL) composition professionals need an understanding of what is involved in second language (L2) writing. They need coherent perspectives, principles, models – tools for thinking about second language writing in general and ESL composition in particular, and for analyzing and evaluating competing views. This chapter attempts to supply some of these tools by focusing on approaches to ESL writing instruction – identifying what they are, what they are not, and what they might be. In particular, this chapter offers for consideration: (1) an interpretation of (and brief commentary on) developments in ESL composition instruction during the period 1945–1990; (2) some tentative models meant to provide a coherent context for understanding, describing, and evaluating approaches to the teaching of L2 writing; (3) an evaluation of existing approaches in terms of these models; and (4) suggestions, growing out of this evaluation, for future directions in ESL composition theory, research, and practice.

Historical sketch

There is no doubt that developments in ESL composition have been influenced by and, to a certain extent, are parallel to developments in the teaching of writing to native speakers of English.[1] However, the unique context of ESL composition has necessitated somewhat distinct perspectives, models, and practices.

The history of ESL composition since about 1945 – the beginning of the modern era of second language teaching in the United States – can be viewed as a succession of approaches or orientations to L2 writing, a cycle in which particular approaches achieve dominance and then fade, but never really disappear. This discussion will focus on the origins,

---

1 See Berlin (1987, esp. Ch. 5–8) and North (1987) for comprehensive and detailed accounts of contemporary developments in L1 composition instruction from two distinct perspectives.

principles, methods, and implications of the four most influential approaches of this period: controlled composition, current-traditional rhetoric, the process approach, and English for academic purposes.

1. *Controlled composition*

Controlled composition (sometimes referred to as guided composition) seems to have its roots in Charles Fries's oral approach, the precursor of the audiolingual method of second language teaching. Undergirding controlled composition are the notions that language is speech (from structural linguistics) and that learning is habit formation (from behaviorist psychology). Given these basic notions, it is not surprising that from this perspective writing was regarded as a secondary concern, essentially as reinforcement for oral habits. Accordingly, in his *Teaching and Learning English as a Second Language* (1945), Fries addressed writing as an afterthought, stating that "even written exercises might be part of the work" (p. 8) of the second language learner.

Some, like Erazmus (1960) and Brière (1966), believed that these written exercises should take the form of free composition – that is, writer-originated discourse – to extend the language control of the student and to promote fluency in writing. However, such free composition was soundly rejected by others, like Pincas (1962), who believed it to be a "naive traditional view ... in direct opposition to the expressed ideals of scientific habit-forming teaching methods" (p. 185). She developed this point by explaining that "the reverence for original creativeness dies hard. People find it difficult to accept the fact that the use of language is the manipulation of fixed patterns; that these patterns are learned by imitation; and that not until they have been learned can originality occur in the manipulation of patterns or in the choice of variables within the patterns" (p. 186).

Pincas seemed to echo the majority opinion, one that focused primarily on formal accuracy and correctness, of employing rigidly controlled programs of systematic habit formation designed to avoid errors ostensibly caused by first language interference and to positively reinforce appropriate second language behavior. The approach preferred practice with previously learned discrete units of language to talk of original ideas, organization, and style, and its methodology involved the imitation and manipulation (substitutions, transformations, expansions, completions, etc.) of model passages carefully constructed and graded for vocabulary and sentence patterns.[2]

2 For more on the principles and practices of controlled composition, see the work of Dykstra (1964), Pincas (1964), Danielson (1965), Moody (1965), Praninskas (1965), Spencer (1965), Dykstra and Paulston (1967), Paulston (1967, 1972), Rojas (1968), Ross (1968), Horn (1974), and Paulston and Bruder (1976).

In essence, in the controlled composition model, writing functions as "the handmaid of the other skills" (listening, speaking, and reading), "which must not take precedence as a major skill to be developed" (Rivers 1968: 241) and must be "considered as a service activity rather than as an end in itself" (p. 258). Learning to write in a second language is seen as an exercise in habit formation. The writer is simply a manipulator of previously learned language structures; the reader is the ESL teacher in the role of editor or proofreader, not especially interested in quality of ideas or expression but primarily concerned with formal linguistic features. The text becomes a collection of sentence patterns and vocabulary items – a linguistic artifact, a vehicle for language practice. The writing context is the ESL classroom; there is negligible concern for audience or purpose. While some might feel that the controlled composition approach is no longer operative in ESL composition, my own feeling is that it is still alive and well in many ESL composition classrooms and textbooks, even though it is addressed only infrequently these days in the professional literature (typically for ritual condemnation).

Current-traditional rhetoric

The mid-sixties brought an increasing awareness of ESL students' needs with regard to producing extended written discourse. This awareness led to suggestions that controlled composition was not enough; that there was more to writing than building grammatical sentences; that what was needed was a bridge between controlled and free writing. This vacuum was filled by the ESL version of current-traditional rhetoric, an approach combining the basic principles of the current-traditional paradigm[3] from native-speaker composition instruction with Kaplan's theory of contrastive rhetoric. In this theory Kaplan, defining rhetoric as "the method of organizing syntactic units into larger patterns" (1967: 15), suggested that ESL writers "employ a rhetoric and a sequence of thought which violate the expectations of the native reader" (1966: 4). Thus, because first language interference was seen as extending beyond the sentence level, "more pattern drill, . . . at the rhetorical level rather than at the syntactic level" (1967: 15) was called for. It was necessary

3 One of the most commonly cited characterizations of the current-traditional paradigm is that of Richard Young. He states that its overt features include "the emphasis on the composed product rather than the composing process; the analysis of discourse into words, sentences and paragraphs; the classification of discourse into description, narration, exposition, and argument; the strong concern with usage (syntax, spelling, punctuation) and with style (economy, clarity, emphasis); the preoccupation with the informal essay and the research paper; and so on" (1978: 31). See also Berlin and Inkster (1980) for a succinct yet thorough account of the paradigm's historical origins and philosophical assumptions.

"to provide the student with a form within which he may operate" (1966: 20).

The central concern of this approach was the logical construction and arrangement of discourse forms. Of primary interest was the paragraph. Here attention was given not only to its elements (topic sentences, support sentences, concluding sentences, and transitions), but also to various options for its development (illustration, exemplification, comparison, contrast, partition, classification, definition, causal analysis, and so on). The other important focus was essay development, actually an extrapolation of paragraph principles to larger stretches of discourse. Addressed here were larger structural entities (introduction, body, and conclusion) and organizational patterns or modes (normally narration, description, exposition, and argumentation), with exposition typically seen as the pattern most appropriate for use by university-level second language writers.

Classroom procedures associated with this view of writing instruction focus students' attention on form. At their simplest, they ask students to choose among alternative sentences within the context of a given paragraph or longer discourse. Another variety involves reading and analyzing a model and then applying the structural knowledge gained to a parallel piece of original writing. The most complex types ask students (already provided with a topic) to list and group relevant facts, derive topic and supporting sentences from these facts, assemble an outline, and write their compositions from that outline.[4]

In short, from the perspective of this version of current-traditional rhetoric, writing is basically a matter of arrangement, of fitting sentences and paragraphs into prescribed patterns. Learning to write, then, involves becoming skilled in identifying, internalizing, and executing these patterns. The writer fills in a preexisting form with provided or self-generated content. The reader is easily confused and perhaps vexed by unfamiliar patterns of expression. The text is a collection of increasingly complex discourse structures (sentences, paragraphs, sections, etc.), each embedded in the next largest form. The implicit context for writing is an academic one, with the instructor's judgment presumed to mirror that of the community of educated native speakers.[5] Though current traditional practices have been regularly and vigorously attacked and inveighed against in the literature for a number of years now, their continuing influence is clearly reflected in many of the most well-known

4 Additional discussion of the rationale and procedures for the ESL version of current-traditional rhetoric can be found in Arapoff (1967, 1968, 1969), Carr (1967), Kaplan (1970, 1972), Taylor (1976), and Dehghanpisheh (1979).
5 See Leki (this volume) and Cohen and Cavalcanti (this volume) for further discussion of the ways in which teachers sometimes act as or are viewed by students as the judges of student writing.

and popular contemporary ESL composition textbooks. Indeed, one could make a strong case for the notion that the current-traditional approach is still dominant in ESL writing materials and classroom practices today.

The process approach

The introduction of the process approach to ESL composition seems to have been motivated by dissatisfaction with controlled composition and the current-traditional approach. Many felt that neither approach adequately fostered thought or its expression – that controlled composition was largely irrelevant to this goal and the linearity and prescriptivism of current-traditional rhetoric discouraged creative thinking and writing. Those who, like Taylor (1981), felt that "writing is not the straightforward plan–outline–write process that many believe it to be" (pp. 5–6) looked to first-language composing process research for new ideas, assuming with Zamel (1982) that "ESL writers who are ready to compose and express their ideas use strategies similar to those of native speakers of English" (p. 203). The assumptions and principles of this approach were soon enunciated. The composing process was seen as a "non-linear, exploratory, and generative process whereby writers discover and reformulate their ideas as they attempt to approximate meaning" (Zamel 1983a: 165). Guidance through and intervention in the process were seen as preferable to control – that is, the early and perhaps premature imposition of organizational patterns or syntactic or lexical constraints. Content, ideas, and the need to communicate would determine form. In essence, "composing means expressing ideas, conveying meaning. Composing means thinking" (Raimes 1983a: 261).

Translated into the classroom context, this approach calls for providing a positive, encouraging, and collaborative workshop environment within which students, with ample time and minimal interference, can work through their composing processes. The teacher's role is to help students develop viable strategies for getting started (finding topics, generating ideas and information, focusing, and planning structure and procedure), for drafting (encouraging multiple drafts), for revising (adding, deleting, modifying, and rearranging ideas); and for editing (attending to vocabulary, sentence structure, grammar and mechanics).[6]

From a process perspective, then, writing is a complex, recursive, and creative process or set of behaviors that is very similar in its broad

6 See also Zamel (1976, 1983b, 1987), Raimes (1978, 1983b,c, 1985), Watson (1982), Hughey et al. (1983), Spack (1984), Hamp-Lyons (1986), Liebman-Kleine (1986), Krapels (this volume), and Kroll (in press) for further treatment of the process approach in an ESL context.

outlines for first and second language writers.[7] Learning to write entails developing an efficient and effective composing process. The writer is the center of attention – someone engaged in the discovery and expression of meaning; the reader, focusing on content, ideas, and the negotiating of meaning, is not preoccupied with form. The text is a product – a secondary, derivative concern, whose form is a function of its content and purpose. Finally, there is no particular context for writing implicit in this approach; it is the responsibility of individual writers to identify and appropriately address the particular task, situation, discourse community, and sociocultural setting in which they are involved. Although the process approach has been generally well and widely received in ESL composition, it is not without its critics. These critics have perceived theoretical and practical problems and omissions of the approach and have suggested that the focus of ESL composition be shifted from the writer to the reader – that is, the academic discourse community.

English for academic purposes

To date, much of the aforementioned criticism of the process approach has come from proponents of an English for academic purposes orientation, which seems as much a reaction to the process approach as an attempt to construct a new and distinct perspective on ESL composition. One major part of this criticism is that the process approach does not adequately address some central issues in ESL writing. Reid (1984a, b) has suggested that the approach neglects to seriously consider variations in writing processes due to differences in individuals, writing tasks, and situations; the development of schemata for academic discourse; language proficiency; level of cognitive development; and insights from the study of contrastive rhetoric.

   Critics also question whether the process approach realistically prepares students for academic work. According to Horowitz (1986a), the approach "creates a classroom situation that bears little resemblance to the situations in which [students' writing] will eventually be exercised" (p. 144). He goes on to suggest that a process orientation ignores certain types of important academic writing tasks (particularly essay exams) and that what he sees as two basic tenets of the process approach – "content determines form" and "good writing is involved writing" – do not necessarily hold true in many academic contexts. Horowitz further states that a process-oriented approach "gives students a false impression of how university writing will be evaluated" (p. 143). In essence, he asserts that the process approach overemphasizes the individual's psychological

---

7 Friedlander (this volume) discusses process strategies of a group of Chinese ESL writers, for example.

functioning and neglects the sociocultural context, that is, the realities of academia – that, in effect, the process approach operates in a sociocultural vacuum.

The alternative proposed involves a primary focus on academic discourse genres and the range and nature of academic writing tasks, aimed at helping to socialize the student into the academic context and thus "ensure that student writing falls within ... [the] range ... of acceptable writing behaviors dictated by the academic community" (Horowitz 1986b: 789). The suggested instructional methodology aims at recreating the conditions under which actual university writing tasks are done and involves the close examination and analysis of academic discourse formats and writing task specifications; the selection and intensive study of source materials appropriate for a given topic, question, or issue; the evaluation, screening, synthesis, and organization of relevant data from these sources; and the presentation of these data in acceptable academic English form.[8]

In brief, from an English for academic purposes orientation, writing is the production of prose that will be acceptable at an American academic institution, and learning to write is part of becoming socialized to the academic community – finding out what is expected and trying to approximate it. The writer is pragmatic and oriented primarily toward academic success, meeting standards and requirements. The reader is a seasoned member of the hosting academic community who has well-developed schemata for academic discourse and clear and stable views of what is appropriate. The text is a more or less conventional response to a particular task type that falls into a recognizable genre. The context is, of course, the academic community and the typical tasks associated with it. While the English for academic purposes approach has gained many adherents of late, some perceive its emphasis on writing in various disciplines (particularly in scientific and technical fields) as questionable. These critics see a humanities-based approach with a primary focus on general principles of inquiry and rhetoric as more viable and appropriate. (See Spack's 1988 critique and the reactions of Braine 1988 and Johns 1988.)

Analysis and discussion

Although the foregoing account of developments in teaching ESL composition does, to a certain extent, indicate a move toward a more com-

---

8 Canseco and Byrd (1989), Horowitz (1986c, d), Johns (1986), Reid (1984c, 1985, 1987, 1989), and Shih (1986) are other useful sources that address writing in English for academic purposes.

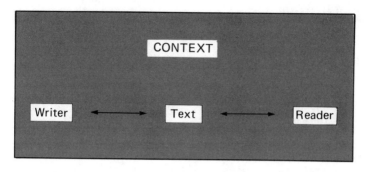

Figure 1   Elements of second language writing

plete understanding of the phenomenon of L2 writing, it also illustrates the workings of a rather unproductive approach cycle. This cycle – a result of the desire for a simple answer to a complex question – seems to be comprised of five phases: (1) an approach is conceptualized and formulated in a rather limited fashion; (2) it is enthusiastically (some would say evangelically) promoted; (3) it is accepted uncritically; (4) it is rejected prematurely; and (5) a shiny new (but not always much improved) approach takes its place.

This merry-go-round of approaches has a number of negative effects on the discipline: It generates more heat than light and does not encourage consensus on important issues, preservation of legitimate insights, synthesis of a body of knowledge, or principled evaluation of approaches. It is not surprising that such a situation engenders a great deal of confusion and insecurity among ESL composition teachers.

How can this situation be improved? I offer two suggestions. The first is that we begin to evaluate approaches to the teaching of ESL composition in a principled manner by considering what is involved in L2 writing, characterized here as purposeful and contextualized communicative interaction, which involves both the construction and transmission of knowledge. The basic elements that need to be addressed are (1) the L2 writer (the person – in terms of personal knowledge, attitudes, and characteristics; cultural orientation; language proficiency; motivation, etc. – as well as the process); (2) the L1 reader – perhaps the primary audience for academically oriented, college-level ESL writers (with regard to the person and the reading process); (3) the L2 text (in terms of genre, aims, modes, discourse structures, intersentential phenomena, syntax, lexis, and print-code features); (4) the contexts for L2 writing (cultural, political, social, economic, situational, physical); and (5) the interaction of these elements in a variety of authentic ESL settings (see Figure 1).

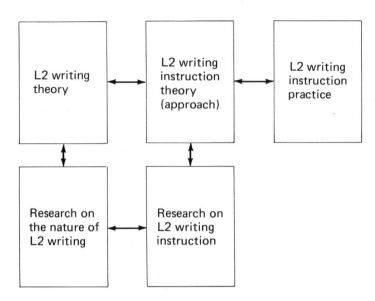

Figure 2   Relationship of theory, research, and practice in L2 writing instruction

My second suggestion is that we consider the place or role of approaches (theories of L2 writing instruction) within a coherent model of the interrelationship of ESL writing theory, research, and practice. The following questions must be asked:

1. Is a given approach informed by an appropriate and adequate theory of L2 writing?[9]
2. Is that L2 writing theory supported by credible (valid and reliable) empirical research?
3. Is the approach itself supported by valid and reliable research? That is, to what extent have programs based on the approach been shown to be efficient and effective in improving students' writing? (See Figure 2.)

How do the aforementioned approaches fare in light of these considerations? With regard to the elements of L2 writing, these approaches seem narrowly construed, each privileging and largely limiting its atten-

9 An appropriate and adequate theory of L2 writing, in my view, is one that, at a minimum, regards writing as an interactive activity; is reasonably comprehensive and internally consistent; reflects an understanding of historical developments in the field; is informed by current work in relevant disciplines; and is sensitive to the cultural, linguistic, and experiential differences of individuals and societies.

tion to a single (albeit important) element of writing.[10] Controlled composition focuses on the lexical and syntactic features of a text, whereas
ESL current-traditional rhetoric focuses on discourse-level text structures. The process approach attends to the writer's composing behaviors;
the English for academic purposes approach focuses on the reader, in
the form of the academic discourse community.

Are any of these approaches sufficiently grounded in appropriate and
adequate theory and credible research? It seems that they are not. This
situation reflects the limits of theory and research in ESL composition
at present. There simply are no comprehensive theories of L2 writing,
and it does not seem prudent to assume that theories of first language
writing alone will suffice. The existing body of empirical research on
the nature of L2 writing is fairly substantial and growing rapidly. However, while there is much of value in many of these studies, it is necessary
to note that they (1) are primarily small-scale and exploratory; (2) are
somewhat uneven in quality and diffuse in terms of focus, methodology,
and orientation – and thus are not easily compared or synthesized; and
(3) often have not been conceived, conducted, or interpreted within
adequate models of L2 composition. Finally, published research on the
relative effectiveness of different approaches when applied in the classroom is nearly nonexistent.

Conclusion

To summarize, it seems that viable approaches to the teaching of ESL
composition need to be based on a broader, more comprehensive con-
ception of what L2 writing involves. This bigger picture must, at least,
meaningfully account for the contributions of the writer, reader, text,
and context, as well as their interaction. In addition, approaches need
to be guided by realistic theories and convincing research. This implies
formulating adequate and appropriate theories of L2 writing; conducting
credible research to support these theories; developing adequate and
appropriate approaches (theories of L2 writing instruction) based on
viable theories of the nature of L2 writing; and conducting credible
research on the relative effectiveness of these approaches when applied
in the classroom.

The course of action that has been proposed is ambitious but re-
alizable, especially given the enthusiasm, dedication, preparation, and
creative efforts of today's ESL writing theorists, researchers, and prac-
titioners. Such action is essential for the development of more viable,
realistic theories of ESL writing and writing instruction; the establish-

10 See Johns (this volume) for a different perspective on this point.

ment and maintenance of the credibility of ESL composition professionals; and, most importantly, the academic and personal success of ESL students.

References

Arapoff, N. (1967). Writing: A thinking process. *TESOL Quarterly, 1,* 33–39.
  (1968). Controlled rhetoric frames. *English Language Teaching, 23,* 297–304.
  (1969). Discover and transform: A method of teaching writing to foreign students. *TESOL Quarterly, 3,* 297–304.
Berlin, J. (1987). *Rhetoric and reality: Writing instruction in American colleges, 1900–1985.* Carbondale: Southern Illinois University Press.
Berlin, J., and Inkster, R. (1980). Current-traditional rhetoric: Paradigm and practice. *Freshman English News, 8,* 1–5, 14.
Braine, G. (1988). A reader reacts. *TESOL Quarterly, 22,* 700–702.
Brière, E. (1966). Quantity before quality in second language composition. *Language Learning, 16,* 141–151.
Canseco, G., and Byrd, P. (1989). Writing required in graduate courses in business administration. *TESOL Quarterly, 23,* 305–316.
Carr, D. (1967). A second look at teaching reading and composition. *TESOL Quarterly, 1,* 30–34.
Danielson, D. (1965). Teaching composition at the intermediate level. In V. Allen (Ed.), *On TESOL 1964* (pp. 143–145). Champaign, Ill.: National Council of Teachers of English.
Dehghanpisheh, E. (1979). Bridging the gap between controlled and free composition: Controlled rhetoric at the upper intermediate level. *TESOL Quarterly, 13,* 509–519.
Dykstra, G. (1964). Eliciting language practice in writing. *English Language Teaching, 19,* 23–26.
Dykstra, G., and Paulston, C. (1967). Guided composition. *English Language Teaching, 21,* 136–141.
Erazmus, E. (1960). Second language composition teaching at the intermediate level. *Language Learning, 10,* 25–31.
Fries, C. (1945). *Teaching and learning English as a second language.* Ann Arbor: University of Michigan Press.
Hamp-Lyons, L. (1986). No new lamps for old yet, please. *TESOL Quarterly, 20,* 790–796.
Horn, V. (1974). Using the "Ananse Tales Technique" for composition. *TESOL Quarterly, 8,* 37–42.
Horowitz, D. (1986a). Process not product: Less than meets the eye. *TESOL Quarterly, 20,* 141–144.
  (1986b). What professors actually require: Academic tasks for the ESL classroom. *TESOL Quarterly, 20,* 445–462.
  (1986c). The author responds to Liebman-Kleine. *TESOL Quarterly, 20,* 788–790.
  (1986d). The author responds to Hamp-Lyons. *TESOL Quarterly, 20,* 796–797.

Hughey, J.; Wormuth, D.; Hartfiel, V.; and Jacobs, H. (1983). *Teaching ESL composition: Principles and techniques.* Rowley, Mass.: Newbury House.

Johns, A. (1986). Coherence and academic writing: Some definitions and suggestions for teaching. *TESOL Quarterly, 20,* 247–266.

(1988). Another reader reacts. *TESOL Quarterly, 22,* 705–707.

Kaplan, R. (1966). Cultural thought patterns in intercultural education. *Language Learning, 16,* 1–20.

(1967). Contrastive rhetoric and the teaching of composition. *TESOL Quarterly, 1,* 10–16.

(1970). Notes toward an applied rhetoric. In E. Lugton (Ed.), *Preparing the EFL teacher: A projection for the seventies* (pp. 45–74). Philadelphia: Center for Curriculum Development.

(1972). *The anatomy of rhetoric: Prolegomena to a functional theory of rhetoric.* Philadelphia: Center for Curriculum Development.

Kroll, B. (In press). Teaching writing in the ESL context. In M. Celce-Murcia (Ed.), *Teaching English as a second or foreign language,* 2nd ed. New York: Newbury House/Harper & Row.

Liebman-Kleine, J. (1986). In defense of teaching process in ESL composition. *TESOL Quarterly, 20,* 783–788.

Moody, K. (1965). Controlled composition frames. *English Language Teaching, 19,* 146–155.

North, S. (1987). *The making of knowledge in composition: Portrait of an emerging field.* Upper Montclair, N.J.: Boynton/Cook.

Paulston, C. (1967). The use of model passages in a program of guided composition. In B. Robinett (Ed.), *On TESOL 1966* (pp. 149–153). Washington, D.C.: TESOL.

(1972). Teaching writing in the ESOL classroom: Techniques of controlled composition. *TESOL Quarterly, 6,* 33–59.

Paulston, C., and Bruder, M. (1976). *Teaching English as a second language: Techniques and procedures.* Cambridge, Mass.: Winthrop.

Pincas, A. (1962). Structural linguistics and systematic composition teaching to students of English as a second language. *Language Learning, 12,* 185–194.

(1964). Teaching different styles of written English. *English Language Teaching, 18,* 74–81.

Praninskas, J. (1965). Controlled writing. In V. Allen (Ed.), *On TESOL 1964* (pp. 146–148). Champaign, Ill.: National Council of Teachers of English.

Raimes, A. (1978). *Problems and teaching strategies in ESL composition.* Arlington, Va.: Center for Applied Linguistics.

(1983a). Anguish as a second language? Remedies for composition teachers. In A. Freedman, I. Pringle, and J. Yalden (Eds.), *Learning to write: First language/second language* (pp. 258–272). London: Longman.

(1983b). Tradition and revolution in ESL teaching. *TESOL Quarterly, 19,* 535–552.

(1983c). *Techniques in teaching writing.* Oxford: Oxford University Press.

(1985). What unskilled writers do as they write: A classroom study. *TESOL Quarterly, 19,* 229–258.

Reid, J. (1984a). The radical outliner and the radical brainstormer: A perspective on composing processes. *TESOL Quarterly, 18,* 529–533.

(1984b). Comments on Vivian Zamel's "The composing process of advanced ESL students: Six case studies." *TESOL Quarterly, 18,* 149–159.

(1984c). ESL composition: The linear product of American thought. *College Composition and Communication, 35,* 449–452.

(1985). The author responds. *TESOL Quarterly, 19,* 398–400.

(1987). ESL composition: The expectations of the academic audience. *TESOL Newsletter, 21* (2), 34.

(1989). English as a second language composition in higher education: The expectations of the academic audience. In D. Johnson and D. Roen (Eds.), *Richness in writing: Empowering ESL students* (pp. 220–234). New York: Longman.

Rivers, W. (1968). *Teaching foreign language skills.* Chicago: University of Chicago Press.

Rojas, P. (1968). Writing to learn. *TESOL Quarterly, 2,* 127–129.

Ross, J. (1968). Controlled writing: A transformational approach. *TESOL Quarterly, 2,* 253–261.

Shih, M. (1986). Content-based approaches to teaching academic writing. *TESOL Quarterly, 20,* 617–648.

Spack, R. (1984). Invention strategies and the ESL college composition student. *TESOL Quarterly, 18,* 649–670.

(1988). Initiating ESL students into the academic discourse community: How far should we go? *TESOL Quarterly, 22,* 29–52.

Spencer, D. (1965). Two types of guided composition exercise. *English Language Teaching, 19,* 156–158.

Taylor, B. (1976). Teaching composition to low level ESL students. *TESOL Quarterly, 10,* 309–313.

(1981). Content and written form: A two-way street. *TESOL Quarterly, 15,* 5–13.

Watson, C. (1982). The use and abuse of models in the ESL writing class. *TESOL Quarterly, 17,* 165–187.

Young, R. (1978). Paradigms and problems: Needed research in rhetorical invention. In C. Cooper and L. Odell (Eds.), *Research on composing: Points of view* (pp. 29–47). Urbana, Ill.: National Council of Teachers of English.

Zamel, V. (1976). Teaching composition in the ESL classroom: What we can learn from research in the teaching of English. *TESOL Quarterly, 10,* 67–76.

(1982). Writing: The process of discovering meaning. *TESOL Quarterly, 16,* 195–209.

(1983a). The composing processes of advanced ESL students: Six case studies. *TESOL Quarterly, 17,* 165–187.

(1983b). In search of the key: Research and practice in composition. In J. Handscombe, R. Orem, and B. Taylor (Eds.), *On TESOL '83: The question of control* (pp. 195–207). Washington, D.C.: TESOL.

(1987). Recent research on writing pedagogy. *TESOL Quarterly, 21,* 697–715.

2 L1 composition theories: implications for developing theories of L2 composition

Ann M. Johns

In the 1980s, English as a second language (ESL) composition research and teaching developed and matured to an extent never imagined by the oral/aural proponents of the 1960s and early 1970s (see Silva's chapter in this volume). So far, however, most of this research and pedagogy has been drawn, in bits and pieces, from research in first language (L1) composition, which in turn is based upon L1 theory. Unfortunately, there has as yet been little discussion of the development of coherent and complete theories of ESL composition as allied to – or separate from – the various theories of L1 composition.

This chapter addresses the issue of ESL composition theory development[1] with two intents. The first is to suggest that a discussion of ESL composition theory should conform to some basic requirements for completeness – that is, it should encompass the values and relationships among basic components in composition (the writer, the topic, etc.). The second purpose of this chapter is to present three approaches to composition theory, drawn from L1 literature, for consideration by teachers. Zebroski (1986: 57) suggests that "if we write and teach writing, we have a theory of writing by definition." As teachers, we will benefit from becoming aware of our theories and the assumptions that underlie them.

Because L1 theory is rich in both history and substance (see, e.g., Fulkerson 1979), it is necessary to select one of several comprehensive models from which to work in order to classify essential components. One well-known, evolving model is presented by Berlin (1982, 1987, 1988), who suggests that all complete rhetorical theories and, by extension, all approaches to teaching composition must consider the following: (1) the writer (or "knower"), (2) the audience (or reader), (3) reality and truth, and (4) the sources of language in written texts.

In the discussion that follows, Berlin's four components become the

---

1 Throughout this chapter, theories of rhetoric, theories of composition, and theories of teaching composition are intermingled. Though these three categories of theory are carefully separated in most of the L1 literature, the admixture here is intentional, since as teachers, we mix the three frequently in our thinking and planning.

organizing principles for a presentation of three categories of approach
to composition theory: *the process approaches, the interactive views,* ✓
and the social constructionist views.[2]

The writer

Process approaches

One topic that must be considered in every theory is the *writer*. In one
cluster of L1 theories, the writer is viewed as originator of written text,
and the *process* through which the writer goes to create and produce
discourse is the most important component in the theory. Faigley (1986)
identifies two groups within the process camp, the expressivists and the
cognitivists. Expressivism, which developed in the first decades of the
twentieth century, reached its zenith in the late 1960s and early 1970s,
when the individual expression of honest and personal thought became
a popular trend in teaching writing. Writing was considered "an art, a
creative act in which the process – the discovery of the true self – is as
important as the product – the self discovered and expressed" (Berlin
1988: 484).

Leaders of the expressivist movement – Donald Murray, Ken Ma-
crorie, William Coles, Peter Elbow, and others – have published
widely, advocating classroom techniques that encourage students to
take power over their own prose. Elbow, perhaps the most famous of
the group (see, e.g., *Writing without teachers,* 1973; *Embracing contraries,* 1981; *Writing with power: Techniques for mastering the
writing process,* 1981b), speaks of writing as a kind of "magic" that
can be performed by anyone who is involved in and believes in his
or her "tale" (1981b: 369).

Teachers advocating the expressivist view are nondirective; they facilitate classroom activities designed to promote writing fluency and
power over the writing act. Their textbooks contain assignments designed to encourage self-discovery, such as journal writing and personal
essays, through which students can "first write freely and uncritically
so that [they] can get down as many words as possible" (Elbow 1981b:
7). Much of our current discussion of the use of journals, especially to
produce topics for essays (Sullivan and Van Becker 1982; Urzua 1986),
stems from the contributions of the expressivists.

It is the cognitivist, or "writing as problem-solving," group that has

2 There is considerable debate about whether any of these views can be considered
 "theories"in the true sense, because some of the theoretical components are implied,
 or, more importantly, because there are competing approaches within each camp
 (Coe 1987).

had more effect upon ESL research and teaching, however. There are two key words in cognitivist discussions: *thinking* and *process*. The first, which identifies higher-order thinking skills with problem-solving, is the theme of Flower's textbook *Problem-solving Strategies for Writing* (1985, 1989). This book requires students to plan extensively. Planning includes defining the rhetorical problem, placing it in a larger context, making it operational, exploring its parts, generating alternative solutions, and arriving at a well-supported conclusion. Once the problem has been identified and the paper has been planned, students continue the *writing process* by translating their plans and thoughts into words, and by reviewing their work through revising and editing. *Problem-solving Strategies* . . . is based upon research by Hayes and Flower (1983) that employed think-aloud protocols and other techniques: it revealed that complex writing processes are not linear or formulaic but rather individual and recursive.

Spack (1984) and Zamel (1983), studying ESL writers, corroborated Hayes and Flower's findings about the writing process for their populations. More recently, Raimes (1987: 459–460) compared ESL students' composing processes with other researchers' findings on L1 basic writers, and concluded that the two groups of students had much in common. Both Krapels (this volume) and Friedlander (this volume) continue the discussion of ESL writing process research.

Thus the writer's mental processes are of central importance to cognitivists. If mature, these processes are in concert with other components of theory: "For cognitive rhetoric, the structures of the mind are in perfect harmony with the structures of the material world, the minds of the audience, and the units of language" (Berlin 1988: 480).

The influence of the process approaches, especially of cognitive views, upon modern ESL classrooms cannot be exaggerated. In most classrooms, ESL teachers prepare students to write through invention and other prewriting activities (see e.g., Lauer 1970), encourage several drafts of a paper, require paper revision at the macro levels, generally through group work (see, e.g., Johns 1986a), and delay the student fixation with and correction of sentence-level errors until the final editing stage. Therefore, the goal of a teacher, in this view, is to produce good writers who "not only have a large repertoire of powerful strategies, but they have sufficient self-awareness of their own process to draw on these alternative techniques as they need them. In other words, they guide their own creative process" (Flower 1985: 370).

Interactive approaches

A second, lesser-known view of the writer envisions the writer as a person involved in a dialogue with his or her audience (Bakhtin 1973). In this approach, text is what an individual creates through a dialogue with another conversant; thus, both the writer and reader take responsibility for coherent text (see, e.g., Eisterhold, this volume).

Hinds (1987) has provided some useful insights into the writer-reader relationship in various languages, suggesting metaphors for this "middle-of-the-road" view. He refers to English as a "writer-responsible" language, "since the person primarily responsible for effective communication is the writer" (1987: 143). However, "in Japan, perhaps in Korea and certainly in Ancient China, there is a different way of looking at the communication process. In Japan, it is the responsibility of the reader to understand what the author intended to say" (1987: 144).

In ESL classes, then, those teachers who take an interactive view can speak of English as "writer-responsible"; student writers must make their topics, their arguments, their organization and transitions clear to the reader. Specifically, the writers producing English expository prose should pre-reveal the form of the text (e.g., "The problem to be discussed in the paper . . . ") and the content (e.g., " . . . is pollution.") within the first paragraphs of their texts (Meyer 1977), provide generalizations at appropriate points in the discourse, and maintain and develop topics in a manner accessible to the reader (Connor and Farmer, this volume). Other features of "writer-responsible" text include organization of the discourse in a manner familiar to the reader, appropriate use of cohesion, and direct explication of information (Singer 1984).

The social constructionist view

Two roles of the writer have now been discussed: the writer as *creator*, whose cognitive processes are the focus of theory and practice, and the writer as *interactant*, who dialogues with the reader. A third role of the writer appears in the social constructionist literature. Here, the written product is considered a social act that can take place only within and for a specific context and audience (Coe 1987). For the proponents of the social constructionist views, the language, focus, and form of a text stem from the community for which it is written. Inspired more than twenty years ago by Kuhn's *Structure of Scientific Revolutions* (1970), social constructionists have argued that "reality, knowledge, thought, facts, texts, selves and so on are constructs generated by communities of like-minded peers" (Bruffee 1986: 774).

In the extreme version of this view, the writer is, in Rorty's words (1982), "shoved around by physical reality" (quoted in Bruffee 1986: 776). Bruffee notes that

social construction assumes that the matrix of thought is not the individual self but some community of knowledgeable peers and the vernacular knowledge of that community. That is, social construction understands knowledge and the authority of knowledge as community-generated, community-maintaining symbolic artifacts. (1986: 777)

Thus, for social constructionists, knowledge, language, and the nature of discourse are determined for the writer by the "discourse community" for whom the writer is producing text. Since "discourse community" is a term that ESL teachers will commonly hear, an extended definition is given below. Swales (1990) has provided a recent and carefully constructed six-part definition, inspired by his work with advanced ESL students, that is in keeping with the social constructionist view:

1. A discourse community has a broadly agreed upon set of common public goals. [Sometimes these goals are implicit, unfortunately. For students, implicitly shared goals of academic discourse communities are often difficult to fathom.]
2. A discourse community has mechanisms for intercommunication among its members. [These can include meetings – e.g., TESOL – newsletters and journals, letters to the editor or to other members of the community.]
3. A discourse community uses its participatory mechanisms primarily to provide information and feedback. [Journals, for example, are created for these purposes, though unfortunately, most students have little opportunity to participate in the community at this level.]
4. A discourse community utilizes and hence possesses one or more genres in the communicative furtherance of its aims. [Genres can vary considerably, from letters and journal articles to posters and memos. For ESL writers at the graduate level, these genres become increasingly important; for undergraduates and students in primary and secondary schools, "school-based writing" – e.g., for essay examinations – is more common.]
5. The discourse community has some specific vocabulary. [Prominent members of the community can and do add to this vocabulary.]
6. A discourse community has a threshold level of members with a suitable degree of relevant content and discoursal expertise.

Those who hold the social constructionist view acknowledge that becoming an accepted member of an academic discourse community presents particular problems for "basic writers," with whom ESL students have a great deal in common in terms of "outsider" status. Patricia Bizzell (1987), perhaps the most vocal proponent of the concerns of "outsiders," notes that students from other than "Standard English" cultures must develop "multiple literacies" (p. 131); they must work with a cultural and discourse repertoire much broader than those de-

veloped by students from "Standard English" cultures. Often, ESL and
basic writing students are seen as failures. Academic faculty contend
that

a large number of students...are incompetent in the form of literacy
preferred in school. This 'academic literacy,' as I call it, entails the ability to
use Standard English and think academically...Hence to be an 'academic
illiterate' is to be unpracticed in Standard English and inept in 'critical
thinking.' (Bizzell 1987: 131)

Bizzell and others who write about the social constructionist nature
of discourse suggest two approaches for teaching writers who are "outsiders." The first, preferred by Bizzell, is based on the premise that
students should not be forced to acquire academic literacy and become
part of the academic discourse community. Instead, it is the academy
that must change to adapt to the many cultures that the students represent. Other, seemingly more realistic, teachers and researchers attempt
to understand both what academic literacy means and how best to
introduce it into English for academic purposes (EAP) classes (see, e.g.,
Horowitz 1986; Huckin 1987).

This second group is composed of two subgroups, each with a different
approach to teaching the language of academia. One is the "general
academic" group, who base their teachings upon the belief that there is
a general set of tasks and a basic academic language that ESL teachers
should present to students (see, e.g., Spack 1988), and that task and
language transferal can take place after a student has been presented
with the common core of academic language and conventions. It is the
duty of the researcher, then, to discover these transferable tasks and to
provide opportunities for task practice in ESL classrooms (Johns 1988).
A second group of ESL specialists maintain that understanding of general
tasks will not suffice in many instances, for each classroom and each
discourse community has unique characteristics that must be ferreted
out. Connor and Johns (1989), for example, found that approaches to
argumentation differ considerably between businesspeople and engineers; Swales (1984) notes the predictable characteristics of scientific
introductions; Huckin (1987) speaks of special features of scientific articles. This juxtaposition and confusion of approaches to academic literacy underscores a persistent need for additional theory and research
to justify positions and realize them in EAP classrooms.

The audience

The three visions of the writer that have been introduced are reflected,
quite naturally, in the several views of *audience* appearing in the L1

literature. For the expressivists, who contend that writing is an individual act, it is the competent writer who establishes purpose, meaning, and form; in so doing the writer "creates" an audience that conforms to the writer's text and purposes (Nystrand 1986: 61). This view of audience parallels Ede and Lunsford's (1984) concept of "audience invoked," in which "the audience in written discourse is a construction of the writer, a created fiction" (p. 160). Teachers espousing expressivism encourage students to write with honesty, for themselves. Others may appreciate and critique their writing as long as the central purpose for producing text is to provide an avenue for creativity and individual expression. Therefore, "the goal of writing should be to move toward a condition in which we don't necessarily need an audience to write and speak well" (Elbow 1981b: 190).

For the second and more influential group in the process camp, the cognitivists, the issue of audience becomes a more complicated one. Though the focus of their approaches is the writer's cognitive structures and the process through which the writer goes to create text, understanding how a sense of audience is developed in the writer's mind is also a major concern (Kroll 1978). Flower (1979), discussing the inability of college writers to succeed in their classes, attributes their problems to their failure to move cognitively from "writer-based" to "reader-based" prose. She suggests that students be urged to appeal to their readers' needs and interests in order to mature as writers. For these reasons, Berlin (1987) refers to the cognitivists as "transactional" and would undoubtedly argue that, in terms of the audience component, they are closer to the interactive philosophies, discussed later, than to expressivists.

Though audience theory as it appears in the L1 literature has generally been neglected in ESL, the concept of interactivity of reader and text, which appears frequently in ESL reading literature, can be extended to create a middle ground in a theory of audience in writing. In ESL reading literature (see, e.g., Carrell, Devine, and Eskey 1988), the reader is seen as someone who possesses both formal and content schemata (Carrell 1983), which are activated by the text as the reading process begins. Coherence of text is thereby established through the fit between the schemata of the reader (or audience) and the organization, content, and argument of the text. The schema theory literature makes increasingly clear the complexity of the relationship between writers and readers and the necessity for a complex model of audience. Ede and Lunsford (1984) suggest that the ideal model must "balance the creativity of the writer with the different, but equally important, creativity of the reader" (p. 16). Discussions of schema theory and reading have appeared frequently in ESL publications. However, only recently have the implications of this theory made inroads into ESL writing classes (see, e.g., Hillman and Kessell 1986; Johns 1986b).

A third view of audience, propounded by those who contend that writing is principally a social act (i.e., the social constructionists), is one in which the expert reader, an initiated member of the discourse community, is all-powerful. When the writer, like most ESL students, is an "outsider" (Bizzell 1987), the reader/audience has the power to accept or reject writing as coherent, as consistent with the conventions of the target discourse community. In an academic context, the faculty audience is particularly omniscient, for they set the entire classroom agenda and have the final word on paper grading. The social constructionists are most closely allied to Ede and Lunsford's (1984) concept of "audience addressed," in which "knowledge of this audience's attitudes, beliefs, and expectations is not only possible...but essential" (p. 156).

Reality and truth

In addition to considering the nature of the writer, of writing, and the role of audience, L1 composition theories and research often include a view of *reality and truth*. This feature is important to composition pedagogy as well, because "in teaching writing, we are tacitly teaching a version of reality and the student's place and mode of operation within it" (Berlin 1982: 766). In the cognitive approaches, reality and truth reside in the writer's mind. This vision of the real corresponds to the Platonic view, in which "truth is discovered through internal apprehension, a private vision of the world which transcends the physical" (Berlin 1982: 771). Not surprisingly, the "internal truth" hypothesis also appears among the expressivists, the most radical of the process groups, for whom "all good writing is personal, whether it be an abstract essay or a private letter" (Miller and Judy 1978: 12).

A second view is evident in the work of those who believe that reality and truth reside in both the writer, who attempts to establish them through the text, and the readers, who process, in their schemata, their own vision of reality and truth, modifiable through comprehension and acceptance of the writer's story or argument. In this version of interactivity between writer and text, the writer attempts to appeal to the reader through a reality upon which the writer and the reader can agree, and to convince the reader of a particular argument within this reality. However, if this appeal is unsuccessful, the reader will reject the truth value of the text; coherence between writer (and text) and reader will not be established. One of the most empathetic of interactive views can be found in the discussions of Rogerian argumentation, in which the purpose of a writer's argument is to "increase communication in both directions, eliminate any suspicion on the part of the reader that she is misunderstood and acknowledge shared goals" (Ewald 1986: 7).

A third view of reality and truth is held by the social constructionists, who believe that the nature of text is determined by the community for which it is written. This reality is best understood through genre studies and discussion of discourse communities (see Swales 1990). Academic discourse communities, for example, have their own conventions for establishing the "truth" – for example, through developing hypotheses and analyzing data, and for maintaining or extending it through the discourse community.

An ESL teacher's view of reality and truth, like his or her view of the other components discussed here, will undoubtedly influence the focus of classroom activities and assignments. If, for example, the teacher believes that reality resides in the individual, then he or she will encourage students to be creative and to find their own topics and organization for their texts. If the teacher believes that reality is negotiated between reader and writer, he or she will assist students in developing arguments that are sensitive to another reader's views and counterarguments. If, on the other hand, the teacher takes a social constructionist stand, he or she will begin with the rules of discourse in the community for which the student writers are producing text. These rules, not the students' own, will become the standards for teaching and evaluating writing for the class.

The language component

The final feature to be considered in a complete theory is *language*, which is influenced by, or influences the other features of a theory (i.e., the nature of the writer, the audience, and reality and truth). In the expressivist and cognitivist views, which focus upon the writer and the writing process, "form and language come from content – and are a result of what the reader wants to say" (Miller and Judy 1978: 15). The language of a composition, then, is the writer's own, stemming from prior experience and the creative urge.

In the second view, taken from principles of interactivity, language that draws from the content schemata of both reader and writer is appropriate. The writer must make concessions to the language of the reader; and likewise, the reader must concede to the writer his or her language, or L2 language limitations, and previous background, employing these to instantiate and modify the reader's content schemata. If language new to the reader is used, the writer leads the reader through the text in a manner that assists comprehension, allowing for gradual revision of the reader's previously held schemata.

The social constructionist views language as an outgrowth of the discourse community for which a text is written. The "outsider" writer's alternatives for language use are therefore severely constrained. ESL students often run into major difficulties attempting to use the language of a discourse community when they do not fully understand the context for language use or the audience addressed. However, academic faculty insist that students learn to "talk like engineers," for example, surrendering their own language and modes of thought to the requirements of the target community.

Though there are many lessons to be learned from the long history of L1 composition theory and research, two should be most evident from the preceding discussion. First, any viable theory of ESL composition must be complete; that is, it must include, at the very least, the four elements mentioned by Berlin, in addition to other features necessitated by the nature of second language learning and use (e.g., contrastive rhetoric). Second, and fully as important, because world views among theorists, researchers, and teachers in both the first language and ESL differ in terms of these basic elements, no single, comprehensive theory of ESL composition can be developed on which all can agree. As in the case of L1 theories, there are those in ESL who focus upon the learner as creator of language or the cognitive elements of the writing process; and there are others who, like the social constructionists, will be concerned primarily with the audience and conventions and language of the discourse community to which the audience belongs.

It is hoped that by classifying and discussing approaches to L1 theory this chapter will provoke thinking about theory development in ESL. Equally important, it is hoped that teachers will recognize their theoretical positions.[3] Zebroski (1986), in an article arguing for the importance of theory to writing instructors, discusses how taking theory seriously has assisted him as a teacher:

Theory has helped me to excavate and to uncover my own assumptions about writing. It has aided me in crafting a more coherent and unified course structure. It has encouraged me to try out some new methods of teaching writing. It has helped me to relinquish control and to emphasize classroom community. (p. 58)

Fully as important as teacher acknowledgment and use of a complete and coherent theory is the development of mature theories by students:

---

3 There should be no question about where I stand. Note the number of pages devoted to social constructionism as compared to the pages devoted to process approaches and interactive views.

The primary objective of a writing course is to encourage students, through a variety of experiences and by means of writing assignments that require reflection upon these experiences, to arrive at a more explicit and conscious "theory" of writing that can guide them and help them to better understand and control their own behavior. (Zebroski 1986: 58–59)

For Berlin, whose influence permeates this chapter, composition theories, by their nature, reflect ideologies, often influenced by the conditions of a historical period. It is these ideologies that provide the "language to define the self, other subjects, the material world and the relation of all of these to each other. Ideology is thus inscribed in language practices, entering all features of our experience" (1988: 479).

With the notable exception of work by Auerbach (Auerbach and Burgess 1985; Auerbach 1989), little has been said in major ESL publications about ideology and its connections to theory and practice. In the future, our profession would benefit from a more careful examination of theories and the ideologies they reflect, and of the classroom practices that result.

References

Auerbach, E. (Ed.) (1989). Non-traditional materials for adult ESL. *TESOL Quarterly, 23*, 321–335.

Auerbach, E., and Burgess, D. (1985). The hidden curriculum in survival ESL. *TESOL Quarterly, 19*, 475–494.

Bakhtin, M. M. (1973). *Marxism and the philosophy of language*, trans. L. Matejka and I. R. Titunik. New York: Seminar Press.

Berlin, J. A. (1982). Contemporary composition: The major pedagogical theories. *College English, 44*, 765–777.

(1987). *Rhetoric and reality: Writing instruction in American colleges, 1900–1985*. Carbondale: Southern Illinois University Press.

(1988). Rhetoric and ideology in the writing class. *College English, 50*, 477–494.

Bizzell, P. (1987). Language and literacy. In T. Enos (Ed.), *A sourcebook for basic writing teachers* (pp. 125–137). New York: Random House.

Bruffee, K. A. (1986). Social construction: Language and the authority of knowledge; A bibliographical essay. *College English, 48*, 773–790.

Carrell, P. L. (1983). Some issues in the role of schemata, or background knowledge, in second language comprehension. *Reading in a Foreign Language, 1*, 81–92.

Carrell, P.; Devine, J.; and Eskey, D. (Eds.) (1988). *Interactive approaches to second language reading*. New York: Cambridge University Press.

Coe, R. M. (1987). An apology for form: Or, who took the form out of process? *College English, 49*, 13–28.

Connor, U., and Johns, A. (1989). Argumentation in academic discourse communities: There are differences. Paper presented at the 23rd Annual TESOL Convention, San Antonio, Texas, March.

Ede, L., and Lunsford, A. (1984). Audience addressed, audience invoked: The role of audience in composition theory and pedagogy. *College Composition and Communication, 35,* 155–171.

Elbow, P. (1973). *Writing without teachers.* New York: Oxford University Press.

(1981a). *Embracing contraries: Explorations in Learning and Teaching.* New York: Oxford University Press.

(1981b). *Writing with power: Techniques for mastering the writing process.* New York: Oxford University Press.

Ewald, H. (1986). The "model" reader: Audiences within genres. Paper presented at the 37th Annual Conference on College Composition and Communication, New Orleans, La., March.

Faigley, L. (1986). Competing theories of process: A critique and a proposal. *College English, 48,* 527–542.

Flower, L. (1979). Writer-based prose: A cognitive basis for problems in writing. *College English, 41,* 19–38.

(1985). *Problem-solving strategies for writing,* 2nd ed. San Diego: Harcourt Brace Jovanovich.

(1989). *Problem-solving strategies for writing,* 3rd ed. San Diego: Harcourt Brace Jovanovich.

Fulkerson, R. (1979). Four philosophies of composition. *College Composition and Communication, 30,* 343–348.

Hayes, J. R., and Flower, L. (1983). Uncovering cognitive processes in writing: An introduction to protocol analysis. In P. Mosenthal, L. Tamar, and S. A. Walmsley, (Eds.), *Research in writing* (pp. 206–220). New York: Longman.

Hillman, L., and Kessell, B. (1986). *Thinking, reading and writing integrated,* Book II. New York: Holt, Rinehart & Winston.

Hinds, J. (1987). Reader vs. writer responsibility: A new typology. In U. Connor and R. B. Kaplan (Eds.), *Writing across languages: Analysis of L2 text* (pp. 141–152). Reading, Mass: Addison-Wesley.

Horowitz, D. (1986). What professors actually require: Academic tasks for the ESL classroom. *TESOL Quarterly, 20,* 445–462.

Huckin, T. (1987). Surprise value in scientific discourse. Paper presented at the 38th Annual Conference on College Composition and Communication, Atlanta, Ga., March.

Johns, A. M. (1986a). Coherence and academic writing: Some definitions and suggestions for teaching. *TESOL Quarterly, 20,* 247–266.

(1986b). The ESL student and the revision process: Some insights from schema theory. *Journal of Basic Writing, 5* (Fall), 70–80.

(1988). The discourse communities dilemma: Identifying transferable skills for the academic milieu. *English for Specific Purposes, 7,* 55–60.

Kroll, B. M. (1978). Cognitive egocentrism and the problem of audience awareness in written discourse. *Research in the Teaching of English, 12,* 269–281.

Kuhn, T. S. (1970). *The structure of scientific revolutions,* 2nd ed. Chicago: University of Chicago Press.

Lauer, J. (1970). Heuristics and composition. *College Composition and Communication, 21,* 396–404.

Meyer, B.J.F. (1977). The structure of prose: Effects on learning and implications for educational practice. In R. C. Anderson, R. J. Spiro, and W. E. Montague

(Eds.), *Schooling and the acquisition of knowledge* (pp. 179–208). Hillsdale, N.J.: Erlbaum.

Miller, J., and Judy, S. (1978). *Writing and reality.* New York: Harper & Row.

Nystrand, M. (1986). *The structure of written communication: Studies in reciprocity between writers and readers.* Orlando: Academic Press.

Raimes, A. (1987). Language proficiency, writing ability, and composing strategies: A study of ESL college student writers. *Language Learning, 37,* 439–467.

Rorty, R. (1982). Hermeneutics, general studies and teaching. *Synergos: Selected papers from the synergos seminars,* Vol. 2. Fairfax, Va.: George Mason University Press.

Singer, H. (1984). Friendly texts. In E. K. Dishner, T. W. Bean, J. E. Readance, and D. W. Moore (Eds.), *Content area reading: Improving classroom instruction* (pp. 114–127). Dubuque, Iowa: Kendall Hunt.

Spack, R. (1984). Invention strategies and the ESL college composition student. *TESOL Quarterly, 18,* 649–670.

(1988). Initiating ESL students into the academic discourse community: How far should we go? *TESOL Quarterly, 22,* 29–52.

Sullivan, N., and van Becker, D. (1982). *Journal to essay: A sequential program in composition.* Dubuque, Iowa: Kendall Hunt.

Swales, J. (1984). Research into the structure of introductions to journal articles and its application to teaching academic writing. In R. Williams, J. Swales, and J. Kirkman (Eds.). *Common ground: Shared interests in ESL and communication studies* (pp. 77–86). Oxford: Pergamon Press.

(1990). *Genre analysis: English in academic and research settings.* Cambridge: Cambridge University Press.

Urzua, C. (1986). A child's story. In P. Rigg and D. S. Enright (Eds.), *Children and ESL: Integrated perspectives* (pp. 93–112). Washington, D.C.: TESOL.

Zamel, V. (1983). The composing processes of advanced ESL students: Six case studies. *TESOL Quarterly, 17,* 165–187.

Zebroski, J. T. (1986). The uses of theory: A Vygotskian approach to composition. *The Writing Instructor, 5* (Winter), 57–67.

3 An overview of second language writing process research

Alexandra Rowe Krapels

Not too long ago, second language acquisition theorist Stephen Krashen claimed that "studies of second language writing are sadly lacking" (1984: 41). To be sure, to that date, few studies had yet been shared with the second language research community, but many studies were being conducted at that time, and shortly thereafter these studies became a part of the growing body of literature on second language (L2) writing research. Of particular concern here is research on second language writing processes. This chapter provides an overview of L2 writing process research, including (1) its relationship to first language (L1) research, (2) a survey of L2 studies, (3) a summary of recurring issues, and (4) suggestions for future research. A few product-based studies are also included because they corroborate the findings of process-oriented research and because many L2 studies include both product- and process-based data (see Connor 1987).

The relationship of L1 research to L2 research

Second language composition textbooks abound, and, as Silva points out in the first chapter of this volume, approaches to teaching L2 writing exist in plenty, supported by ardent, even "evangelical," advocates and readily accessible materials. Second language composition instruction is, then, well established and much of it follows theory. However, L2 composition teaching has generally not been based on theoretically derived insights gained from L2 composition research, because until the 1980s there was not much L2 research to draw upon in building theory or planning classes.

Second language composition specialists have found guidance, nevertheless, in first language composition research, which has a history dating to the early 1900s (Haynes 1978). Shortly after the mid-point in the twentieth century, L1 composition research in English-speaking countries expanded from focusing on studies investigating the effect of some pedagogical treatment on student writers' products to exploration of the act of writing itself. Braddock, Lloyd-

Jones, and Schoer (1963) issued the call for L1 writing process research in the United States. Hillocks (1986) has provided the best summary of L1 studies to date in his detailed and critical account of research on all different kinds of L1 writers.

Emig's (1971) landmark L1 research, *The Composing Processes of Twelfth Graders,* was the first major study to respond to the shift in composition orientation from product to process and to some of the research questions posed by Braddock et al. (1963), as well as to their suggestions regarding scientifically sound methodology. With her study, Emig established what has become the primary research design for conducting research into the writing process. Using a case study approach, Emig analyzed the writing processes of eight high school seniors, above average students who were not randomly selected. She met with her subjects four times and gathered data from "composing-aloud" audiotapes (her own notes were taken while observing the subjects writing) and interviews in which "each subject gave a writing autobiography" (p. 30), and answered questions on his or her writing process for a particular piece of writing. Emig also collected the students' preliminary notes, outlines, and final written products. In addition to providing a research design for the investigation of writing processes, Emig's study fostered "the development of what might be called 'science consciousness' in composition research" (Voss 1983: 279), an attitude and an approach that both L1 and L2 researchers have maintained.

Second language process-oriented research lagged behind process-oriented theory and practice among L2 composition specialists. Basing their comments on developments in L1 composition, Zamel (1976) and Raimes (1979) recommended treating L2 writing as a process in the L2 classroom − thereby decreasing the focus on surface-level errors and achieving correctness. They encouraged their colleagues to learn from first language composition theory, practice, and research and to apply effective L1 techniques to L2 writing instruction. Since that time, second language writing teachers have begun to conduct their own investigations of L2 writing processes and of the use of process-oriented pedagogy with second language learners.

In general, second language composition researchers have adopted L1 writing process research designs, and more often than not their findings have concurred with those of their L1 counterparts. Some L2 studies also use the analysis criteria of L1 studies; two frequently used L1 schemes are those developed by Perl (1978), who developed a coding scheme for categorizing writing process behaviors, and Faigley and Witte (1981), who designed a system for studying the influence of revision on meaning. Pianko's (1979) L1 study has also influenced the research designs of some L2 writing process studies in that Pianko's writing tasks have been used in some L2 studies. In fact, according to Zamel (1984),

"research into second language composing processes seems to corroborate much of what we have learned from research in first language
writing" (p. 198).

"Corroborate" is the key term here because it underscores the need
for L2 writing researchers to be aware of L1 writing research and then
to test L1 findings in an L2 context. First language writing process
research has informed second language research, but L2 researchers must
be careful not to let L1 studies guide or determine their investigations
of second language writing processes, because the research contexts are
not the same.

A survey of second language writing process studies

The following survey is presented in rough chronological order, grouping, as far as is possible, those studies that have addressed similar research
questions or have been similarly designed. This organization reveals how
L2 writing process research has developed. On the whole, early L2
studies attempt to describe all aspects of L2 composing processes. Early
L2 researchers are apparently trying to grasp whatever they can about
the nature of L2 composing, especially concerning which behaviors seem
to be successful or unsuccessful in producing effective L2 compositions.
Later L2 researchers focus on specific composing behaviors, specific types
of L2 writers, or features unique to L2 composing. Particular research
themes recur throughout the body of L2 writing process research, and
any single study usually provides insight into several of these themes,
summarized later in this chapter.

Chelala (1981) conducted one of the first second language writing
process studies, using a case study approach to investigate composing
and coherence. Her two Spanish-speaking subjects, both "professional"
women, composed aloud four times and were interviewed twice. Using
Perl's coding scheme to analyze the subjects' tapes of composing aloud
and several previously developed methods to analyze the coherence of
their written products, Chelala identified effective behaviors and ineffective behaviors. Included among the latter were using the first language
for prewriting and switching back and forth between the first and second
language, findings that contradict those of later studies (e.g., Lay 1982;
Cumming 1987; Friedlander, this volume).

In another early L2 writing process study on rhetorical concerns and
composing, Jones (1982) also investigated the written products and writing processes of two L2 writers, designating one "poor" and the other
"good," thus distinguishing between effectiveness and ineffectiveness in
writing, as Chelala (1981) had done. Unlike Chelala's subjects, Jones's

students had different profiles: The poor writer, a Turkish speaker, was a graduate-level student, whereas the good writer, a German speaker, was a freshman-level writer. Also, the poor writer demonstrated somewhat less L2 grammar proficiency than the good writer. The subjects "composed aloud" as they produced a self-generated narrative and revised a paragraph of kernel sentences. Jones analyzed the composing strategies by noting two composing behaviors: writing or generating text and reading the text already generated. His findings indicated that writing strategies affected writers' rhetorical structures. According to Jones, the poor writer was bound to the text at the expense of ideas, whereas the good writer allowed her ideas to generate the text. Jones concluded that the poor writer had never learned how to compose, and this general lack of competence in composing, rather than a specific lack in L2 linguistic competence, was the source of her difficulty in L2 writing.

Jacobs (1982) also made the point that factors beyond linguistic competence determined the quality of students' writing in her study of the writing of eleven graduate students – six native and five nonnative speakers of English. The students' written work, thirteen essays each, and interviews with them about arranging information comprised Jacobs's data. Jacobs functioned as writing teacher for all the students who were taking a premedical course. Although Jacobs's study was primarily based on product analysis, her findings relate to process-oriented research, particularly to the notion that linguistic competence does not affect composing competence among second language writers. She observed that the "high predication load" of academic writing tasks resulted in two writing problems: "integrative thinking" and "phrasing for correctness and readability" (p. 63). She found that there was an apparent inverse relationship between integrative thinking and grammatical accuracy among her subjects, and she conjectured that this relationship related to a student's development as a writer. Finally, her study revealed no significant differences between L1 and L2 subjects.

Zamel (1982) also found that competence in the composing process was more important than linguistic competence in the ability to write proficiently in English, as Jones (1982) and Jacobs (1982) had indicated. Her subjects were eight university-level "proficient" L2 writers (p. 199), one of whom was a graduate student. Her data consisted of interviews about her subjects' "writing experiences and behaviors" (p. 199), which were retrospective accounts of writing processes, and the students' multiple drafts for the production of one essay each. Zamel found that the writing processes of her L2 subjects were like those of the subjects described in L1 studies. She concluded that L2 composing processes indicated that L1 process-oriented writing instruction might also be effective for teaching L2 writing. Zamel maintained that when students understood and experienced composing as a process, their written products would improve.

Zamel's (1983) study of six advanced L2 students provided more support to a theme that was developing among L2 writing process studies – that L2 writers compose like L1 writers. For this study, Zamel again used a case study approach, observing her subjects while they composed, interviewing them upon conclusion of their writing, and collecting all of their written materials for the production of one essay each, which they had unlimited time to complete. Direct observation differentiated the research method of this study from that of Zamel's (1982) earlier study. Her subjects were her own university-level students, designated as skilled or unskilled as a result of evaluations of their essays by other L2 composition instructors. The skilled L2 writers in her study revised more and spent more time on their essays than the unskilled writers. In general, they concerned themselves with ideas first, revised at the discourse level, exhibited recursiveness in their writing process, and saved editing until the end of the process – all writing strategies similar to those of skilled L1 writers, as described in L1 writing process studies (e.g., Pianko 1979; Sommers 1980). Zamel's (1983) unskilled L2 writers revised less and spent less time writing than the skilled writers. They focused on small bits of the essay and edited from the beginning to the end of the process, very like the unskilled writers in Sommers's (1980) report of her L1 writing process study, which investigated revising strategies. Zamel (1983) also investigated how writing in a second language influenced the composing process. Her subjects "did not view composing in a second language in and of itself [as] problematical" (p. 179), thereby indicating that writing in a second language did not have a major impact on the composing process in general. She maintained that the skilled writers in her study "clearly understand what writing entails," whereas the unskilled writers did not (p. 180), a conclusion similar to that of Jones (1982).

Trying to gain insight into her students' composing process, Pfingstag (1984) investigated the composing-aloud protocol of one of her undergraduate students – a native Spanish speaker with an intermediate level of English proficiency, as measured by the Michigan Placement Test, and an apparent lack of composing competence, in that he did "very little planning" and had a narrow range of strategies for generating ideas on a topic (p. 1). She then did a 20-minute composing-aloud session to model effective composing strategies for the student. According to Pfingstag, the student's subsequent composing-aloud protocol exhibited improved composing strategies, which she attributed to her using the protocol as a pedagogical as well as a research tool.

Hildenbrand's (1985) case study also offered suggestions on how teachers might help their L2 students improve their writing. Hildenbrand daily observed her Spanish-speaking subject write in two community college courses. Findings indicated that the subject's preferred writing mode – creative, personal writing – conflicted with the academic mode expected of her, thereby hindering her writing process. Once again, factors beyond the L2 writer's linguistic competence were found to impede the student's composing process.

Jones (1985) set out to investigate further the factors that might constrain second language writers. He videotaped nine advanced L2 students while they wrote three different compositions. Each composition was of a different discourse type – "personal experience," "description," and "generalization" (p. 102) – and the topics were drawn from Pianko's (1979) L1 writing process study. Each subject was given unlimited time to complete each composition. Jones also interviewed the subjects on their writing processes for each composition and on their opinions about how their L2 writing processes differed from their L1 processes. Applying Krashen's monitor theory to analyze the writing behaviors of two subjects in this study, Jones reported that "monitoring does not lead to improved writing" (1985: 112), and he maintained that monitoring was, then, a factor constraining the L2 writing process. He speculated that monitor use among L2 learners might result from instructional methods. Jones's study, like Zamel's (1982, 1983) studies, provided support for the use of process-oriented composition pedagogy in L2 classes, especially in light of the call for L2 classrooms to be places enabling the acquisition of English rather than just the learning of English, an emerging "paradigm shift" discussed by Raimes (1983).

Another study providing support for process-oriented teaching of second language writing was Rorschach (1986). Rorschach's three advanced L2 subjects wrote one essay each, to which teachers responded. Then the students revised their essays. Data consisted of external raters' evaluations of the students' essays and interviews with the students about why they wrote and revised as they did. Findings indicated that reader awareness led the writers to focus on correctness rather than content. Rorschach concluded that her study calls into question composition teaching that concentrates on form, a conclusion that agrees with Jones's speculation about the relationship between instruction and overusing the monitor. (For a discussion of the effects of feedback on content versus form, see Fathman and Whalley, this volume.)

The studies of Hildenbrand (1985), Jones (1985), and Rorschach (1986), then, implied that certain L2 instructional approaches might not develop the composing competence that was intended – indeed, that certain teaching hindered the development of L2 writers. Furthermore, Jones (1985) commented, "It is worth noting that many of the proposals for improving first language composing are also effective in helping second language learners develop acquired linguistic competence" (p. 114).

Providing support for Jones's comment, the studies of Diaz (1985, 1986) and Urzua (1987) articulated the benefits of process-oriented composition teaching for L2 learners. Diaz's (1985) first task was to establish a process-oriented classroom environment; then she observed what happened to the students and their writing. Based on hypotheses that grew out of her classroom-based ethnographic study, Diaz concluded "that not only are process strategies and techniques strongly indicated and recommended for ESL students, but also when used in secure, student-centered contexts, the benefits to these students can go beyond their development as writers" (1986: 41), thus recalling Jones's (1985) remark. Urzua (1987) came to much the same conclusion about the benefits of process-oriented teaching with L2 writers when she reported the progress of four children, two fourth graders and two sixth graders, over six months' time. Like Diaz, she set out to assess process-oriented composition pedagogy in an L2 context. Urzua's data consisted of "transcripts of peer response sessions, weekly compositions, and twice-weekly dialogue journals" (p. 279). She observed that the children acquired three significant composing skills: "(a) a sense of audience, (b) a sense of voice, and (c) a sense of power in language" (p. 279). Diaz's and Urzua's studies strongly indicated that what had proved effective in L1 classrooms was also effective in L2 classrooms.

Additional research provided specific information on L2 college-level basic writers, one type of writer often targeted in L1 composition research (e.g., Perl 1978). Zamel (1983) found that unskilled L2 writers wrote like unskilled L1 writers and that the lack of composing competence in L1 was reflected in students' L2 writing ability. Brooks's (1985) study indicated that writing competence was separate from oral proficiency and that lack of L1 cognitive academic development, a somewhat broader concept than writing competence, affected L2 learners' composing skills. Analysis of questionnaires, audiotapes of student discussions, and multiple drafts of three essays written by each student led Brooks to propose three developmental levels for L2 writers, which recalled Jacobs's (1982) comments about her subjects. Brooks's levels were primarily based on the amount of experience L2 learners had with writing. Brooks offered suggestions on how L2 writers could proceed through the stages she identified in order to improve their writing skills. Brooks's conclusions were reminiscent of a first language writing process study conducted by Pianko (1979), who also concluded that the problems of unskilled writers may result from "a truncated writing process" (p. 20).

Raimes (1985b) offered even more information on unskilled L2 writers. The eight subjects in her study were deemed "unskilled" by their performances on a holistically scored university-wide writing test, a measure similar to that used to assess the writing proficiency of Zamel's (1983) subjects. In addition to these data on writing proficiency, Raimes collected data from the students' scores on the Michigan Proficiency Test, the students' responses to a lengthy questionnaire on their "background, education, and experience with and attitude toward English and writing" (p. 235), and composing-aloud audiotapes made for the production of one essay each. The students had 45 minutes to complete the essay, although some exceeded the time allotted. Raimes found that her subjects' composing competence did not correspond with their linguistic competence, a recurrent finding in L2 writing research. With most of her subjects, she observed very little planning before or during writing, a behavior previously observed among unskilled L1 and L2 writers (e.g., Perl 1978; Zamel 1983). However, she also observed that her subjects, unlike the unskilled writers in previous studies, paid less attention to revising and editing than she had expected and that they seemed to reread their work to let an idea germinate. Raimes conjectured that L2 writers might not be "as concerned with accuracy as we thought they were, that their primary concern is to get down on paper their ideas on a topic" (p. 246).

Furthermore, whereas Zamel (1982, 1983) pointed out similarities in the writing behaviors of L2 and L1 writers, Raimes (1985b, 1987) found differences when she compared her subjects to the L1 subjects of Pianko (1979) and especially Perl (1978). Raimes (1985b) reported that her subjects wrote more, exhibited more commitment to the writing task, produced more content, and paid less attention to errors than Perl's subjects. Such a comparison was possible because of Raimes's research design. She used a writing task that Pianko had used in her study and adapted Perl's coding scheme to analyze the protocols resulting from the composing-aloud sessions. Raimes (1987) concluded that L2 writers were different from L1 writers in that L2 writers "did not appear inhibited by attempts to edit and correct their work" (p. 458). Before Raimes, L2 researchers had underscored the likenesses between L1 and L2 writers, both skilled and unskilled. Raimes agreed that likenesses certainly existed, but differences between L1 and L2 writers existed as well, and for this reason, Raimes suggested the adaptation rather than the wholesale adoption of L1 writing instruction. She also recommended the use of the composing-aloud protocol as an effective pedagogical strategy, as Pfingstag (1984) had before.

In another report, Raimes (1985a) discussed the variety among second language writers. Her research led her to maintain that the L2 writer was no definable type, for L2 writers represented a variety of types, backgrounds, and needs. Raimes's obvious but very important observation is the very factor that makes the investigation of L2 writing processes so provocative. The L2 composition class may represent at least half a dozen strikingly different cultures, very different educational backgrounds, ages ranging from sixteen to sixty, and very different needs for being able to write in a foreign language.

Raimes's (1985a, 1987) findings indicate that the act of writing in a second language is somehow different from that of writing in a first language and that there may be a relationship between the two processes. These differences have not yet been fully examined in second language writing process research, but some studies have begun to explore differences between L1 and L2 writers, have included consideration of the role of first language use in second language writing, have compared L1 and L2 writing processes, and have investigated the influence of L1 writing processes on L2 writing processes.

Although product-based, Edelsky's (1982) research deserves mention because her longitudinal study supports a finding common to the L2 studies described thus far – that when writing in a second language, writers call on what they know about writing in their first language. Unlike most of the other researchers discussed, Edelsky used very young children as subjects, specifically 26 first, second, and third graders enrolled in a bilingual program. She collected as data four different writing samples from each of her subjects over the period of one school year. She found that knowledge of L1 writing "forms the basis of new hypotheses rather than interferes with writing in another language," and she implied that fundamental L1 composing processes were applied to L2 composing (p. 227).

Considering the use of both L1 and L2 in the study of the writing processes of second language learners, Lay (1982) analyzed the compositions and accompanying composing-aloud audiotapes of four adult, Chinese-speaking L2 students. She also interviewed her subjects about their writing backgrounds and current attitudes toward writing. Although intending to produce L2 compositions, Lay's subjects incorporated the first language into their L2 composing processes. Her study pointed out that, first, "when there are more native language switches (compared to the same essay without native language switches), the essays in this study were of better quality in terms of ideas, organization and details" and that, second, "certain topics induce more native language switches" (p. 406). The first finding runs counter to that of Chelala (1981).

Jones and Tetroe (1987) analyzed protocols to study the L1 and L2 planning behaviors of six Spanish-speaking L2 writers, all of whom were preparing for graduate study. Collecting data over a six-month period, they observed great variety among their subjects in the amount of native language use in L2 writing, as well as "some decrease in [writing] performance" when writing in the second language. They proposed that composing in a second language used "cognitive capacity" that would be used for other tasks when writing in the native language (p. 53). They concluded that a lack of L2 vocabulary resulted in first language use in composing, and "that the quality, though not the quantity, of planning transfers from L1 to L2" (p. 56). Therefore, as Lay's (1982) work had earlier suggested, certain features in one's first language writing process transfer to, or are reflected in, those same features in one's second language writing process.

Martin-Betancourt (1986) also considered the use of first language in second language writing processes. Analyzing the protocols of Puerto Rican college students, she concluded that the L2 writing process was similar to the L1 process, with the exception of two composing behaviors – using more than one language and translating. Martin-Betancourt indicated that her subjects' writing processes involved solving linguistic problems and that use of the first language in L2 writing added to the problems, especially in vocabulary. Raimes (1985a) also mentioned the problem of inadequate vocabulary among her L2 subjects and commented that this was also a problem for L1 writers. Concerning L1 use in L2 writing, Martin-Betancourt (1986) found inconsistencies among her subjects in that some relied on Spanish very little while others used Spanish frequently, sometimes even incorporating translation into their second language writing processes.

Gaskill's (1986) case study on revising in Spanish and English set out to compare L1 and L2 composing processes by having four undergraduate subjects write in both Spanish and English. Using Faigley and Witte's (1981) analysis scheme, Gaskill analyzed videotapes of the students composing and their written products, and concluded that writing and revising processes in English resembled those in Spanish. In a similar study, Hall (1987) used four subjects and relied on videotapes and multiple drafts for generating data. Hall also interviewed the subjects and had them fill out postwriting questionnaires, concluding that a single system was used to revise across languages. Hall also found that advanced L2 writers use both L1 and L2 knowledge and experience when revising.

In her study of L1 and L2 writing, Arndt (1987) reported similar findings, that is, that "the composing strategies of each individual writer were found to remain consistent across languages" (p. 257). Her six Chinese-speaking subjects were all graduate-level students. Basing her research design and analysis scheme on those of Perl, Arndt was surprised to observe that, although the L1 and L2 writing processes of each individual writer were generally similar, the writers as a group exhibited very different writing processes, a finding that recalled Raimes's (1985b) comment on the great variety among L2 writers, and that these processes were unrelated to their level of writing proficiency. Like Raimes, Arndt also discovered slight differences in L1 and L2 writing processes, especially related to vocabulary. Finally, Arndt's finding indicated "that all L2 writers, proficient or otherwise in terms of writing as activity, need more help with the demands of writing-as-text" (p. 265).

Although Zamel's (1982) study did not investigate L1 composing per se, one of her subjects, a graduate student, incorporated translation into her L2 writing process. According to Zamel, this subject was "the most proficient writer" in her study (p. 201). However, Zamel's other subjects did not depend on translation to write in English; indeed, they scorned such a procedure, one saying, "It would be like being pulled by two brains" (p. 201). This student's comment corresponded with Johnson's (1985) findings. Johnson reported that her six subjects felt that the use of first language when writing in a second language was ill advised for advanced L2 learners. Even so, they generally tended to rely on their first language when they were generating ideas about a culture-bound topic. This finding concurred with that of Burtoff's (1983) product-based study on Japanese, Arabic, and native speaker discourse strategies, which considered ninety compositions written by freshmen and concluded that the writing prompt or topic affected how writers arranged their compositions, in that the more culture-bound the topic, the more different the discourse structures were. The studies of Lay (1982), Burtoff (1983), and Johnson (1985) all indicated that certain topics elicited more first language use in second language composing than other topics did.

Cumming (1987) reported that all six of his Francophone Canadian adult subjects tended to use their first language for generating content for the three writing tasks they were given, which were personal, expository, and academic. Cumming drew his data from composing-aloud tapes, observational notes taken while the students wrote, questionnaires on the subjects' educational and personal background as well as their assessments of their L1 writing, external raters' holistic evaluation of the subjects' L1 writing expertise, and subjects' performances on ESL proficiency tests. Cumming observed that whereas the inexpert writers consistently used L1 to generate ideas, the expert writers used L1 for both generating content and checking style, particularly with regard to diction. In fact, according to Cumming, the expert writers in his study did a lot of thinking in French, a finding contrary to that of Johnson (1985).

Friedlander (this volume) also provided information about the role of first language use in generating content. His findings indicated that using the topic-related language to plan content resulted in better planning and better compositions. Also, Friendlander's data indicated that translating did not constrain writers, either in time or quality, as they produced L2 texts.

Just what the influence of one's first language may be on one's second language writing process has just begun to be explored. Galvan's (1985) ethnographic study involved ten doctoral students of education in investigating the cultural and linguistic factors in composing processes. Galvan drew data from interviews, direct observations, and assessments of writing skills as well as levels of bilingualism and biculturalism. He found that his participants' second language writing was generally influenced by both their first language thinking and culture and their second language thinking and culture. He stated that moving between two languages and two cultures caused his participants' composing processes to be full of pauses and doubts.

Campbell (this volume) examined both the products and the composing processes of L1 and L2 students to compare the way in which they incorporated information from reading into their academic writing, a research focus similar to that of Jacobs (1982). Unlike Jacobs, who had observed nothing to distinguish the academic writing of her L1 and L2 subjects, Campbell found some differences – that the L2 writers planned less and depended more on the reading than the L1 writers.

Second language writing process issues

This survey of second language writing process studies reveals several recurrent motifs concerning both research design and research findings.

Research designs

1. All studies reflect a keen awareness of L1 writing process research as a guiding force.
2. Most studies rely on case study as a research methodology, resulting in a small number of subjects (often from four to six) in any single writing process study (e.g., Lay 1982; Zamel 1983; Gaskill 1986).
3. The subjects of most published studies are usually females (e.g., Chelala 1981; Jones 1982; Hildenbrand 1985), advanced second language learners (e.g., Zamel 1982, 1983; Jones 1985; Rorschach 1986), undergraduate students (e.g., Brooks 1985; Raimes 1985a,b, 1987; Gaskill 1986), native speakers of either Spanish (e.g., Chelala 1981; Martin-Betancourt 1986; Jones and Tetroe 1987) or Chinese (e.g., Lay 1982; Arndt 1987; Friedlander, this volume), and "subjects of convenience," who are sometimes the researcher's own students and therefore not chosen randomly (e.g., Zamel 1983; Pfingstag 1984; Raimes 1985a).
4. The writing tasks of studies vary in number, from one (e.g., Zamel

1982) to the total number required for a course (e.g., Jacobs 1982); in discourse mode – narrative/descriptive, expository, and/or argumentative; in topic type – personal/nonpersonal and culture bound/non-culture bound; and in time allotted for completing a task, from twenty minutes (e.g., Pfingstag 1984) to as much time as needed (e.g., Jones 1985). Those studies that include more than one writing task combine different discourse modes and topic types (e.g., Jones 1985; Cumming 1987).

5. The data of most studies are gathered from both process- and product-oriented sources. Data on the composing process consist of direct observations (e.g., Zamel 1983), audiotaped (e.g., Raimes, 1985a,b, 1987) or videotaped (e.g., Gaskill 1986) protocols based on composing-aloud sessions, and retrospective accounts of composing drawn from interviews (e.g., Zamel 1982) or questionnaires (e.g., Hall 1987). Interviews or questionnaires also provide data on subjects' education and background as writers (e.g., Raimes 1985a,b, 1987). Product-oriented data consist of multiple drafts (e.g., Zamel 1982), holistic assessments of subjects' composing skill (usually L2) (e.g., Rorschach 1986), and/or subjects' scores on standardized English proficiency tests (e.g., Cumming 1987).

Research findings

1. A lack of competence in writing in English results more from the lack of composing competence than from the lack of linguistic competence (e.g., Jones 1982; Zamel 1982; Raimes 1985a).
2. The composing processes of "unskilled" L2 writers are similar to those of "unskilled" L1 writers; likewise, the composing processes of "skilled" L2 writers are similar to those of "skilled" L1 writers. Therefore, differences between L1 and L2 writers relate to composing proficiency rather than to their first languages (e.g., Zamel 1983).
3. A finding closely related to item (2) is that one's first language writing process transfers to, or is reflected in, one's second language writing process (e.g., Edelsky 1982; Gaskill 1986; Jones and Tetroe 1987).
4. The composing processes of L2 writers are somewhat different from the composing processes of L1 writers, a finding that contradicts item (2) (e.g., Raimes 1985a,b, 1987; Arndt 1987).
5. First language use when writing in a second language, a fairly common strategy among L2 writers, varies (e.g., Martin-Betancourt 1986; Cumming 1987; Friedlander, this volume). (Some studies, in fact, offer contradictory findings on this issue.)
6. Using L1 when writing in L2 frequently concerns vocabulary and

enables the L2 writer to sustain the composing process (e.g., Raimes 1985a; Martin-Betancourt 1986; Arndt 1987). L1 use is often an inventional (e.g., Johnson 1985), sometimes an organizational (e.g., Lay 1982), and occasionally a stylistic strategy (e.g., Cumming 1987).

7. Certain writing tasks, apparently those related to culture-bound topics, elicit more first language use when writing in a second language than other tasks do (Lay 1982; Burtoff 1983; Johnson 1985).

These motifs and the research reports surveyed reveal contradictions in second language writing research, which may result from premature generalizing on the part of the researchers. Case study research usually yields data and findings with limited generalizability, given the fact that such research permits few subjects and often precludes randomization of subject selection. In an assessment of college-level writing process research conducted from 1982 to 1987, Silva (1988) states:

> The interpretation of findings appears to be one of the most problematic areas in this body of research. While some researchers were very careful, modest, tentative, and reasonable, just as many were not. There seem to be more than a few instances of over- and misinterpretation of evidence here; these include unjustified cause and effect inferences – both implicit and explicit; unjustified generalization from very small samples to large subgroups or the entire population of ESL writers; suggested implications for the classroom not well supported by the evidence provided; and sweeping claims that go way beyond findings in support of a particular popular approach or orientation to writing instruction. (p. 6)

These problematic findings point to the robust nature of second language writing process research. Contradictory findings invite further research, vital to resolve contradictions and clarify uncertainties regarding how L2 writers compose. There exists a wide range of L2 writers to learn about – experienced and inexperienced, graduate and undergraduate, male and female, as well as writers from every culture around the world. To date, studies have investigated the composing processes of approximately 100 subjects; not only is this a small sample, but the representativeness of these subjects is unclear because of inconsistencies in some of the research reports.

Discussing these inconsistencies, Silva (1989) examined 22 studies, coding and then assessing 24 features as satisfactory or unsatisfactory. His analysis could be interpreted as charging that some L2 writing process research lack rigor. However, his analysis reveals two positive trends, both of which have developed since 1984. First, there has been a marked improvement in both consistency and completeness in reporting subject and task variables, analyzing data, and presenting findings. Second, more researchers have been prudently cautious about both generalizing beyond their studies and claiming cause-and-effect relationships. In a very short time, second language writing process research has matured, and each new study has contributed to the overall growth in the body of knowledge concerning second language writing.

Suggestions for future research

Logistics

Analysis of existing second language writing process studies indicates directions for future research designs and research reports. At present, lack of comparability across studies impedes the growth of knowledge in the field. The research designs of future studies should replicate the best and most appropriate designs of prior studies so that findings can be compared. Furthermore, the research reports should include more information about subject and task variables, because then the studies enable comparative analysis across studies, thereby increasing potential for generalizability. Studies cannot contribute significantly to the body of knowledge if very different research designs are used across studies. Lack of comparability affects generalizability, which in turn decreases the significance of a study's findings. Although composing research literature has questioned the credibility and validity of protocol analysis (Cooper and Holzman 1983; Voss 1983), the L2 studies that have used it have consistently mined more useful data than those studies that have not, because the data are then comparable across studies. This comparability leads to the kind of generalizable conclusions needed to build research-based theory.

Second language researchers should also consider increasing their repertoire of research methods. Once again, L2 writing researchers can look for guidance from their L1 colleagues who have used ethnography to increase their understanding of writing processes. Ethnography takes the researcher out of the artificial environment of the laboratory and into the real space of writing, the collective consciousness of people making and then sharing meaning, so that both researcher and subject become participants in the research process. Kantor, Kirby, and Goetz (1981) present ethnography as possibly being "the design of choice for many language, composition, literature and reading studies, particularly those which question basic assumptions about the growth of writing and reading abilities in the classroom" (p. 293). Zamel (1987) has also recommended that L2 researchers consider ethnography as a research method (see Watson-Gegeo 1988). Of course, ethnographic studies lack direct comparability with experimental studies because the designs are very different. Even so, ethnography can produce increased insight into second language composing because it requires the kind of in-depth inquiry that is lacking in some L2 writing research.

Substance

The aforementioned research findings also indicate directions for future L2 writing process research. For example, very little research has yet involved beginning language learners. With beginners, one must question the first research finding listed, that a lack of competence in writing in English results more from the lack of composing competence than from the lack of linguistic competence.

As pointed out earlier, research findings have been contradictory regarding the similarity of L1 and L2 writing processes. These opposing conclusions may result from different research designs. Resolving the contradictions requires replicating research designs. Furthermore, if differences exist, further research is needed to articulate these differences. As Silva (1988) concluded in his review of L2 writing research, "It is perhaps time to move away from documenting similarities... and to focus more attention on how they [L1 and L2 writing processes] are different. The area that would seem to hold the most promise and value in this regard is the interaction of first and second languages and cultures in L2 writing" (p. 6). The role that contrasting rhetorical preferences may play in L2 composing processes offers rich potential for research.

One of the differences already noted is L1 use in L2 writing. Although several studies indicate that the writing task influences L1 use, findings have otherwise been mixed. Some second language writers seem to depend more on first language use than others. Is this difference merely a result of individual preferences or do external factors have some relation to L1 use in L2 writing? Do L1 rhetorical preferences have any impact on L2 writing processes? What are the roles of writing in students' native cultures and in their lives, and do these roles affect L2 writing processes? What is the effect of multilingual literacy on L3 composing processes? Does the writer's cultural background, especially the writer's education in an L1 environment, influence L1 use in L2 composing?

The question of how L2 students have learned or acquired writing as a language skill is, then, significant to L2 writing process research. English L1 writing process researchers primarily operate within the familiar milieu of the North American educational system, but L2 writing process researchers do not. Although they may be able to discover how their subjects were previously taught English, it is very difficult to know how these subjects were taught writing, or indeed whether they were actually "taught" writing at all. The International Study of Achievement in Written Composition, conducted by the Curriculum Laboratory of the University of Illinois (1980), has contributed data drawn from sixteen countries that address this issue (see Purves 1988).

The third research finding on the list also calls for additional research, especially concerning transfer of composing ability across languages. A student's L1 composing competence needs some sort of assessment (Zamel 1983: 172). Although L1 writing process research usually includes information about the subjects' competence in writing at the beginning of the study and often includes some discussion of their previous experiences in writing, L2 writing process research does not as yet typically include comparable data on the subjects' level of L1 writing. Without such information, any conclusion on L2 composing competence is tentative, at best, because research thus far hints that L1 composing competence somehow affects L2 composing.

Conclusion

Although much has already been learned about second language writing processes, so much more lies undiscovered. Early L2 studies pointed out similarities between L1 and L2 composing. More recent studies have questioned these similarities and have presented differences to be considered in future research. The details of these differences remain unclear. Even so, each study provides new knowledge; each study offers new questions to ask and new areas to explore. As a field of research, then, the second language composing process is rich with potential and full of vitality.

Yet untouched is the area of universal notions of composing – beyond the similarities and/or differences of L1 and L2 composing. L1 writing researchers cannot hope to broach this important and exciting subject because their pool of subjects represents only a small segment of people, all of whom speak only one language. Instead of looking outside for guidance, L2 researchers can look within their own group, to others like themselves who work within a multilingual context and who are confronted with the interplay among languages. Syntacticians are seeking grammatical universals, and discourse analysts are exploring discourse universals. L2 composition researchers are in a position to lead the way in considering the universals of composing.

References

Arndt, V. (1987). Six writers in search of texts: A protocol based study of L1 and L2 writing. *ELT Journal, 41,* 257–267.
Braddock, R.; Lloyd-Jones, R.; and Schoer, L. (1963). *Research in written composition.* Champaign, Ill.: National Council of Teachers of English.

Brooks, E. (1985). Case studies of the composing processes of five "unskilled" English-as-a-second-language writers. Unpublished doctoral dissertation, New York University.

Burtoff, M. (1983). The logical organization of written expository discourse in English: A comparative study of Japanese, Arabic, and native speaker strategies. Unpublished doctoral dissertation, Georgetown University.

Chelala, S. (1981). The composing process of two Spanish-speakers and the coherence of their texts: A case study. Unpublished doctoral dissertation, New York University.

Connor, U. (1987). Research frontiers in writing analysis. *TESOL Quarterly, 21,* 677–696.

Cooper, M., and Holzman, M. (1983). Talking about protocols. *College Composition and Communication, 34,* 284–293.

Cumming, A. (1987). Decision making and text representation in ESL writing performance. Paper presented at the 21st Annual TESOL Convention, Miami, April.

Curriculum Laboratory. (1980). *IEA International Study of Achievement in Written Composition.* Urbana: University of Illinois.

Diaz, D. (1985). The process classroom and the adult L2 writer. Unpublished doctoral dissertation, Columbia University Teachers College.

   (1986). The adult ESL writer: The process and the context. Paper presented at the 76th Annual NCTE Convention, San Antonio, Texas, Nov.

Edelsky, C. (1982). Writing in a bilingual program: The relation of L1 and L2 texts. *TESOL Quarterly, 16,* 211–228.

Emig, J. (1971). *The composing processes of twelfth graders.* Urbana, Ill.: National Council of Teachers of English.

Faigley, L., and Witte, S. (1981). Analyzing revision. *College Composition and Communication, 32,* 400–414.

Galvan, M. (1985). The writing processes of Spanish-speaking bilingual/bicultural graduate students: An ethnographic perspective. Unpublished doctoral dissertation, Hofstra University.

Gaskill, W. (1986). Revising in Spanish and English as a second language: A process oriented study of composition. Unpublished doctoral dissertation, University of California, Los Angeles.

Hall, C. (1987). Revision strategies in L1 and L2 writing tasks: A case study. Unpublished doctoral dissertation, University of New Mexico.

Haynes, E. (1978). Using research in preparing to teach writing. *English Journal, 67* (1), 82–88.

Hildenbrand, J. (1985). Carmen: A case study of an ESL writer. Unpublished doctoral dissertation, Columbia University Teachers College.

Hillocks, G., Jr. (1986). *Research on written composition: New directions for teaching.* Urbana, Ill.: ERIC Clearinghouse on Reading and Communication Skills and the National Conference on Research in English.

Jacobs, S. (1982). *Composing and coherence: The writing of eleven pre-medical students.* Linguistics and Literacy Series 3. Washington, D.C.: Center for Applied Linguistics.

Johnson, C. (1985). The composing process of six ESL students. Unpublished doctoral dissertation, Illinois State University.

Jones, S. (1982). Attention to rhetorical form while composing in a second language. In C. Campbell, V. Flashner, T. Hudson, and J. Lubin (Eds.),

Proceedings of the Los Angeles Second Language Research Forum, Vol. 2 (pp. 130–143). Los Angeles: University of California at Los Angeles.

(1985). Problems with monitor use in second language composing. In M. Rose (Ed.), *Studies in writer's block and other composing process problems* (pp. 96–118). New York: Guilford Press.

Jones, S., and Tetroe, J. (1987). Composing in a second language. In A. Matsuhashi (Ed.), *Writing in real time: Modelling production processes* (pp. 34–57). Norwood, N.J.: Ablex.

Kantor, K.; Kirby, D.; and Goetz, J. (1981). Research in context: Ethnographic studies in English education. *Research in the Teaching of English, 15,* 293–305.

Krashen, S. D. (1984). *Writing: Research, theory, and applications.* Oxford: Pergamon Institute of English.

Lay, N. (1982). Composing processes of adult ESL learners. *TESOL Quarterly, 16,* 406.

Martin-Betancourt, M. (1986). The composing processes of Puerto Rican college students of English as a second language. Unpublished doctoral dissertation, Fordham University.

Perl, S. (1978). Five writers writing: Case studies of the composing processes of unskilled college writers. Unpublished doctoral dissertation, New York University.

Pfingstag, N. (1984). Showing writing: Modelling the process. *TESOL Newsletter, 18,* 1–3.

Pianko, S. (1979). A description of the composing process of college freshman writers. *Research in the Teaching of English, 13,* 5–22.

Purves, A. C. (Ed.) (1988). *Writing across languages and cultures: Issues in contrastive rhetoric.* Newbury Park, Cal.: Sage Publications.

Raimes, A. (1979). *Problems and teaching strategies in ESL composition.* Language in Education: Theory and Practice 14. Arlington, Va.: Center for Applied Linguistics.

(1983). Tradition and revolution in ESL teaching. *TESOL Quarterly, 17,* 535–552.

(1985a). An investigation of the composing processes of ESL remedial and nonremedial students. Paper presented at the 36th Annual CCCC Convention, Minneapolis, Minn., March.

(1985b). What unskilled writers do as they write: A classroom study of composing. *TESOL Quarterly, 19,* 229–258.

(1987). Language proficiency, writing ability, and composing strategies: A study of ESL college student writers. *Language Learning, 37,* 439–468.

Rorschach, E. (1986). The effects of reader awareness: A case study of three ESL student writers. Unpublished doctoral dissertation, New York University.

Silva, T. (1988). Research on the composing processes of college-level ESL writers: A critical review. Paper presented at the 39th Annual CCCC Convention, St. Louis, Missouri, March.

(1989). A critical review of ESL composing process research. Paper presented at the 23rd Annual TESOL Convention, San Antonio, Texas, March.

Sommers, N. (1980). Revision strategies of student writers and experienced adult writers. *College Composition and Communication, 31,* 378–388.

Urzua, C. (1987). "You stopped too soon": Second language children composing and revising. *TESOL Quarterly, 21,* 279–304.

Voss, R. (1983). Janet Emig's "The composing processes of twelfth graders": A reassessment. *College Composition and Communications, 34,* 278–283.

Watson-Gegeo, K. A. (1988). Ethnography in ESL: Defining the essentials. *TESOL Quarterly, 22,* 575–592.

Zamel, V. (1976). Teaching composition in the ESL classroom: What we can learn from research in the teaching of English. *TESOL Quarterly, 10,* 67–76.

(1982). Writing: The process of discovering meaning. *TESOL Quarterly, 16,* 195–209.

(1983). The composing processes of advanced ESL students: Six case studies. *TESOL Quarterly, 17,* 165–187.

(1984). In search of the key: Research and practice in composition. In J. Handscombe, R. Orem, and B. P. Taylor (Eds.), *On TESOL '83: The question of control* (pp. 195–207). Washington, D.C.: TESOL.

(1987). Recent research on writing pedagogy. *TESOL Quarterly, 21,* 697–715.

4 Coaching from the margins: issues in written response

Ilona Leki

How best to respond to student writing is part of the broader question of how to create a context in which people learn to write better or more easily. To that end, teachers have tinkered with all aspects of the context: the number of assignments, the types of assignments, the nature of the relationship between teacher and student, and so on. This chapter addresses issues surrounding another aspect of the writing context, types of written responses to student writing. Although students often write responses to papers by their peers, the focus of this chapter is limited to responses written by teachers.

Murray (1968) tells the story of an advertising executive who received written reports from his staff. Since he sometimes felt that the reports were not well written, he developed a response strategy to improve his employees' writing. He took written reports home, and the next day returned the reports to their authors in his private office saying, "Is this the best you can do?" The authors sheepishly took the reports back, worked on them, and resubmitted them. The boss once again took them and the next day again asked, "Is this really the best you can do?" This continued until the authors finally said, "Yes, it is the best we can do!" And the boss answered, "Good, then I'll read it."

While this way of responding to writing may have its merits, the more common way is to read whatever student writers offer and then, to paraphrase Grant-Davie and Shapiro (1987), behave with the same combination of a sense of responsibility and a sense of helplessness as the coach of a football team, booing and cheering while pacing the margins of the student's paper, shouting encouragement and tactical advice. Or worse, the teacher may, at the end of the paper, write the postmortem, like a coroner diagnosing the cause of death. It is also not uncommon for composition teachers to spend a great deal of time annotating papers, following what Hairston (1986) calls the conventional wisdom that responding properly to student writing means making meticulous and copious comments on student papers and holding conferences in the belief that student writing improves "in direct proportion to the amount of time teachers spend on their papers" (p. 117).

Writing teachers and students alike do intuit that written responses can have a great effect on student writing and attitude toward writing – such a great effect, in fact, that the response a writer gets may be the final arbiter of whether a writer will continue to write at all. Written comments are time consuming, but teachers continue to write comments on students' papers because we sense that our comments help writers improve; because written comments *seem* more feasible and more thorough than conferences on every paper; and because, for most writing teachers, our jobs require us not only to evaluate our students' writing but to be able to justify our evaluations.

What constitutes improvement

Before the issue of written responses to student writing can be explored, the goals in teaching writing to second language students need to be considered. Does L2 writing need to be error free or merely free of global errors that impede understanding? Is a legitimate goal for L2 students' writing that it be clear, though perhaps prosaic (Brodkey 1983), or must these students develop a vivid and varied style? Have we done our job when our L2 students can produce formally correct writing, or should we aim primarily at helping our students grow intellectually as they struggle with the import of their ideas (Knoblauch and Brannon 1984)? To what extent do we need to consider our students' own varied purposes in learning to write in the second language? Most would agree that the expectations, goals, and past writing experiences of L2 students are different from those of native speakers, yet unfortunately, most of the research on responding to student writing deals with native speakers. Thus, many important questions about our goals in teaching writing to L2 students remain unresolved.[1]

Written commentary on student papers is, of course, intended to produce improvement, but what constitutes improvement is not so clear. Much of the research on intermediate draft interventions only looks at improvements in students' subsequent drafts of the same piece of writing. In other words, there is little information on long-term improvement in writing. Furthermore, even looking at subsequent drafts yields inconclusive findings since, as both anecdotal and research evidence show, postintervention drafts are not always an improvement over preintervention drafts (Beach 1979). If we encourage students to rethink what they have written, to be willing to take risks both intellectual and linguistic, then backsliding is perhaps inevitable; perhaps "to expect that risk-taking and improvement can

---

1 For other perspectives see Silva (this volume) and Johns (this volume), who also discuss various roles writing goals can play in the design of ESL writing classes.

occur simultaneously is unrealistic and inappropriate" (Cynthia Onore, cited in Horvath 1984: 139). Because of their interest in nonprescriptive interventions, Knoblauch and Brannon (1984) point out that "whether or not a second draft represents improvement over a first in some objective sense is not only extremely difficult to determine but is also irrelevant to the value of the process itself," a process in which "a writer's control of personal choices and opportunity to discover personal meanings are more important for growth than local textual 'improvement,' superficial or otherwise" (p. 133). For this reason the authors feel that "there are no optimal responses, only more and less honest ones" (p. 132).

While Knoblauch and Brannon's interesting perspective on improvement may well be pertinent for L1 writers, the peculiar situation of L2 writers makes adoption of their attitudes somewhat more problematic for the L2 writing teacher. An element of prescription appears necessary in responses to L2 student papers because L2 students have a smaller backlog of experience with English grammatical or rhetorical structure to fall back on, not having had the same exposure to those structures as native speakers have had. Unlike basic writers, for example, L2 students do not automatically correct written errors when asked to read their texts aloud, a phenomenon noted among native speakers (Butler 1980).

Thus, it is important to keep in mind that, while they may be different for L1 and L2 writing classes, the goals we set for our writing classes go a long way toward determining how we will respond to our students' writing.

The persona of the writing teacher

Another issue central to the question of how to respond to student writing is what role writing teachers play in relation to student writing. The role of the writing teacher is schizophrenic, split into three incompatible personas: teacher as real reader (i.e., audience), teacher as coach, and teacher as evaluator (see Cowan 1977). Some educators advocate responding to student writing as real readers, not as writing teachers, questioning or commenting on the writing only when we might genuinely do so if we were reading a published text. But given the unequal power inherent in the roles of teacher and student, it is unrealistic to pretend that teachers can read student texts in the same way as we read texts we select for ourselves. Furthermore, since the job of a writing teacher is to teach writing, the teacher is constantly forced away from the content of the text toward the way the content is presented. L2 students in particular expect and require greater intervention than that of a real reader – intervention offering suggestions, options, or other ways of looking at what they have said (see, e.g., Radecki and Swales 1988).

An even more profound schizophrenic split that writing teachers, particularly process-oriented writing teachers, experience is that of trying to be at the same time the coach and the evaluator of student writing. For example, if a teacher has collaborated with students rather than teach/evaluate, and the students' work is then judged insufficient by the standards of that educational setting, the teacher has, in a sense, betrayed the students by not intervening more heavily. Short of refusing to evaluate student papers on the basis of quality, however that may be defined in a given context, teachers must continue to live in this contradiction of trying to be both collaborator and judge.

This schizophrenia has a profound impact on our students. We teach our students that having a clear sense of audience helps the writer decide what to say and how to say it. As long as a teacher is evaluating a student's performance, it does not matter how much we try to persuade ourselves and our students that the audience is their classmates or the university community; the students know very well that whoever gives the grade is the audience, an audience who will decide something very important about their futures. Because this is true, appropriation of the students' writing by the teacher, at least to some extent, becomes almost inevitable, because teachers *want* students to do well.

The effect of written commentary

Nevertheless, for both L1 and L2 students, the most pressing of the issues surrounding written responses, overriding and encompassing all others, is whether or not written responses to student writing do any good. Is the improvement that our comments effect short term or long term? How does written commentary affect students' self-confidence and self-esteem? Of the small amount of research that exists on responding to L2 writing, most focuses, in one form or another, on the effects of treating error (Semke 1984; Zamel 1985; Robb, Ross, and Shortreed 1986; Fathman and Whalley, this volume). Yet these studies and research on native speaker writing reveal depressingly little evidence to indicate that careful annotation of papers actually helps student writers improve.

Many L1 research projects examining types of written responses have criticized teachers for being too general (rubber stamping students' papers with remarks like "be specific" [Sommers 1982]), for being too specific (giving students advice that is so text specific that they cannot use it on subsequent writing), and for focusing too heavily on surface features (Searle and Dillon 1980).

Knoblauch and Brannon (1981) review research responding to these criticisms and testing numerous hypotheses on better ways for teachers to respond to student writing. They cite studies contrasting responses of praise with responses of criticism; contrasting the effect of oral responses with that of written responses; contrasting end commentary with side comments; contrasting copious response with brief response; contrasting response only to error with response to content; contrasting outright correction of errors with naming errors and with offering rules; contrasting explicit suggestions for change with implicit suggestions for change. In each case, the researchers were forced to the conclusion that *none* of these different ways of responding to student writing produced significant improvements in students' subsequent writing. Hillocks (1986) similarly reviews dozens of research findings. He writes, "The results of all these studies strongly suggest that teacher comment has little impact on student writing" (p. 165). And further, "The available research suggests that teaching by written comment on compositions is generally ineffective" (p. 167).

In L2 research, despite a general move in the profession away from focus on errors to focus on content and communication, Zamel (1985) has revealed that the annotations of ESL writing teachers are apparently intended to catch every error the students make, and that despite that intention, the teachers miss errors; that sometimes minor errors are corrected and much more significant problems causing serious ambiguity in meaning go uncorrected; and that the content of the writing is ignored in favor of what has been called "prose decorum." Zamel concludes that this type of marking is not helpful to student writers. Other research looking at error correction of this type supports the view that despite attention to errors in teachers' written responses to L2 writing, the errors persist (Hendrickson 1976; Semke 1984; Robb et al. 1986), although Fathman and Whalley (this volume) show that specific feedback on grammatical error has a greater effect on the improvement of grammatical accuracy than general feedback on content has on the improvement of content (see also Cardelle and Corno 1981).

Perhaps even more significant is research suggesting that these errors are much less disturbing to content-area professors than the perceived lack of maturity of thought and of rhetorical style in the L2 students' writing (Santos 1988), a problem of course not addressed by teacher response to surface error.

Student reactions to written commentary

What might explain the failure of careful annotations to improve student writing? One body of research exploring student responses to annotations on their papers suggests several possibilities. Students may not read the annotations. In a survey of native speaker students, Burkland and Grimm (1986) report that if there is a grade on a paper, these students read the grade and simply discard the paper, often in disgust at the injustice of receiving a low mark for an essay they had worked hard on. Other research shows that even native English speaking students often simply do not understand the meaning of comments on their papers (King 1979; Hahn 1981). Furthermore, even when students have managed to decipher a comment, they often have no idea how to respond to it. Sperling and Freedman (1987), reporting on their "good girl" writer, analyze alterations she made in response to teacher annotations and conclude that, although she made the alteration correctly, she had no idea what the principle behind the teacher's directive might have been and therefore was unable to correct the same type of error in another part of her paper. Finally, Smith (1982) found that without training, her students were not able to identify which of three versions of a single paper was the original, a first improved revision, and the final version.

There is also evidence of student hostility arising from the cooptation of their words or their ideas by their teacher's commentary (Lynch and Klemans 1978: 170; Burkland and Grimm 1986: 245; Sperling and Freedman 1987: 357). These students expressed unwillingness to surrender the content of their papers to the teacher. They spoke of resenting the teachers' suggestions that the content of a paper was weak, immature, or superficial; they expressed hostility at the idea that someone else had the right to put a grade on their thoughts.

Although some research (Gee 1972) shows that students have better attitudes toward writing if they receive positive feedback, in another study to determine the effect of praise on student writing and on student attitudes, L1 student writers responded that praise neither helped them improve nor made them want to improve more (Burkland and Grimm 1986).

Second language research reveals a slightly different picture of student reactions. In a study of L2 writers, Cohen and Cavalcanti (this volume) show that these students generally received the kind of written response they wanted from their English teachers. Another survey of ESL students (Leki 1986) revealed that these students' wanted to have every error marked and mostly approved of written clues from the teacher to enable them to correct their errors themselves. Like their native speaker counterparts, however, these students also expressed lack of interest in teacher reaction to the content of their papers. Students reported that such commentary did not help their writing improve, whereas directives on development and organization and indications of errors did help their writing (see also Fathman and Whalley, this volume).

In a study of North American students learning German, Semke (1984) reports some evidence that while students expressed hostility at having errors pointed out for them to correct, supportive comments without indication of errors had a positive influence on students' attitudes (p. 201).

Thus, while research into student reaction to written commentary gives us some clues as to why written annotations on student papers generally fail to improve student writing, this research remains inconclusive.

Possible directions for appropriate feedback

Given the enormous amount of time and energy poured into written commentary on student papers, the picture that emerges from research on the usefulness of this commentary is problematic. Comments of praise do not appear to be useful to students; critical comments have not helped student writing improve; written comments are difficult for students to interpret if only because weak writers are probably also weak readers (Butler 1980); and finally, written comments are difficult for students to act upon. But insights from research have also emerged (see, e.g., Anson 1989 and Moxley 1989).

Knoblauch and Brannon (1981) try to explain the lack of success in affecting student writing by looking at the assumptions of the research itself and at the broader instructional context in which the teachers' responses are made. A great deal of research has focused only on comments teachers make on students' papers without considering the on-going dialogue between student and teacher – which might have, for example, established an environment in which written commentary is received with hostility. Furthermore, they say, if research has failed to establish that annotations on student papers help them improve their writing, it may well be that the problem is not the annotation but the entire teaching environment. In this environment student papers are evaluated in an activity "resembling literary criticism" (Knoblauch and Brannon 1981: 2) and then laid aside, and new compositions are begun in which presumably the students will be able to remember and draw upon comments teachers made on previous papers. Knoblauch and Brannon (1981) write: "Our assumption has been that evaluating the product of composing is equivalent to intervening in the process" (p. 2). The two conclusions they draw are: (1) we need to look not at responses written on final drafts but rather at responses written on intermediate drafts, and at how those drafts were reshaped as a result of the teacher's comments, and (2) we need to look at the ongoing dialogue between students and teachers.

Despite a fairly large amount of information, at least in L1 writing, on the effects of teacher responses (Sperling and Freedman 1987: 344), examples of appropriate feedback and subsequent student action are rare in the literature on teacher response, and what examples exist again appear primarily in the writing on native speakers. Knoblauch and Brannon (1984) publish one example of an inappropriate way to respond to a student's paper followed by a preferable, less prescriptive, response. Lees (1979) combines a brief, pointed critical comment with an additional, sequential assignment for a graduate student whose paper violated its own stated criteria for good writing. Butler's delightful article (1980) on responding to the writing of remedial writers describes his responses as simply indicating how well he is able to understand the student's ideas. Considering the gratitude expressed by Semke's (1984) subjects writing in German, perhaps simply indicating that the reader understood the L2 writer's ideas is not too brief a response. Finally, Ziv's excellent article (1984) on the effect of her categorized responses to the work of four of her freshmen allows us to see at least the direction these students would take based on her notations. Her research shows that when the teacher intervenes as the student is writing and revising, the final product shows improvement over the intermediate drafts.

Recent results of an NCTE National Writing Project survey by Freedman (1987) reveal that writing teachers considered successful agree that intervening during the writing process helps student writers improve. Thus, multiple drafting with comments on intermediate drafts is an obvious first step away from making each assignment into an isolated miniature test (see also Hillocks 1982).

Another potentially even more productive but relatively unexplored step in L2 writing is the writing equivalent of Krashen's narrow reading (1985), that is, sequenced assignments in which each assignment in a term is related to an ongoing project. Teachers' comments on the individual segments of such a writing project become meaningful and significant because they become incorporated into the next assignment, not just into a revision of one paper.

The next step in looking at the broader educational context in which students write and teachers respond consists of respecting the students' right to their own expression through writing. If we do not want to appropriate a student's paper to ourselves by marking it in accord with our own mental image of the Ideal Text to which a paper seeks to conform, then we need to compare the paper to some other text – one that corresponds to the student's intentions in a given piece of writing.

How can we know what those intentions might be, especially with inexperienced L2 writers? The easiest way is to engage students in dialogue on those intentions. There is some research (Rubin 1985) to show that while students are not good evaluators of their own writing and lack even the vocabulary to describe their work, they have an excellent grasp of what mental processes they went through as they wrote, what they did as they wrote, what they experienced, and what they wanted their reader to experience. Asking students to analyze each piece of writing they do is one way to take advantage of these insights. Brannon and Knoblauch (1982) suggest having students write a paragraph-by-paragraph analysis of what they were trying to do in a piece of writing. Then, a classmate similarly analyzes the piece one paragraph at a time. In this way writers can compare their own intentions with the effect the writing had on a reader.

A less time-consuming alternative requires students to answer questions on their work in order to give the teacher a clearer understanding of how each student conceived of his or her own project in the text. Students indicate what they liked best in what they have written, whether any part was particularly easy or hard to write, what they feel the least sure of in what they have written, what the most important thing was that they wanted the reader to find out or see from reading the paper, and what they would change in the paper if they had more time. The value of this last question is that it communicates to the student that although we must sometimes work under a deadline and finally turn in a paper in whatever form it may be at the time, in a sense, a paper is never really a final draft. Jenkins (1987) has her students respond in writing to the comments she has made on their papers, thus giving the students the opportunity to enter into written dialogue with the teacher.

A final issue in responding to student writing is grades. Many writing teachers experience intense discomfort when forced to evaluate students with whom they feel they have been collaborating. Various approaches to solving this problem tinker with the grading system: not grading writing based on quality but rather on the completion of a minimum number of assignments; the portfolio approach,[2] not grading papers but rather grading overall performance in a class; grading on the basis of a few limited required improvements. Other solutions focus on types of writing classes: for example, writing across the curriculum or content-based programs, in which L2 teachers collaborate with content-area teachers and all writing assignments are done for the content-area teacher. In a variation of this approach, the role of coach is assigned to the students' classroom teacher and the role of evaluator to another. The evaluator looks only at final drafts of the students' writing and does no more than evaluate, writing no comments or corrections at all. What-

---

2 The portfolio approach is based on assembling a representative sample of the student's best work, usually final drafts but sometimes including an in-class "timed" essay. At the end of the term, the entire portfolio is evaluated for a grade rather than assigning a grade to each paper separately or using some sort of grade-averaging system. See Belanoff and Dickson (in press) for a full discussion of issues related to using a portfolio approach.

ever the solution to grading, this issue is inescapable for most of us and colors all other aspects of responding appropriately and effectively to student writing.

It is obvious that writing teachers need effective and efficient ways to respond to student writing without becoming what Hairston (1986) calls "composition slaves." Student writers need and deserve responses to their writing. We now have some idea of which responses improve writing and which are wasted effort. But research results have been inconclusive, sometimes contradictory, and, in L2 writing, sparse. We need more research, especially in L2 writing, to look not only at teachers' written responses but at combinations of classroom settings, course goals, and grading procedures in order to discover what forms our responses can most profitably take.

References

Anson, C. M. (Ed.) (1989). *Writing and response: Theory, practice, and research*. Urbana, Ill.: National Council of Teachers of English.

Beach, R. (1979). The effects of between-draft teacher evaluation versus student self-evaluation on high school students' revising of rough drafts. *Research in the Teaching of English, 13*, 111–119.

Belanoff, P., and Dickson, M. (Eds.) (In press). *Portfolio grading: Process and product*. Upper Montclair, N.J.: Boynton/Cook Heinemann.

Brannon, L., and Knoblauch, C. H. (1982). On students' rights to their own texts: A model of teacher response. *College Composition and Communication, 33*, 157–166.

Brodkey, D. (1983). An expectancy exercise in cohesion. *TESL Reporter, 16*, 43–45.

Burkland, J., and Grimm, N. (1986). Motivating through responding. *Journal of Teaching Writing, 5*, 237–247.

Butler, J. (1980). Remedial writers: The teacher's job as corrector of papers. *College Composition and Communication, 31*, 270–277.

Cardelle, M., and Corno, L. (1981). Effects on second language learning of variations in written feedback on homework assignments. *TESOL Quarterly, 15*, 251–261.

Cowan, G. (1977). The rhetorician's personae. *College Composition and Communication, 28*, 259–62.

Freedman, S. W. (1987). *Response to student writing*. Urbana, Ill.: National Council of Teachers of English.

Gee, T. C. (1972). Students' responses to teacher comments. *Research in the Teaching of English, 6*, 212–219.

Grant-Davie, K., and Shapiro, N. (1987). Curing the nervous tick: Reader-based response to student writing. Paper presented at the 38th Annual Conference on College Composition and Communication, Atlanta, Ga., March.

Hahn, J. (1981). Students' reactions to teachers' written comments. *National Writing Project Network Newsletter, 4*, 7–10.

Hairston, M. (1986). On not being a composition slave. In C. W. Bridges (Ed.),

Training the new teacher of college composition (pp. 117–124). Urbana, Ill.: National Council of Teachers of English.

Hendrickson, J. (1976). The effects of error correction treatments upon adequate and accurate communication in the written compositions of adult learners of ESL. Unpublished doctoral dissertation, Ohio State University.

Hillocks, G., Jr. (1982). The interaction of instruction, teacher comment, and revision in teaching the composing process. *Research in the Teaching of English, 16,* 261–278.

(1986). *Research on written composition: New directions for teaching.* Urbana, Ill.: ERIC Clearinghouse on Reading and Communication Skills and the National Conference on Research in English.

Horvath, B. K. (1984). The components of written response: A practical synthesis of current views. *Rhetoric Review, 2,* 136–156.

Jenkins, R. (1987). Responding to student writing: Written dialogues on writing and revision. *The Writing Instructor, 6,* 82–86.

King, J. A. (1979). Teacher comments on student writing: A conceptual analysis and empirical study. Unpublished doctoral dissertation, Cornell University.

Knoblauch, C. H., and Brannon, L. (1981). Teacher commentary on student writing: The state of the art. *Freshman English News, 10,* 1–4.

(1984). *Rhetorical traditions and the teaching of writing.* Upper Montclair, N.J.: Boynton/Cook.

Krashen, S. (1985). The power of reading. Plenary presented at the 19th Annual TESOL Convention, New York, March.

Lees, E. O. (1979). Evaluating student writing. *College Composition and Communication, 30,* 370–374.

Leki, I. (1986). ESL student preferences in written error correction. Paper presented at the Southeast Regional TESOL Conference, Atlanta, Ga., Oct.

Lynch, C., and Klemans, P. (1978). Evaluating our evaluations. *College English, 4,* 166–180.

Moxley, J. (1989). Responding to student writing: Goals, methods, alternatives. *Freshman English News, 17,* 3–11.

Murray, D. M. (1968). *A writer teaches writing: A practical method of teaching composition.* Boston: Houghton Mifflin.

Radecki, P. M., and Swales, J. M. (1988). ESL student reaction to written comments on their written work. *System, 16,* 355–365.

Robb, T.; Ross, S.; and Shortreed, I. (1986). Salience of feedback on error and its effect on EFL writing quality. *TESOL Quarterly, 20,* 83–95.

Rubin, L. (1985). Uneven performance: What students do and don't know about their own writing. *The Writing Instructor, 4,* 157–167.

Santos, T. (1988). Professors' reactions to the academic writing of nonnative-speaking students. *TESOL Quarterly, 22,* 69–90.

Searle, D., and Dillon, D. (1980). The message of marking: Teacher written response to student writing at intermediate grade levels. *Research in the Teaching of English, 14,* 233–242.

Semke, H. D. (1984). The effects of the red pen. *Foreign Language Annals, 17,* 195–202.

Smith, G. L. (1982). Revision and improvement: Making the connection. In R. Sudol (Ed.), *Revising: New essays to teachers of writing* (pp. 132–139). Urbana, Ill.: ERIC Clearinghouse on Reading and Communication Skills.

Sommers, N. (1982). Responding to student writing. *College Composition and Communication, 33,* 148–156.

Sperling, M., and Freedman, S. W. (1987). A good girl writes like a good girl. *Written Communication, 4,* 343–369.

Zamel, V. (1985). Responding to student writing. *TESOL Quarterly, 19,* 79–101.

Ziv, N. (1984). The effects of teacher comments on the writing of four college freshmen. In R. Beach and L. S. Bridwell (Eds.), *New directions in composition research* (pp. 362–380). New York: Guilford Press.

5 Second language writing: assessment issues

Liz Hamp-Lyons

The field of writing assessment has developed considerably in the last quarter of the century. Twenty years or so ago, many if not most people in North America (to a lesser extent in Great Britain and Australia) believed that writing could be validly tested by an indirect test of writing. As we enter the 1990s, however, they have not only been defeated but also chased from the battlefield. This change is the result of social pressure from schools, colleges, and parents, who argued that failure to learn and practice writing reasonable lengths of text in school was leading to declining literacy levels and to a college-entry population that could not think critically about intellectual ideas and academic material. In 1970 researchers had begun to respond to these social pressures, but there were serious questions about the levels of reliability that could be achieved on a direct test of writing (these same questions had been primarily responsible for the disfavor writing had fallen into as a test method from the 1940s on). What was happening in the field of writing assessment then was the kind of transatlantic conflict of philosophies that we have become familiar with in many areas of English as a second language (ESL) teaching. North American research emphasized the failure of direct writing tests to achieve score reliability levels that could compete with score reliabilities on multiple choice items, and many, perhaps even most people became convinced of the hopelessness of direct writing assessment. Meanwhile, in Great Britain educators such as Wiseman (1949), Wiseman and Wrigley (1958), and Britton et al. (1975) were strong opponents of standardized testing, and they spearheaded studies and education reports to ensure that the nation knew the dangers of discounting writing. They also worked to discover ways of increasing the level of score reliability obtainable on a direct writing test, and ultimately their work provided models for developments in direct writing assessment in North America.

As a result of many careful studies, the score reliability usually achieved on a direct test of writing has been raised to around .80 (commonly regarded as a satisfactory level for decision-making purposes), and has been stabilized as a result of a large number of careful research projects and the development of professional training practices for essay readers. There has also been progress in achieving some level of validity for writing tests, beyond the very obvious validity that comes from simply testing writing through writing rather than through an indirect measure. But there are still plenty of unresolved issues in first language writing assessment, as we shall see later.

In second language writing assessment also, direct testing of writing has become the order of the day once again. The final nail in the coffin of indirect measurement of ESL writing was driven in by the TOEFL program,[1] which in 1986, after heavy and increasing pressure from the ESL professional community and from admissions agencies, introduced the Test of Written English (TWE) as a separately reported direct test of writing to be taken, optionally, with the TOEFL. Before taking that step, ETS carried out rigorous reliability studies (Carlson et al. 1985). Other reliability studies have been conducted, usually in fairly restricted settings and for fairly narrow purposes (e.g., Mullen 1980; Jacobs et al. 1981; Weir 1983; Robinson 1985). Jacobs et al. (1981), Carlson et al. (1985), and Hamp-Lyons (1987) also report careful development of training procedures for essay readers. But as in first language writing assessment, many issues remain unresolved, and most of these are validity issues.

Validity

As with most assessment contexts, with writing assessment we can consider four kinds of validity: face validity, content validity, criterion validity, and construct validity. The simplest validity is *face validity*, or what looks to an intelligent outsider as if it is valid. Direct tests of writing have always had good face validity, even in the heyday of the psychometric-structuralist era. Bridgeman and Carlson (1983) discovered as a result of their large-scale survey of higher education institutions in the United States that judgments based on actual writing samples were highly valued by college admissions officers. Criper and Davies (1988), as a result of a large-scale study of university faculty across the United Kingdom, found that the most frequently asked-for piece of information in addition to test scores (where a direct writing test score was already reported among the battery of results) was an actual writing sample. Similarly, at the University of Michigan, a large public university with 24,000 undergraduates at the Ann Arbor campus, where data were collected, Keller-Cohen and Wolfe (1987) found that written work forms

---

1 The TOEFL is the Test of English as a Foreign Language and is administered by the Educational Testing Service (ETS) in Princeton, New Jersey.

part of the course expectations in over 70% of courses within the undergraduate curriculum as a whole, and that 97% of faculty surveyed ($N = 700+$) agreed that skill in writing is important or very important for college study. Clearly, judgments based on actual writing samples are frequently made, and highly regarded by faculty and admissions officers, whatever their actual reliability or validity.

We need to go beyond face validity, however. If writing tests are to do more than permit crude, short-term decisions about who goes into which writing class, we need to ensure that writing tests are construct-valid. *Construct validity* means that the test reflects the psychological reality of behavior in the area being tested; a construct-valid test is designed to measure certain human responses. Construct validity is especially important in educational contexts, where the backwash, or impact on what happens in the classroom, resulting from a test is (or should be) a key criterion in judging whether a test is "bad" or "good." Strong arguments for the construct validity of direct writing tests have been made by Jacobs et al. (1981), for example:

The direct testing of writing emphasizes the *communicative* purpose of writing . . . (it) utilizes the important intuitive, albeit subjective, resources of other participants in the communicative process – the *readers* of written discourse, who must be the ultimate judges of the success or failure of the *writer's* communicative efforts. (p. 3)

The problem with this is that it remains at an abstract level: To achieve construct validity it is necessary to set up studies that will demonstrate construct validity through empirical evidence for the hypothesized set of behaviors and relationships, or to engage in a priori construct validation at such a level of detail and specificity that the constructs described can be recognized in a posteriori behavior. We urgently need serious research into the construct validity of direct tests of writing.

A type of validity commonly associated with writing tests at the college level is *content validity*: it is often claimed, for example, that if the students are history majors, we should give them a writing test that asks them to write about history. The simplistic argument is that if we ask them to discuss, for example, the significance of the Crimean War for modern military tactics, they will do better than if we ask them to discuss the problems of environmental pollution, or of utilization of space resources. But this takes no account of the fact that they may not have studied nineteenth century European history, or that if they had, the course may not have included military strategy. The problem here is one of infinite regress. The problems with content validity (which, taken further toward their logical conclusions, resurface as "mastery learning" and "domain referencing") are better solved by attention to construct validity – that is, to defining what it is that writers do when they write history, and to finding ways to test that without depending on any specific content. In this way, writers are freed to select the content themselves, and thus display their knowledge or lack thereof, their ability to select from what they know to forward an argument, or their ability to capitalize on what they do know while underplaying those aspects of content where they are lacking. Thus, the competent writer finds a kind of content validity for himself or herself.

Another kind of validity is *criterion validity*. This refers to the measurable relationship, usually correlational, between a particular test of writing and various other measures. As with all criterion validity studies, the key problem when we try to look at the criterion validity of a writing test is the identification of a reasonable criterion measure against which the writing test is to be compared. *Concurrent validity* is validity established by comparison with other test scores collected at or about the same time (e.g., Flahive and Snow 1980). *Predictive validity* is validity established by comparison with other test scores collected at a significantly later time (e.g., Pitcher and Ra 1967; Criper and Davies 1988). Studies over the years have shown that writing tests often correlate highly with "objective" measures, and this was the argument used by ETS for many years for not testing writing directly. But the old maxim says, "a correlation does not a causation make," and many of us have felt dissatisfied with non-causal explanations. If scores on multiple choice grammar, vocabulary, or other skills tests are highly correlated with writing test scores, why is that? Few ESL professionals these days are prepared to accept that we can test writing by any means other than writing: They believe that correlations of .80 with other tests, leaving as they do 36% of the variance in test score unaccounted for (correlation = r; variance = r^2), leave unrevealed the most interesting part of the writer's repertoire. So far, predictive validity studies, such as the correlation of test scores with outcomes, have proved unhelpful too (Criper and Davies 1988), since in most academic contexts a student's success or failure in obtaining a degree is based on many factors other than written performance, and the predictor (that is, the writing test) and the criterion (that is, the degree result) are so far apart as to fall prey to many intervening variables, and predictive indicators (that is, the writing test results) are consciously confounded by teachers, who work to overcome predictions of failure for their students (Hamp-Lyons 1988a).

In my view, then, construct validity is the overarching validity which subsumes and, in some sense, assumes all the others, and it is this view of validity that governs the rest of this chapter. Of course reliability is important, but as every introductory testing textbook tells us, reliability is a necessary but not sufficient condition for an ethical test.

It is convenient to think of four components of a direct test of writing for which validity must be established: the task, the writer, the scoring procedure, and the reader(s). Each of these components will be addressed in turn. I will then argue for an approach to writing assessment that takes account of who the learner is, the context the learner has come from, and the context in which the learner must work toward educational success. The chapter closes with a consideration of writing assessment, an activity necessarily concerned with written products, in the light of current thinking about composing processes.

The task

There has probably been more work done on task validity in ESL writing assessment than in L1 writing assessment. The work of Horowitz (1986a,b) comes particularly to mind, but useful work has also been done by Swales (1982), Johns (1981), and Kroll (1979); and Weir (1983) surveyed large numbers of college faculty and also engaged in observational studies in a range of contexts, in a study that has yet to be matched for in-depth data gathering. Bridgeman and Carlson (1983) also conducted a very large survey but did not couple it with observations, although they did conduct interviews of a small subset of survey respondents. The approach in all these studies, to a greater or lesser degree, has been to argue, or to assume, that valid tasks for direct tests of writing in English as a second language are tasks that are reported or observed to occur in the contexts in which the writers being assessed will need to write.

In psychometric terms, variables of the task component of the writing test are those elements that must be manipulated and controlled to give every test taker the opportunity to produce his or her best performance. Task variables include length of time to write; use of paper and pen, typewriter, or word processor; as well as a large number of variable elements that make up the topic, or prompt, itself (Hamp-Lyons 1986; Ruth and Murphy 1988). Of the variables that have been identified empirically as affecting a writer's test score, the topic variable has been the most controversial. In the L1 literature, Hartog (1936), Hartog et al. (1941), Braddock, Lloyd-Jones, and Schoer (1963), Britton et al. (1975), Poetker (1977), Hirsch and Harrington (1981), Applebee (1982), Freedman and Calfee (1983), and Pollitt et al. (1985) have all claimed that content quality and quantity in an essay are significantly affected by the topic of the question. In contrast, Brossell and Hoetker Ash (1984) found the topic of the question to have little influence on scores, and

Robert Rentz (personal communication), in a very large study of writing in grades 3 through 11 carried out for the Georgia Board of Regents, found no significant differences among a large number of topics (although he has never published his work).

In the developmental research leading to the TWE, Carlson et al. (1985) found correlations of .66 to .73 between topics administered to ESL writers, with correlations of the same magnitude between topics of the same type (as defined by their study) and topics of different types; they concluded that there was no significant difference between the way one topic was ranking students compared to another. Spaan (1989) chose two MELAB (Michigan English Language Battery) prompts with apparently very different parameters, and found that students in an experimental group received very similar scores on both prompts. Reid (this volume) analyzed a corpus of TWE essays using the computer series Writer's Workbench and found significant quantitative variations on several features of student texts written across topic types, although she does not report relationships between these differences and actual score levels. Reid raises important questions about whether lack of score differences across topics and topic types is a feature of the topics themselves or of some aspect of the scoring procedure. Hamp-Lyons (in press) argues that the scoring procedure, and indeed the scorers themselves, do in fact account for the lack of differences. As is so often the case, the solution one prefers will depend on one's choice of statistics and on the expectations one started with. In the Carlson et al. (1985) study, for example, even after the care and sophistication of treatment we expect from ETS, the correlations, uncorrected for reader unreliability but with some reader unreliability washed out because they worked with "total score," still account for only about 50% of the variance in writer performance across topics (that is, topics correlated at about .7 both within and across topic types). While these figures are typical of good writing assessment programs, they are not very robust.

The "topic variable" is itself a complex of variables, since, for example, the expected content not only can vary but always will; the input provided can vary from only a two-line task to a well-supported task (Pollitt et al. 1985) to a task with plentiful resources provided (Hamp-Lyons 1986); and the mode and the kind of response expected can also vary (Ruth and Murphy 1988). Clearly, topic variation is of particular importance, outside of writing assessment itself, to the proponents of English for specific purposes (ESP), for whom the genres of writing tasks and examination questions are of both theoretical and practical interest (see, for example, Swales 1982; Horowitz 1986b). Further, it is a central tenet of ESP that second language learners will be advantaged, linguistically and academically, by programs of language teaching and testing that focus on their disciplinary knowledge. There are few studies which attempt to show empirically that this is the case, although Alderson and Urquhart (1983) provide tentative evidence for such a conclusion in the testing of reading for specific purposes. Hamp-Lyons (1986) set out to test this question empirically for the direct test of "specific purpose writing," which is part of the British Council's English Language Testing Service (ELTS), and found that the situation was too complex for all variables to be controlled and measured. After comparing performances on matched prompts in each writer's discipline with performance on a general prompt, she found more confusion than pattern in the topic effects. She concluded that there was no evidence in the test being investigated to suggest such an advantage, but was unable to say whether this was because no such advantage could exist, or because of problems with the test being investigated. Tedick (in press) investigated a general topic and a discipline-specific topic, and found that students wrote significantly better on the topic in their own discipline, but the use of only two prompts makes generalizability difficult.

Other task variables that have been found empirically to affect L1 writers' performance include purpose (Witte et al. in press); audience (Smith and Swan 1977; Crowhurst and Piche 1979; Rubin and Piche 1979); mode of discourse (Kincaid 1953, Rosen 1969; Perron 1977; Crowhurst and Piche 1979; Freedman and Pringle 1981; Quellmalz, Capell, and Chou 1982; Freedman and Calfee 1983; Pollitt et al. 1985); culture-related expectations (Shuy and Fasold 1973; Hoover and Politzer 1980; White and Thomas 1980); linguistic difficulty level (O'Donnell 1968; Harpin 1976; Brossell and Hoetker Ash 1984; Pollitt et al. 1985); and rhetorical specification (Brossell 1983). Audience, purpose, and mode of discourse are all response expectations – that is, they ask something of the writer, and are thus interactive between writer and task. None of the foregoing studies is with L2 writers: Hirokawa and Swales (1986) looked at effects of modification of formality level of language in the questions on the Academic English Evaluation (AEE), a test given to ESL entrants to the University of Michigan, but their study was small and they found no significant differences. There has, then, been no real investigation of the effect of task variables on the measured writing quality of ESL writers on direct tests of writing.

Researchers have not gone very far yet in attempting to determine what makes questions on essay tests difficult, in L1 or in L2 studies. The work of Ruth and Murphy (1984, 1988) takes a constructivist position: that is, the view that difficulty resides almost wholly in the writer as opposed to the task. In contrast, Pollitt et al. (1985) believe it is possible to identify and predict sources of difficulty in tasks. Currently there is increasing interest in the use of latent trait analysis, usually one of the Rasch analysis family of item-response theory methods, to achieve a statement of the difficulty of essay test items that is not influenced by a person's ability (e.g., Henning and Davidson 1987; Pollitt and Hutchinson 1987). (For a clear introduction to the use of item-response theory in language testing, see Woods and Baker 1985). In the future we may find help in text structure research (e.g., Kozminsky 1977; Meyer 1975; Meyer and Rice, 1982) and document design research (e.g., Swartz, Flowers, and Hayes 1980; Wright 1981), but before that we need a number of rigorous studies that would identify topic-related performance differences, if such exist, and replicate results.

The writer

It is a sad irony that in writing assessment research there is a real tendency for the writer to be forgotten in the difficulties and controversies surrounding such issues as topic choice, construct validity versus reliability, and the like. If there is any justification for this in L1 writing assessment research (which I personally cannot see), there is surely none in L2 writing assessment research. Second language learners are tremendously varied in language background, socioeconomic status, cultural integration, and a spectrum of other factors, all of which should be accounted for in an assessment that is to be humanistically, if not to say psychometrically, defensible.

Every writer's performance varies from occasion to occasion, but there is at present no developed classification of writer variables separate from variables associated with the task, the reader, or the scoring procedure. Audience, purpose, and mode of discourse are examples of response expectations, and the test setter (the classroom teacher or the professional tester) also has response expectations – but these expectations must be fulfilled by the writer. Ballard and Clanchy (in press) and Basham and Kwachka (in press) show how difficult it is for the nonnative writer of English, or the writer who is a user of English as a second dialect, to grasp these expectations. Research with minority users of English, for example by Toelken (1975) and Hale-Benson (1986), suggests that even when these students understand intellectually what is expected, anomie, or cultural imperatives, make it hard for them to conform. To complicate this matter further, teachers do not yet possess the knowledge of culturally determined writing behaviors to be able to teach students what to change in their writing in order to conform to expectations, should they wish to do so – indeed, it is still not generally accepted that written text production is in part culturally determined (Kaplan 1987; Hamp-Lyons 1989). Brossell (1986) pinpoints the problem when he says:

All writers are influenced in writing assessments by innumerable factors related to background and personality. Elements of culture, gender, ethnicity, language, psychology and experience all bear upon the way different people respond to a writing task. Unfortunately, the current level of knowledge about such influences does not allow us to understand the precise ways in which human factors affect writers and their performance on writing assessments. (p. 175)

The situation is made even more complex by the fact that the reader of writing in a writing assessment context is typically not the setter of the test. The reader is coming in on a dialogue of sorts between test setter and writer, and is bringing his or her own expectations (Hamp-Lyons 1988b).

Only recently have we come to understand that all writing, even expository writing on timed essay tests, is personal. Each writer brings the whole of himself or herself to the task at hand. In interpreting a task and creating a response to it, each writer must create a "fit" between his or her world and the world of the essay test topic. There has been very little work done in this area, but Weaver's (1973) work suggests that each writer needs to take the other-initiated test task and transform it into a "self-initiated" topic – that is, make it his or her own. In order to match writer response to test expectations, the writer must follow the steps of attending to, understanding, and valuing the task. If this breaks down, the writer will replace the task with a different or a related one, but will not respond to the topic intended. Hamp-Lyons (1988b) calls this a "challenge" and points out the difficulty that responses like these create in scoring. Work in this area of discourse analysis is just beginning, and it will make little progress until serious ethnographic research into the writer's encounter with the test is conducted, as has been begun in other spheres of L2 language assessment by, for example, Cohen and Cavalcanti (this volume) and Spolsky (1988).

An aspect of writing proficiency that is receiving increasing attention fits with the view of "writer as thinker." Many teachers are currently involved in writing-across-the-curriculum programs and are accustomed to stressing the role of writing in developing critical thinking. There is real interest in models of writing assessment that describe the writer on a cognitive development scale. Researchers such as Elbow (1973), Holland (1976), and Pollitt et al. (1985) have applied models of stages or structures of cognitive development such as those of Piaget (1967), Perry (1970), Peel (1971), or Sutherland (1982) to a description of levels of thinking. This work is, however, in its infancy, and as the work of Jacobs (1982) has shown, writers' evident level of cognitive control may fluctuate depending on the difficulty of the task they are engaged in. Thus, it may be that it is not cognitive development that is being revealed through writing but relative cognitive load of a particular task for a particular individual.

A writer is more, however, than language skills and cognitive capacities. Wilkinson (1983) criticizes models of writing development that are restricted to descriptions of linguistic skills or cognitive abilities; his model includes "affective" and "moral" measures. Ethnographic studies of essay readers (Cooper and Hamp-Lyons 1988; Hamp-Lyons 1989) have shown that readers make judgments about affective and moral facets of the writer: They "read the writer" as they read the text, unless carefully trained not to do so. Wilkinson's inclusion of these dimensions in the judgment process may, then, ease some of the tension engendered in the reader by being barred from incorporating these facets into judgments. Less controversial, perhaps, is the social dimension on writing tests; it can be seen, for example, that black students are frequently disadvantaged by traditional writing tests (White and Thomas 1981). But at present we have almost no understanding of who the writers are whose performance we measure, or of what the interaction is between who they are and what we can expect of them on a writing test.

The scoring procedure

Many educators have objected over the years to direct testing of writing because human evaluators are used and the possibility of human error exists. But this objection (for example, by Moller 1982 and Cooper 1984) is not to the testing itself but to the scoring procedure. Of the three processes common to all tests of writing, (1) *the construction of questions* is clearly subjective, and carried out by humans; (2) *answering questions* is also clearly subjective and carried out by humans, even when human responses are limited by "objective" items; and only (3) *scoring* has both subjective and objective possibilities. Even then, "objective" scoring can be carried out only when humans have decided what the correct answers are. Behind this objection, then, is the imperative that, all else being subjective and uncertain, objectivity should at least be found in the one area where it is theoretically possible.

Even scoring, however, has its complexities. Perkins (1980) provides a useful discussion of scoring procedures. The design of a scoring procedure is, like everything else in testing, a human and therefore a fallible endeavor (see Charney 1984 for an excellent discussion). The best-known scoring procedure for ESL writing at the present time is the ESL Composition Profile (Jacobs et al. 1981), which uses a scale with four steps to judge five different traits, each trait being differentially weighted, with scores reported both separately and in combination. Often, however, programs want to make finer distinctions between levels of writing performance. The scale used for the Test of Written English, which is becoming widely known, has six steps, in accordance with common practice in such major U.S. postsecondary institutions as the City University of New York system, the University of Michigan, and the University of California system. The ASLPR (Australian Second Language Proficiency Ratings) and the ELTS writing test both have scales with nine steps, and the MELAB scale has ten steps.

A true holistic reading of an essay involves reading for an individual impression of the quality of the writing, by comparison with all other writing the reader sees on that occasion. Holistic reading is based on the view that there are inherent qualities of written text which are greater than the sum of the text's countable elements, and that this quality can be recognized only by carefully selected and trained readers, not by any objectifiable means. And yet study after study, the best-known of which is Diederich, French, and Carlton (1961), has found that the judgments made by essay readers under these conditions are unreliable, and that considerable effort must be expended to establish and maintain reliable judgment. Charney (1984) describes the methods usually used for keeping readers in line as "peer pressure, monitoring, and (insistence upon) rating speed" (p. 73). The essay reading system used for the Test of Written English is a modified form of holistic scoring, and the six-step scale has a carefully developed description of performance at each level (Stansfield 1986), as do the MELAB and the ASLPR, while the ELTS, like the ESL Composition Profile, has five separate scoring traits. Using training and daily standardization, which are carried out in large groups of readers without discussion of the reasons for the assignment of individual scores by individual readers, Carlson et al (1985: 57) reported correlations between different readers of the same essay in the TWE research of between .66 and .74 for the same topic. On the MELAB, which is scored by a very small group of readers who read compositions most working days, interrater correlations average above .90.

All reputable writing assessment programs use more than one reader to judge essays – usually two, with a third in case of extreme disagreement, as is the case with the TWE and the ESL Composition Profile (Jacobs et al. 1981), but sometimes more (the Joint Matriculation Board, Manchester, England uses four readers with a fifth in difficult cases). The ELTS has only one reader, due to the difficulty of finding qualified readers in British Council locations around the world and the demand for immediate reporting of results (J. Charles Alderson, personal communication). The rationale generally given for multiple scoring is that multiple judgments lead to a final score that is closer to a "true" score than any single judgment. Yet cases often occur where two readers reach very different judgments: Reader A may assign a score of 2 on a six-point scale, for example, while Reader F may assign a score of 5. If the two scores are averaged, a score of 3.5 will be reported. Yet we can quickly see that 3.5 bears no resemblance to either of the *actual* scores assigned. What often happens in these cases (on the TWE and MELAB, for example) is that a third reader is brought in. The three scores can be handled in different ways: All three may be averaged, or only the two closest scores may be averaged. Let us say that in the foregoing example the third reader, Reader P, gives a score of 3: the reported score may be 2.5 (average of two closest scores) or 3 (average of all three scores, rounded to nearest whole number). In either case, how do we know that the result is in fact a "true" score? In both cases, Reader F's score is effectively discounted; yet reader F is a trained reader whose scores on other essays are treated as valid. Indeed, Reader F may be the third reader of some other essays over which two readers have disagreed. This is a problem, at the intersection of psychometrics and philosophy, that research in writing assessment has so far left unsolved.

If we accept the argument that opened this section, that judgments must be made by human specialists, it should follow that these people are able to do what it is claimed they do. The evidence suggests that, left to their own judgments, they cannot. They cannot agree on the absolute quality or the relative quality of essays, nor can they agree on the specific qualities in essays that make them good, worse, or worst. If their judgments correlate at .70, they are agreeing only 49% of the time; the correlations may be statistically significant, but they leave a good deal of behavior by the two essay readers unexplained. Clearly, we are a long way yet from being able to characterize what it is that we claim to do, explain how and why we are able to do it, and then do it consistently. Cooper and Hamp-Lyons (1988) and Condon and Hamp-Lyons (in press) each attempt to do so for different kinds of writing assessment, but each is only able to make a start. The field of writing assessment, in second and in first language, has not reached that point yet. This is a validity problem as well as a reliability problem. Since we as researchers cannot consistently agree with each other when assessing the same writing samples or even sometimes with our own judgments about the same samples made on different occasions, we cannot be looking at the same thing. That is, we do not share a construct of writing quality. It seems that writing quality is not a simple construct, and until we arrive at scoring procedures that respect that fact we will continue to have both validity and reliability problems.

All of the scoring procedures discussed here are intended to rate the same thing: proficiency in writing. This should mean that they all yield comparable scores, or at least comparable rankings. To the extent that rankings differ, either different constructs are being measured, or measurement error is intervening. In my view, both of these intrusions into valid, reliable writing assessment are occurring. Our constructs of good writing are inadequate and incomplete, and we have severe measurement error in our tests. Our mistake to date has been in focusing our attention on the scoring procedure as the source of measurement error or accuracy; as we shall now see, the reader, the human instrument, is the source of much error.

The reader

As long ago as 1961, Diederich et al. showed that different readers responded to different facets of writing, and did so with some internal consistency. Vaughan (in press), using ethnographic methods and looking at the scoring of L2 writing, made similar findings. Hamp-Lyons (1989) found that essay readers responded to cultural differences in essays, and did so differentially in ways that appeared to be partially attributable to their experiential backgrounds and to their response to the students' linguistic/rhetorical backgrounds. Vann, Lorenz, and Meyer (in press) found that faculty's responses to error in L2 writing could be partially attributed to their discipline and sex, and also to the amount of exposure they had to the writing of nonnative users of English. Newcomb (1977) also found that rater behavior varied and could to some degree be predicted by background variables, such as sex, race, and geographic origin within the United States. Hake (1973) showed that where raters deviated from their own typical response patterns, these deviations could be explained by affective interactions between the rater and the text.

Findings such as these have led to the emphasis on reader training that is now an accepted part of any rigorous writing assessment program. Among the surprisingly few studies of rater training effects are Stalnaker (1934), Newcomb (1977), and Freedman (1979). Most studies, such as Jacobs et al. (1981) and Carlson et al. (1985), do not set up a pre- and posttraining design. It is clear that we need to understand a great deal more than we do at present about the way training should be conducted, what aims it should have, the interaction between the values embodied in training and the values implicit in the task, and the criteria (defined or implied). The work of Robinson (1985) and Vaughan (in press) questions the commonly heard claim that training is effective in bringing readers' responses together. Indications are that the situation is not that simple: The context in which training occurs, the type of training given, the extent to which training is monitored, the extent to which reading is monitored, and the feedback given to readers all play an important part in maintaining both the reliability and the validity of the scoring of essays.

An integrated approach to writing assessment

This brief overview of some of the key issues in L2 writing assessment will illustrate that there are no easy answers. Each aspect – task, writer, scoring procedure, and reader – interacts with the others, creating a complex network of effects which to date has eluded our efforts to control. We will not, I believe, solve the problems of writing assessment until we look at this total picture rather than each facet in isolation. This overview is not exhaustive: My recent research with the Michigan Writing Assessment, a writing test given to all entering undergraduates, including ESL writers, at the University of Michigan, indicates that the social context is important, too: who the group of readers are on a particular day, whether essays are read by instructors in the writing program or by skilled outsiders, how "invested" in a particular stance a reader feels – the list could go on and on. We must use a context-embedded approach, capitalizing on what has so far been seen as the central problem of writing assessment – the fact that in all its stages it is a wholly human endeavor. We need to collect process data as tests are designed and developed, as teams or individuals make decisions about task types and specific tasks, and about scoring procedures, criteria, and score reporting – for test development and validation is a process as any other. We need to collect process data as writers prepare themselves for a writing test, encounter it, and make their response, if we are to understand why they arrive at particular products – for test taking is a process as any other. We need to collect process data as readers are trained to judge essays and as they make decisions about written products and shape their judgments to the parameters of the instrument they are applying – for rating essays is a process as any other. As these studies provide us with insights, we will learn what questions we should be asking, what hypotheses we should be testing, and what else we should know about what has previously been excluded from our perception of the legitimate arena for investigation of writing assessment. As always when we apply the magnifying lens to a phenomenon, we shall learn that what seemed simple is complex, what seemed tidy is in fact a mass of untied ends. But as we tug on those ends the mystery should unravel for us, and we can learn to put back together what we have pulled apart. This is the lesson we are just beginning to learn in studying second language writing acquisition through process methodologies. We need to apply what we have learned to studying writing assessment.

References

Alderson, J. C., and Urquhart, A. (1983). The effects of students' background discipline on comprehension: A pilot study. In A. Hughes and D. Porter (Eds.), *Current developments in language testing* (pp. 121–127). New York: Academic Press.

Applebee, A. (1982). Writing and learning in school settings. In M. Nystrand (Ed.), *What writers know: The language, process and structure of written discourse* (pp. 365–382). New York: Academic Press.

Ballard, B., and Clanchy, J. (In press). Assessment by misconception: Cultural influences and intellectual traditions. In L. Hamp-Lyons (Ed.), *Assessing second language writing in academic contexts.* Norwood, N.J.: Ablex.

Basham, C., and Kwachka, P. (In press). Reading the world differently: A cross-cultural approach to writing assessment. In L. Hamp-Lyons (Ed.), *Assessing second language writing in academic contexts.* Norwood, N.J.: Ablex.

Braddock, R.; Lloyd-Jones, R.; and Schoer, L. (1963). *Research in written composition.* Urbana, Ill.: National Council of Teachers of English.

Bridgeman, B., and Carlson, S. (1983). *Survey of academic writing tasks required of graduate and undergraduate foreign students.* TOEFL Research Report No. 15. Princeton, N.J.: Educational Testing Service.

Britton, J.; Burgess, T.; Martin, N.; McLeod, A.; and Rosen, H. (1975). *The development of writing abilities (11–18).* London: Macmillan.

Brossell, G. (1983). Rhetorical specification in essay examination topics. *College English, 45,* 165–174.

(1986). Current research and unanswered questions in writing assessment. In K. Greenberg, H. Wiener, and R. Donovan (Eds.), *Writing assessment: Issues and strategies* (pp. 168–182). New York: Longman.

Brossell, G., and Hoetker Ash, B. (1984). An experiment with the wording of essay topics. *College Composition and Communication, 35,* 423–425.

Carlson, S.; Bridgeman, B.; Camp, R.; and Waanders, J. (1985). *Relationship of admission test scores to writing performance of native and nonnative speakers of English.* TOEFL Research Reports No. 19. Princeton, N.J.: Educational Testing Service.

Charney, D. (1984). The validity of using holistic scoring to evaluate writing. *Research in the Teaching of English, 18,* 65–81.

Condon, W., and Hamp-Lyons, L. (In press). Portfolios: Progress through problems. In P. Belanoff and M. Dickson (Eds.), *Portfolio grading: Process and product.* Upper Montclair, N.J.: Boynton/Cook Heinemann.

Cooper, G., and Hamp-Lyons, L. (1988). *Looking in on essay readers.* Ann Arbor: University of Michigan English Composition Board.

Cooper, P. (1984). *The assessment of writing ability: A review of research.* Research Report 84–12. Princeton, N.J.: Educational Testing Service.

Criper, C., and Davies, A. (1988). *ELTS: Research reports 1 (i): Final report of the ELTS Validation Project.* London: British Council.

Crowhurst, M., and Piche, G. (1979). Audience and mode of discourse effects on syntactic complexity in writing at two grade levels. *Research in the Teaching of English, 13,* 101–110.

Diederich, P. B.; French, J.; and Carlton, S. (1961). *Factors in judgments of writing ability.* ETS Research Bulletin RB–61–15. Princeton, N.J.: Educational Testing Service.

Elbow, P. (1973) *Writing without teachers.* New York: Oxford University Press.

Flahive, D., and Snow, B. G. (1980). Measures of syntactic complexity in evaluating ESL composition. In J. Oller and K. Perkins (Eds.), *Research in language testing* (pp. 171–176). Rowley, Mass.: Newbury House.

Freedman, S. W. (1979). How characteristics of student essays influence teachers' evaluations. *Journal of Educational Psychology, 71,* 328–338.

Freedman, S. W., and Calfee, R. C. (1983). Holistic assessment of writing: Experimental design and cognitive theory. In P. Mosenthal, L. Tamor, and S. Walmsley (Eds.), *Research in writing: Principles and methods* (pp. 75–98). New York: Longman.

Freedman, A., and Pringle, I. (1981). Writing in the college years: Some indices of growth. *College Composition and Communication, 31,* 311–324.

Hake, R. (1973). Composition theory in identifying and evaluating essay writing. Unpublished doctoral dissertation, University of Chicago.

Hale-Benson, J. (1986). *Black children, their roots, culture and learning styles,* rev. ed. Provo, Utah: Brigham Young University Press.

Hamp-Lyons, L. (1986). Testing second language writing in academic settings. Unpublished doctoral dissertation, University of Edinburgh.

(1987). Performance profiles for academic writing. In K. Bailey, R. Clifford, and E. Dale (Eds.), *Language testing research* (pp. 78–92). Monterey, Cal.: Defense Language Institute.

(1988a). Proficiency, profiling and M2. In D. Porter (Ed.), *ELTS: Research reports 1 (ii): Proceedings of the Invitational Conference on the ELTS Validation Project.* London: British Council.

(1988b). The product before: Task-related influences on the writer. In P. Robinson (Ed.), *Academic writing: Process and product* (pp. 35–46). London: Macmillan/British Council.

(1989). Raters respond to rhetoric in writing. In H. Dechert and G. Raupach (Eds.), *Interlingual processes,* (pp. 229–244). Tubingen: Gunter Narr Verlag.

(In press). Reconstructing "academic writing proficiency." In L. Hamp-Lyons (Ed.), *Assessing second language writing in academic contexts.* Norwood, N.J.: Ablex.

Harpin, W. (1976). *The second "R": Writing development in the Junior school.* London: Allen & Unwin.

Hartog, P. (1936). English composition at the School Certificate Examination; and the "Write anything about something for anybody" theory. In M. Sadler et al. (Eds.), *Essays on examinations.* London: Macmillan.

Hartog, P. et al. (1941). *The marking of English essays.* London: Macmillan.

Henning, G., and Davidson, F. (1987). Scalar analysis of composition ratings. In K. Bailey, R. Clifford, and E. Dale (Eds.), *Language testing research* (pp. 24–38). Monterey, Cal.: Defense Language Institute.

Hirokawa, K., and Swales, J. M. (1986). The effects of modifying the formality level of ESL composition questions. *TESOL Quarterly, 20,* 343–345.

Hirsch, E. D., and Harrington, D. P. (1981). Measuring the communicative effectiveness of prose. In C. Frederikson and J. Dominic (Eds.), *Writing: The nature, development and teaching of written communication*. Vol. 2: *Writing: Process, development and communication* (pp. 189–207). Hillsdale, N.J.: Erlbaum.

Holland, R. M. (1976). Piagetian theory and the design of composing assignments. *Arizona English Bulletin, 19,* 17–22.

Hoover, M., and Politzer, R. L. (1980). Bias in composition tests with suggestions for a culturally appropriate assessment technique. In M. Farr Whiteman (Ed.), *Writing: The nature, development and teaching of written communication*. Vol 1: *Variation in writing*. (pp. 197–204). Hillsdale, N.J.: Erlbaum.

Horowitz, D. (1986a). Essay examination prompts and the teaching of academic writing. *English for Specific Purposes, 5,* 107–120.

(1986b). What professors actually require: Academic tasks for the ESL classroom. *TESOL Quarterly, 20,* 445–462.

Jacobs, H.; Zinkgraf, S.; Wormuth, D.; Hartfiel V. F. ; and Hughey, J. (1981). *Testing ESL composition: A practical approach*. Rowley, Mass.: Newbury House.

Jacobs, S. (1982). *Composing and coherence*. Washington, D.C.: Center for Applied Linguistics.

Johns, A. (1981). Necessary English: An academic survey. *TESOL Quarterly, 15,* 51–57.

Kaplan, R. (1987). Cultural thought patterns revisited. In U. Connor and R. B. Kaplan (Eds.), *Writing across languages: Analysis of L2 text* (pp. 9–22). Reading, Mass.: Addison-Wesley.

Keller-Cohen, D., and Wolfe, A. (1987). *Extending writing in the college of literature, science and the arts: Report on a faculty survey*. Ann Arbor: University of Michigan English Composition Board.

Kincaid, G. L. (1953). Some factors affecting variations in the quality in student writing. Unpublished doctoral dissertation, Michigan State University.

Kozminsky, E. (1977). Altering comprehension: The effect of biasing titles on text comprehension. *Memory and Cognition, 5,* 482–490.

Kroll, B. (1979). A survey of the writing needs of foreign and American college freshmen. *English Language Teaching Journal, 33,* 219–226.

Meyer, B. (1975). *The organization of prose and its effect on recall*. New York: North Holland.

Meyer, B., and Rice, G. E. (1982). The interaction of reader strategies and the organization of text. *Text, 2,* 155–192.

Moller, A. (1982). A study in the validation of proficiency tests of English as a foreign language. Unpublished doctoral dissertation, University of Edinburgh.

Mullen, K. (1980). Evaluating writing proficiency in ESL. In J. Oller and K. Perkins (Eds.), *Research in language testing* (pp. 91–101). Rowley, Mass.: Newbury House.

Newcomb, J. S. (1977). The influence of readers on the holistic grading of essays. Unpublished doctoral dissertation, University of Michigan.

O'Donnell, W. (1968). *An investigation in the role of language in a physics examination*. Monograph No. 7, Moray House Publications. Edinburgh: Oliver & Boyd.

Peel, E. A. (1971). *The nature of adolescent judgment*. London: Staples Press.

Perkins, K. (1980). Using objective methods of attained writing proficiency to discriminate among holistic evaluations. *TESOL Quarterly, 14,* 61–70.

Perron, J. D. (1977). *The impact of mode on written syntactic complexity, Parts 1–3.* Studies in Language Education: Reports 24, 25, 27. Athens: Department of Language Education, University of Georgia.

Perry, W. C. (1970). *Forms of intellectual and ethical development in the college years.* New York: Holt, Rinehart & Winston.

Piaget, J. (1967). *Six Psychological Studies,* trans. A. Tenger and D. Elkind. New York: Random House.

Pitcher, B. and Ra, J. B. (1967). *The relation between scores on the TOEFL and ratings of actual theme writing.* Statistical Report 67–9. Princeton, N.J.: Educational Testing Service.

Poetker, J. S. (1977). Practical suggestions for improving and using essay questions. *High School Journal, 61,* 7–15.

Pollitt, A.; Hutchinson, C.; Entwhistle, N.; and DeLuca, C. (1985). *What makes exam questions difficult? An analysis of 'O' grade questions and answers.* Research Report for Teachers No. 2. Edinburgh: Scottish Academic Press.

Pollitt, A., and Hutchinson, C. (1987). *The Dunning Credit Level Project subject report: English.* Edinburgh: Godfrey Thompson Research Unit.

Quellmalz, E.; Capell, F.; and Chou, C.-P. (1982). Effects of discourse and response mode on the measurement of writing competence. *Journal of Educational Measurement, 19,* 241–258.

Robinson, T. (1985). Evaluating foreign students' compositions: The effects of rater background and of handwriting, spelling and grammar. Unpublished doctoral dissertation, University of Texas at Austin.

Rosen, H. (1969). An investigation of the effects of differentiated writing assignments on the performance in English composition of a selected group of 15/16 year old pupils. Unpublished doctoral dissertation, University of London.

Rubin, D., and Piche, G. (1979). Development in syntactic and strategic aspects of audience adaptation skills in written persuasive communication. *Research in the Teaching of English, 18,* 293–316.

Ruth, L., and Murphy, S. (1984). Designing topics for writing assessment: Problems of meaning. *College Composition and Communication, 35,* 410–422.

   (1988). *Designing writing tasks for the assessment of writing.* Norwood, N.J.: Ablex.

Shuy, R., and Fasold, R. (1973). *Language attitudes: Current trends and prospects.* Washington, D.C.: Georgetown University Press.

Smith, W., and Swan, B. (1977). Adjusting syntactic structures to varied levels of audience. *Journal of Experimental Education, 46,* 29–34.

Spaan, M. (1989). Essay tests: What's in a prompt? Paper presented at the 23rd Annual TESOL Convention, San Antonio, Texas, March.

Spolsky, B. (1988). Facilitating accurate self-assessment of functional language skills. Paper presented at the 10th Annual Language Testing Research Colloquium, Urbana, Illinois, March.

Stalnaker, J. M. (1934). The construction and results of a twelve-hour test in English composition. *School and Society, 39,* 218–224.

Stansfield, C. (1986). A history of the Test of Written English: The developmental year. *Language Testing, 3,* 224–234.

Sutherland, P. A. A. (1982). An expansion of Peel's describer-explainer stage theory. *Educational Review, 36*, 69–76.

Swales, J. (1982). Examining examination papers. *English Language Research Journal, 3*, 9–25.

Swartz, H.; Flower, L.; and Hayes, J. (1980). *How headings in documents can mislead readers.* Technical Report No. 9, Document Design Project. Pittsburgh, Pa.: Carnegie Mellon University.

Tedick, D. (In press). ESL writing assessment: Topic *does* make a difference. *ESP Journal.*

Toelken, B. (1975). Folklore, worldview, and communication. In D. Ben-Amos and K. Goldstein (Eds.), *Folklore: Performance and communication* (pp. 265–286). The Hague: Mouton.

Vann, R.; Lorenz, F.; and Meyer, D. (In press). Error gravity: Faculty response to errors in the written discourse of nonnative users of English. In L. Hamp-Lyons (Ed.), *Assessing second language writing in academic contexts.* Norwood, N.J.: Ablex.

Vaughan, C. (In press). Holistic assessment: What goes on in our minds? In L. Hamp-Lyons (Ed.), *Assessing second language writing in academic contexts.* Norwood, N.J.: Ablex.

Weaver, F. (1973). The composing processes of English teacher candidates: Responding to freedom and constraint. Unpublished doctoral dissertation, University of Illinois.

Weir, C. (1983). Identifying the language problems of overseas students in tertiary education in the United Kingdom. Unpublished doctoral dissertation, University of London.

White, E., and Thomas, L. L. (1980). Racial minorities and writing skills assessment in the California state university and colleges. *College English, 43*, 276–283.

Wilkinson, A. (1983). Assessing language development: The Credition Project. In A. Freedman, I. Pringle, and J. Yalden (Eds.), *Learning to write: First language/second language* (pp. 67–86). New York: Longman.

Wiseman, S. (1949). The marking of English compositions in grammar school selection. *British Journal of Educational Psychology, 19*, 200–209.

Wiseman, S., and Wrigley, J. (1958). Essay reliability: The effect of choice of essay title. *Educational and Psychological Measurement, 18*, 129–138.

Witte, S.; Meyer, P.; Cherry, R.; and Trachsel, M. (In press). *Holistic evaluation: Issues, theory, and practice.* New York: Guilford Press.

Woods, A., and Baker, R. (1985). Item response theory. *Language Testing, 2*, 119–140.

Wright, P. (1981). Five skills technical writers need. *IEEE Transactions on Professional Communication, 24*, 10–16.

6 Reading–writing connections: toward a description for second language learners

Joan Carson Eisterhold

Decisions about English as a second language (ESL) writing class activities are aimed at providing a language environment in which the ESL writer can begin to construct text that is clearly recognizable as written English. Teachers wrestle with the usefulness of classroom work focusing on, for example, transition words, sentence structure, paragraph development, or rhetorical patterns. It is understandable, then, that many of the questions that shape ESL writing classroom practices center on the issue of what constitutes the relevant language input from which second language learners construct their hypotheses about second language (L2) written text. Traditionally the answer has been reading.

Reading in the writing classroom is understood as the appropriate input for acquisition of writing skills because it is generally assumed that reading passages will somehow function as primary models from which writing skills can be learned, or at least inferred. The nature of this reading–writing link, though not well-defined, is often thought to be like Krashen's notions about second language acquisition. In fact, Krashen (1984) claims that the development of writing ability and of second language proficiency occur in the same way: via comprehensible input with a low affective filter. He theorizes that writing competence derives from large amounts of self-motivated reading for interest and/ or pleasure. "It is reading that gives the writer the 'feel' for the look and texture of reader-based prose" (p. 20).

Is there evidence that a relationship between reading and writing exists and, if so, how might it work? Stotsky (1983) surveyed first language correlational studies and found the following:

1. There are correlations between reading achievement and writing ability. Better writers tend to be better readers.
2. There are correlations between writing quality and reading experience as reported through questionnaires. Better writers read more than poorer writers.
3. There seem to be correlations between reading ability and measures of syntactic complexity in writing. Better readers tend to produce more syntactically mature writing than poorer readers.

88

These studies suggest that reading and writing are related, but researchers have only recently begun to explore this connection.

The reading–writing relationship: first language

Studies of the reading–writing relationship suggest three somewhat interrelated hypotheses, which I have chosen to describe as models. The labels that I use to describe the models reflect the direction in which input is understood as transferring from one modality (reading or writing) to the other. This directional perspective is the relevant one for pedagogical concerns, since it helps teachers decide whether reading should precede writing in the classroom or whether writing should precede reading. Thus, casting the models in terms of the direction of transfer highlights this important concern. However, although directionality is the distinguishing characteristic for purposes of labeling, the fundamental differences among the models have to do with the way cognitive processes and mechanisms are involved in the transfer.

The directional hypothesis

The first hypothesis to be considered is that the reading–writing connection is *directional*. That is, reading and writing share structural components such that the structure of whatever is acquired in one modality can then be applied in the other. For example, being able to recognize a rhetorical pattern such as comparison and contrast in a reading passage would presumably allow the reader to eventually reproduce that pattern in writing. What marks the directional model is that this transfer of structural information can proceed in only one direction.

The most common directional model is the reading-to-writing model. The claim here is that reading influences writing, but that writing knowledge is not particularly useful in reading. This is the model typical of many instructional programs. The reading-to-writing model receives support from research such as Eckhoff's (1983) study, in which children's writing was found to reflect the structures and styles of basal readers used in class. Further support for the reading-to-writing direction comes from Taylor and Beach (1984), who looked at the effects of instruction in using text structure to recall expository text and instruction that emphasized writing expository text. They found that instruction in writing influenced neither writing nor reading, but that instruction in reading influenced both.

Additional information about the reading-to-writing directional model comes from Stotsky's (1983) survey of research on reading–writing relationships. The studies she reviewed showed that additional reading was more effective in improving writing than either grammar exercises or extra writing practice. However, contrary to the Taylor and Beach findings, improving writing through reading instruction was found to be generally ineffective. Belanger's (1987) review of reading–writing connections shows that this apparent contradiction might be explained by studies that yielded significant results when students were taught reading strategies by examining structures applicable to both reading and writing (e.g., sentence and paragraph analysis, story schemata, hierarchical summaries). Thus, instruction in reading can be effective in improving writing, but only when it focuses on a common element. However, Belanger also found that there seemed to be no automatic transfer from general reading improvement courses to written composition.

As for a writing-to-reading directional model, Stotsky (1983) found a number of studies that suggest that writing activities can be useful for improving reading comprehension and retention of information (e.g., summarizing, paraphrasing, and outlining). Belanger (1987) further cites studies that show that direct instruction in sentence, paragraph, and discourse structure for writing result in significant improvement in reading.

This research evidence seems to support a directional model in which reading and writing are hypothesized to share structural components that can be acquired in one domain and then applied in the other. However, because most of the transfer involved in these studies required instruction, it cannot be claimed that transfer of structural components from one domain to the other is necessarily automatic.

The nondirectional hypothesis

The second hypothesis of the reading–writing link is that the relationship is *nondirectional*. In this interactive model, reading and writing are said to derive from a single underlying proficiency, the common link being that of the cognitive process of constructing meaning. Shanklin (1982) claims that if reading and writing are both constructive processes, constrained by some underlying competence, then they must be related. She argues that writing, like reading, is a process of "interactive and dynamic activation, instantiation and refinement of schemata" (p. 89). Shanahan (1984) notes that "if reading and writing involve analogous cognitive structures and processes, it is possible that instruction in one would lead to increased ability in the other" (p. 467). Unlike the directional model, transfer in the nondirectional model can occur in either direction. Since there is a single cognitive proficiency underlying both reading and writing, improvement in one domain will result in improvement in the other. Note that the initial significant difference between the directional and the nondirectional models is the claim that skills can transfer in only one direction (reading to writing or writing to reading) for the directional model versus the claim that skills can transfer in either direction for the nondirectional model.

Most of the research on the reading–writing connection has assumed a directional hypothesis, but there is some evidence for the nondirectional, or interactive, model as well. Gordon and Braun's (1982) study investigated the effects for fifth graders of story schema training on reading and writing. They found that the experimental group recalled more text structure (e.g., setting, theme, plot), more text structures in new selections (i.e., it is transferable), and produced more text structure categories in writing. "Present results show that when an instructional method is designed to deliberately enhance and facilitate transfer, children readily apply story schema to related reading and writing tasks" (Gordon and Braun 1982: 267). Their primary claim is that there is a need for explicit instruction to facilitate transfer. However, the fact that this transfer does occur across modalities provides indirect evidence for a nondirectional model.

Hiebert, Englert, and Brennan (1983) investigated the relationship between the recognition and production of different text structures (description, sequence, enumeration, and comparison and contrast) by college students. They found that the reading–writing relationship was significant for all the text structures but description. Furthermore, students' writing performance (they were asked to generate details compatible with a prevailing text) was a better predictor of reading achievement than the ability to recognize details (the reading measure). Thus, sensitivity to text structure was highly related to performance on comprehension measures. Students understood better if they were able to recognize the text structure. This suggests that

> subjects' sensitivity to text structures in the recognition task and their sensitivity to text structures in the production task are moderately related. Although the correlations between the two measures were not strong ones, the ability to recognize related details consistent with topic and text structure in a written passage was related to the ability to generate related details congruent with the topic and text structure in a writing task. Thus, similar knowledge bases about text structures could be hypothesized to underlie reading and writing. (Hiebert et al. 1983: 77)

These studies that seem to support a nondirectional model could, in fact, also be used to support a directional model, since it is the transfer of structural components across domains that researchers claim as evidence for a common cognitive proficiency underlying both reading and writing. However, in a directional model, what is transferred from reading to writing or from writing to reading is understood to be a separate system or knowledge base that is acquired in one domain (reading, for example) and then is transferred to the other (in this case, writing). In a nondirectional model, what is transferred from reading to writing and from writing to reading is understood to be a single underlying system or shared knowledge base that is acquired in either domain (reading or writing) and then is transferred to the other (writing or reading). Thus, although the initial input of information for the reader/writer proceeds similarly in both models (either from reading or from writing), the resulting structures are understood differently depending on the model.

The bidirectional hypothesis

According to the third hypothesis, the reading–writing relationship is *bidirectional*. This is the most complex model, which includes the claim that reading and writing are interactive, but also claims that they are interdependent as well. In this view, "what is learned at one stage of development can be qualitatively different from what is learned at another stage of development" (Shanahan 1984: 467). Shanahan and Lomax (1986) argue that studies of the reading–writing relationship need to consider it as a "constellation of interrelated processes that utilize a number of knowledge bases" (p. 116). Thus, we need to consider the existence of multiple relations as well as the possibility that the nature of the reading–writing relationship might change with development.

Other research studies appear to offer more direct support for the bidirectional model. Shanahan (1984) found in his study of second and fifth graders that reading and writing were significantly related for both groups. He also found that "as students become more proficient, the nature of the reading–writing relationship changes . . . It appears that at any given point of development, reading and writing consist of both dependent and independent abilities" (p. 475). For second graders, the reading–writing relationship was based on word recognition and spelling ability, but by grade five the relationship was based on reading comprehension and several writing variables, especially organizational structure and vocabulary diversity.

Shanahan and Lomax (1986) found the interactive aspect of the model a better fit for their data at the fifth than at the second grade level. Because subjects generally received more reading than writing instruction, the influence of writing on reading begins to wane in upper grades. Shanahan and Lomax also found that the reading–writing model is superior to the writing–reading model, suggesting that more reading information is used in writing than vice versa.

It appears that learning that accrues from writing will be generalizable to reading only so far as writing competency is somewhat commensurate with reading ability. Similarly, this result underlines the need for theories of the reading–writing relationship that are explicit about the sources of particular types of information (i.e., reading or writing) and the directions in which that information is most likely to be used. (Shanahan and Lomax 1986: 122)

This bidirectional model is the most complex as well as the most comprehensive of the three, and allows for separate subsystems as well as some common underlying proficiencies.

Each of these models – the directional, the nondirectional, and the bidirectional – offers a different focus for the reading–writing relationship, and each focus offers the second language writing teacher a valuable perspective on reading–writing interactions in the writing classroom. The directional model focuses on input – reading to writing or writing to reading – in the development of reading and writing skills and suggests the important role that reading must play as information source in the writing class.[1] The nondirectional model focuses on the common underlying cognitive processes involved in reading and writing. This model suggests the way in which writing abilities develop alongside reading abilities, and argues that classroom practices that focus on constructing meaning – either in reading or in writing – will enhance the development of writing abilities. Finally, the bidirectional model focuses on the multiple relations and interrelated processes that seem to constitute the reading–writing relationship. This model points to the possibility that the reading–writing relationship can be qualitatively different at different stages of development. Thus, although these differences remain at this point unspecified, the existence of multiple relations and interrelated processes gives the writing teacher real confidence in an eclectic approach that includes a variety of activities designed to take advantage of the structural and cognitive similarities in reading and writing. See Silva (this volume) and Johns (this volume) for further discussion of what the second language writing teacher must consider in designing classroom approaches.

The reading–writing relationship: second language issues

Each of the models, then, contributes an important perspective on the reading–writing relationship. But these models are constructed from a first language base and do not take into account the additional complexity of the reading–writing relationship for second language learners already literate in their first language. Hypotheses about the reading–

---

1 For a closer look at the use of reading as a source of information, see Campbell (this volume) for a report on a study comparing how native and nonnative students use information from an assigned background reading in preparing a writing assignment.

writing relationship in first language assume a relatively fully developed oral language system as the basis for the developing writing system. However, L2 learners do not bring with them a fully developed (second) language system as the basis for decoding and encoding written language in their second language. At the same time, literate adult second language learners do bring with them already developed first language literacy skills. Thus, the picture is not one of literacy emerging from and supported by oral language, as it is in first language. Rather, for literate adult second language learners, the picture is one of literacy skills seeking support from a language system which, in the early stages at least, is insufficiently developed to allow those learners the full range of literacy practices to which they are accustomed.

The question of how one learns to write (and/or read) in a second language, however, is not answered by explaining that learners simply map first language (L1) literacy skills onto a developing or developed second language system. The issue of language proficiency underlies the issue of second language literacy acquisition but is by no means the only issue. If it were, then literacy acquisition would simply be synonymous with language acquisition. But because learners can acquire a second (or a first) language without becoming literate in that language, it is clear that literacy acquisition is somehow different from language acquisition. Obviously language, the linguistic system, plays a crucial role in adult L2 literacy acquisition, but it is also the case that language proficiency is a necessary but not sufficient condition for literacy acquisition.

The second language reading–writing relationship, then, must be understood in the context of the larger picture of second language literacy acquisition, which requires an account of the role played by first language literacy skills.[2] Ultimately, to answer the question of how reading and writing are related in the second language we need to consider two questions: (1) Do literacy skills affect the acquisition of L2 literacy? and (2) if so, how might L1 reading and writing skills affect the reading–writing interaction in the second language?

Transfer of literacy skills: first language to second language

In trying to understand the process of literacy acquisition in a second language, we must deal with the fundamental psycholinguistic issue of

2 The role of L1 literacy skills in L2 production is well known in the literature on contrastive rhetoric (see, e.g., Grabe and Kaplan 1989). An additional cross-cultural factor is reported by Hinds (1987), who points out that writers need to know what readers expect in a text, and that this understanding of reader expectations may be culturally based.

transfer – more specifically, the transfer of those abilities that enable second language learners to utilize knowledge from one language in acquiring literacy in another (i.e., how much of what we know about literacy in our first language can we use in becoming literate in our second language?). In focusing on transfer, I am not claiming that developmental processes are unimportant. Rather, I am focusing on the importance of the cognitive abilities that adult second language learners bring to the literacy acquisition task.

The strongest case for transfer of language skills has been made by Cummins's (1981) interdependence hypothesis, which states:

> To the extent that instruction in Lx [i.e., Language x] is effective in promoting proficiency in Lx, transfer of this proficiency to Ly will occur provided there is adequate exposure to Ly (either in school or environment) and adequate motivation to learn Ly. (p. 29)

Cummins's claim is that there is an underlying cognitive/academic proficiency that is common across languages which allows the transfer of literacy-related skills across languages. Thus, learning to be literate in a second language may be affected by literacy capabilities in the first language. However, Cummins also suggests that this transfer capability emerges only after individuals attain a threshold level of proficiency sufficient to permit cognitively demanding language use.

Many studies have supported Cummins's claim, and even though most of the research has been with reading, the generalization, based on Cummins's claim, has been that the same pattern would be seen with writing skills. For example, Mace-Matluck et al. (1983) studied English literacy among students of Cantonese language background and found a significant correlation between the literacy level achieved in English and training in Cantonese literacy prior to English instruction. Goldman, Reyes, and Varnhagen (1984) found that higher order skills involved in comprehending stories in the first language appeared to transfer to comprehension of stories in students' second languages. Canale, Frenette, and Belanger (1988) found that, based on holistic scoring methods, students' L1 and L2 writing was positively correlated, suggesting a common underlying proficiency in writing ability across languages. A study investigating reading–writing relationships for Japanese and Chinese speakers in both the first and second language (Carson et al. 1990) suggests that literacy skills can transfer across languages, but that the pattern of transfer seems to vary depending on the language group.

The issue of language, apart from Cummins's notion of a threshold level of proficiency, must also be addressed, given that literacy and language skills are so closely intertwined. Wald (1987) attempts to sort out literacy and language skills even while he claims that both contribute to literacy in English. His findings were that some of the skills that transcend language, that is, that transferred from the first language, include strategies in written and spoken channels for organizing information coherently, and experience using holistic word recognition strategies in reading (bypassing phonological decoding). Language-specific skills included specific syntactic forms for organizing information and experience in recognition of English words, among other factors.

Thus, although Cummins's notion of a common underlying proficiency has been supported by these and other studies, it is not as simple a picture as it first appears. Language proficiency is a limiting factor, and we must be sensitive to the distinction between language skills and literacy skills. If we are going to say that literacy-related skills transfer after a certain language proficiency has been reached, then we must be able to define literacy skills as opposed to language skills (a fine line) before we are able to say what exactly transfers.

Not all the evidence has supported Cummins's claim for transfer of skills, however. McLaughlin (1987) expected that advanced readers would utilize different, more effective reading strategies than would beginning readers, indicating a continual progression in reading skill as readers developed facility with the language. However, he found that although advanced readers were more capable of making semantic and syntactic predictions, they did not perform significantly better than beginning readers.

McLaughlin's results could be interpreted as refuting Cummins's hypothesis, since the readers with advanced language proficiency (presumably having reached a proficiency threshold) were still unable to utilize effective reading skills. The question to be answered is why these advanced readers were still utilizing decoding strategies in situations where their competencies would have allowed them to apply new strategies directed at meaning. McLaughlin "assumed they read this way [utilizing strategies directed at meaning] in their first language. But they had not yet made the shift in strategies in their second language" (p. 63). These second language learners apparently were not transferring reading skills despite the fact that they were advanced language learners. Carson et al. (1990) also found evidence that writing ability does not transfer easily from first to second language, and this finding calls into question Cummins's generalization that reading and writing are skills that transfer easily and behave similarly.[3]

3 In thinking of writing this way, we may be tempted to understand the L2 writing process as influenced by a more or less "translated" L1 process. However, it is simplistic to assume that the complex process of writing in a second language occurs solely in that language. Friedlander (this volume) reports on a study in which students use their first language in planning their L2 writing, and finds that the use

McLaughlin borrows the notion of restructuring from Rumelhart and Norman (1978) to suggest that learners may need to modify organizational structures at points in the learning process.

Our data suggested that various aspects of second language performance have an emergent quality. Learning at such time involves the modification of organizational structures and the adoption of new strategies and procedures. (McLaughlin 1987: 63)

In restructuring, new structures are added to allow for new interpretation of facts. Restructuring is different both from accretion, adding new facts, and from tuning, modifying categories. The important point that Norman and Rumelhart make is that learning is not a unitary process; some is discontinuous.

The implication of McLaughlin's study for Cummins's interdependence hypothesis is that the language proficiency threshold may be a necessary but not a sufficient condition for transferring literacy skills from the first to a second language. If learners do not "restructure," they may not be able to move beyond limited decoding strategies to more effective and efficient strategies and skills, in spite of their language proficiency.

Freedle (1985) would disagree with Cummins's interdependence hypothesis, making a case against automatic transfer of skills by taking the opposite but equally valid perspective that the task of the language learner is to synthesize language skills that originate as separate entities. According to Freedle, there is no automatic transfer of skills from one domain to another. Rather, language subsystems are represented separately, and this implies separate access to underlying cognitive skills. Freedle hypothesizes a cognitive barrier between language use across varieties and across language modes. Given our limited processing ability coupled with our limited ability to merge information, he says that "it is inevitable that language and the cognitive skills associated with it will show a certain degree of nongeneralizability across what appear to be similar situations and similar tasks" (p. 107). What we have, then, are cognitive barriers between registers that can limit our ability to discover and use structural similarities. As evidence of the nongeneralizability phenomena, Freedle points out that Scribner and Cole (1981) found that the cognitive skills underlying literacy skills in Vai and Arabic appeared not to be identical.

Freedle's position is that because of the fragmentary nature of language systems that arise as functionally discrete entities, language skills are necessarily cognitively separated. However, it is the synthesis of these systems that allows transfer of these skills across systems.

of the first language (in planning) can facilitate rather than inhibit the production of better-quality prose in the second language.

For Freedle, the movement is from the many to the one. Cummins, on the other hand, moves from the one to the many, claiming that separate language proficiencies arise out of a common underlying cognitive proficiency.

The positions that I have outlined here allow for three possibilities for transfer of literacy skills across languages:

1. There exists a common underlying proficiency with a threshold level of language proficiency that allows skills to transfer.
2. There exists an underlying proficiency with a threshold level of language proficiency and a cognitive restructuring that allows skills to transfer.
3. There exist separate language systems with a cognitive separation of language skills. Transfer occurs at the point where two previously separated but structurally similar language routines come together.

It is not the case, however, that these three positions are necessarily mutually exclusive. Whatever theoretical model we adopt to explain transfer phenomena, the following must apply: (1) there must be a mechanism by which we can discover similarities between languages, or synthesize; (2) there must be a mechanism by which we can restructure our experience to allow for new interpretations of second language input; and (3) for the sake of cognitive efficiency, there must be a mechanism that allows strategies and information to be shared across languages.

There is evidence, then, that literacy skills can transfer across languages and across modalities, but it appears that such transfer is not necessarily automatic. Variables that affect the probability of transfer include the interaction of language proficiency with cognitive processes. It appears that language proficiency is a necessary but not a sufficient condition for transfer, and it is possible that transfer results from a combination of a threshold level of proficiency combined with some restructuring in Rumelhart and Norman's sense. Language proficiency is most likely a stronger force in transfer across languages than it is in transfer across modalities. The fact that instruction facilitates transfer across modalities (and that general experience in either reading or writing did not result in automatic transfer) argues for the importance of synthesis of separate literacy skills in both the first and second languages. At the same time, it is clear that there must be common underlying proficiencies, both across languages and across modalities, that allow adult learners to draw on already developed knowledge bases and strategies as they develop literacy skills in their second language.

TABLE 1. MODELS OF LITERACY SKILLS TRANSFER

Components	Model A	Model B
Cognitive processes	Common underlying proficiency	Interrelated proficiencies
Language structure	Shared structural components	Separate language systems
——————— *Language proficiency threshold level* ———————		
Transfer mechanism	Restructuring	Synthesis

The reading–writing relationship: second language

It appears that L1 literacy skills can transfer to the second language and are a factor in L2 literacy acquisition. How this transfer of skills might affect the reading–writing interaction in a second language is a more complicated issue. The general process of acquiring L2 writing and reading abilities appears (1) to result from L2 input – reading and writing – in much the same way that L1 abilities develop, but also (2) to be influenced by the transfer of L1 literacy skills that affect the quality of L2 reading and writing quite apart from what can be learned from the second language itself.

The fundamental process involved in both of these strands – the L2 reading–writing relationship and the relationship between L1 and L2 literacy skills – is *transfer*. The research evidence examined here has given different perspectives on the issue of transfer, both inter- and intralinguistically, but there emerge two distinct models, as shown in Table 1. There are three components of these models to consider in a discussion of literacy skills transfer: (1) the cognitive processes involved in writing and reading; (2) the structural components that underlie writing and reading; and (3) the mechanism that allows the processes and structures to transfer, either across languages or across modalities. Because the research clearly shows language proficiency to be a factor (albeit indirectly for the L2 reading–writing relationship), a threshold level is indicated before the transfer mechanism can be employed successfully. Model A suggests a more holistic view of literacy in which reading and writing share common underlying cognitive processes and common structural components in both the first and second language. In this model, restructuring (modification of organizational structures and adoption of new strategies and procedures) must occur before transfer can be successful. Model B presents a view of literacy in which reading and writing are characterized by interrelated cognitive processes and separate language systems. Because the processes and structures are discrete, synthesis must occur before transfer will be successful.

These models reflect research that indicates that transfer of skills is not automatic, either across languages or across modalities. What this means for the L2 reading–writing relationship is that teaching is important to facilitate transfer, whether learners are restructuring or synthesizing skills. The models and hypotheses discussed here do not indicate a specific program for utilizing reading in the writing classroom. However, they clearly indicate that the relationship between reading and writing should be exploited and that writing teachers need to be explicit in their teaching of that relationship. Writing teachers who are sensitive to the role that first language reading and writing abilities play in developing second language literacy skills, and also to the role that reading ability in the second language plays in the development of second language writing skills, will be better prepared to help L2 learners utilize those relationships to become proficient second language writers.

References

Belanger, J. (1987). Theory and research into reading and writing connections: A critical review. *Reading-Canada-Lecture, 5,* 10–18.

Canale, M.; Frenette, N.; and Belanger, M. (1988). Evaluation of minority student writing in first and second language. In J. Fine (Ed.), *Second language discourse: A textbook of current research* (pp. 147–165). Norwood, N.J.: Ablex.

Carson, J. E.; Carrell, P. L.; Silberstein, S.; Kroll, B.; and Kuehn, P. A. (1990). Reading-writing relationships in first and second language. *TESOL Quarterly, 24,* 245–266.

Cummins, J. (1981). The role of primary language development in promoting educational success for language minority students. In *Schooling and language minority students: A theoretical framework* (pp. 3–49). Office of Bilingual Bicultural Education, California State Department of Education, Sacramento. Los Angeles: Evaluation, Dissemination and Assessment Center, California State University.

Eckhoff, B. (1983). How reading affects children's writing. *Language Arts, 60,* 607–616.

Freedle, R. O. (1985). Achieving cognitive synthesis of separate language skills: Implications for improving literacy. In C. N. Hedley and A. N. Baratta (Eds.), *Contexts of reading* (pp. 107–126). Norwood, N.J.: Ablex.

Goldman, S. R.; Reyes, M.; and Varnhagen, C. K. (1984). Understanding fables in first and second languages. *Journal of the National Association for Bilingual Education (NABE), 8,* 35–66.

Gordon, C. J., and Braun, G. (1982). Story schemata: Metatextual aid to reading and writing. In J. A. Niles and L. A. Harris (Eds.), *New inquiries in reading research and instruction* (pp. 262–268). Rochester, N.Y.: National Reading Conference.

Grabe, W., and Kaplan, R. B. (1989). Writing in a second language: Contrastive rhetoric. In D. M. Johnson and D. H. Roen (Eds.), *Richness in writing: Empowering ESL students* (pp. 263–283). New York: Longman.

Hiebert, E. H.; Englert, C. S.; and Brennan, S. (1983). Awareness of text structure in recognition and production of expository discourse. *Journal of Reading Behavior, 15,* 63–79.

Hinds, J. (1987). Reader versus writer responsibility: A new typology. In U. Connor and R. B. Kaplan (Eds.), *Writing across languages: Analysis of L2 text* (pp. 141–152). Reading, Mass.: Addison-Wesley.

Krashen, S. (1984). *Writing: Research, theory and applications.* Oxford: Pergamon Institute of English.

McLaughlin, B. (1987). Reading in a second language: Studies with adult and child learners. In S. R. Goldman and H. T. Trueba (Eds.), *Becoming literate in English as a second language* (pp. 57–70). Norwood N.J.: Ablex.

Mace-Matluck, B. J.; Dominguez, D.; Holtzman, W.; and Hoover, W. (1983). *Language and literacy in bilingual instruction.* Austin, Texas: Southwest Educational Development Laboratory.

Rumelhart, D. E., and Norman, D. A. (1978). Accretion, tuning, and restructuring: 3 modes of learning. In J. Cotton and R. Klatzky (Eds.), *Semantic factors in cognition* (pp. 37–53). Hillsdale, N.J.: Erlbaum.

Scribner, S., and Cole, M. (1981). *The psychology of literacy.* Cambridge, Mass.: Harvard University Press.

Shanahan, T. (1984). Nature of the reading–writing relation: An exploratory multivariate analysis. *Journal of Educational Psychology, 76,* 466–477.

Shanahan, T., and Lomax, R. G. (1986). An analysis and comparison of theoretical models of the reading–writing relationship. *Journal of Educational Psychology, 78,* 116–123.

Shanklin, N.K.L. (1982). *Relating reading and writing: Developing a transactional theory of the writing process.* Bloomington: Indiana University School of Education.

Stotsky, S. (1983). Research on reading/writing relationships: A synthesis and suggested directions. *Language Arts, 60,* 627–642.

Taylor, B., and Beach, R. W. (1984). The effects of text structure instruction on middle-grade students' comprehension and production of expository text. *Reading Research Quarterly, 19,* 134–146.

Wald, B. (1987). The development of writing skills among Hispanic high school students. In S. R. Goldman and H. T. Trueba (Eds.), *Becoming literate in English as a second language* (pp. 155–185). Norwood N.J.: Ablex.

SECTION II:
CONSIDERATIONS FOR WRITING
INSTRUCTION

Several of the theoretical considerations that underlie second language writing instruction have been reviewed in Section I, providing an overview of the field. Section II features seven chapters describing a variety of empirically based studies. Each focuses on a different aspect of writing and/or the writing classroom, examining concepts and practices writing teachers need to know to best function in the classroom. These foci may be viewed as constraints on the writer or teacher that shape both composing behavior and course design. Each of the chapters reports on research findings that are directly connected to the insights about writing presented in Section I of the book, and each addresses still other key questions in the field. The options presented are just some of the many areas writers and writing teachers continue to explore as we learn more about this complex field.

Can using one's native language in composing assist the second language writer?

Chapter 7, by Alexander Friedlander, explores one constraint on the second language writer, namely, the language in which one chooses to carry out prewriting activities. Language can be seen as a constraint because lack of complete control over the linguistic code might limit a writer's possibility of exhibiting mastery over the discourse skills required to produce a particular type of text, a theory examined in a number of the studies summarized by Alexandra Rowe Krapels in her review of composing process research in Chapter 3. The influence of one's first language on the process of composing in one's second language has a number of dimensions, and Friedlander focuses on how topic information might be stored in memory and how writers might best access that information. He reports on a study involving essays planned in either Chinese or English and then written in English by a group of Chinese ESL students. He hypothesizes that Chinese writers will write more effectively on a Chinese topic if they first plan in Chinese, whereas they will write more effectively on an American topic if they first plan in English.

How can text analysis assist writers in the revision process?

The composing process is also an element that underlies the focus of Chapter 8, but it is presented from a teaching perspective rather than from a composing perspective, with a view toward how teachers might best train students to improve their revision skills in a process-based curriculum. Ulla Connor and Mary Farmer present a linguistically based text analysis strategy that can be utilized to help students consider discourse-level features of their texts. They investigate the applicability of Lautamatti's "topical structure analysis" as a tool in understanding text structure. Briefly, topical structure analysis (Lautamatti 1978) serves to identify the relationship between sequences of sentences by examining the topic and comment in each successive sentence. Connor and Farmer provide a number of specific examples to show how topical structure analysis works and then discuss how to train students to analyze and improve their own writing by using this framework as a guideline for revision. Because topical structure analysis operates on the discourse level of texts, Connor and Farmer claim it is particularly useful in helping students attain textual coherence in their writing, one of the components that can mark a "written discourse accent" (McKay 1989) when violated and lead to lack of academic success.

Do written products exhibit different levels of proficiency in different skill areas?

Chapter 9 introduces preparation time as another constraint on the writer. Barbara Kroll's study examines the writing produced by the same subjects under two different conditions: essays written in class under pressure of time and essays written at home over a 10- to 14-day period. She measures the essays along two dimensions: (1) the type, range, and frequency of grammatical errors; and (2) the adherence of the essays to principles of organization and coherence. She then compares the essays written at home to those written in class. Results of this study suggest that despite some individual gains, time does not buy very much for students in the improvement of either their control over syntax or their organizational skills. Further, the level of performance in the areas of syntax and organization is not interdependent, so that "good" essays might be written in "bad" English and "bad" essays might be written in "good" English.

Do teachers and students agree on the role written feedback can and should play?

In Chapter 10, Andrew D. Cohen and Marilda C. Cavalcanti report on three separate small-scale studies which investigate the relationship between the feedback teachers provide on compositions, student processing and assessment of teacher feedback, and also the match between the teachers' declared agendas for responding to writing and their actual feedback provided on student papers. Their discussion touches on some of the issues raised by Ilona Leki in her review of feedback issues in Chapter 4. All three of their studies were conducted in Brazil; one study dealt with feedback that native Portuguese speakers received on their Portuguese L1 compositions, and the other two studies examined feedback on foreign language compositions. Cohen and Cavalcanti recommend that teachers and students need to work more on establishing agreement between their separate agendas for feedback and on expanding the repertoire of strategies students might employ in deriving maximal benefit from the feedback they do receive. Their research methodology is in keeping with Yorio's (1989) call for teachers to listen to what students think of our teaching methodology and to help them understand why we make the choices we do.

What kind of written feedback leads to improvement in student revisions?

In Chapter 11, Ann Fathman and Elizabeth Whalley focus on the nature of written feedback and its effect on revision. They compare essays written by four different groups of ESL students; each group received a different type of feedback. Following the return of their original essays, students in all four groups rewrote their essays, and then both sets of essays were evaluated for grammatical accuracy and quality of the content. While Fathman and Whalley point out that revision in and of itself has a positive effect on the quality and accuracy of student writing, Cohen and Cavalcanti point out that student revision of essays is not a standard practice in Brazil. Findings from both the Cohen and Cavalcanti study and the Fathman and Whalley study can help guide writing teachers in making informed choices about appropriate and effective pedagogical approaches to providing feedback on written work, and to a richer understanding of how "what a teacher says to a student about writing is saturated with the teacher's values, beliefs and models of learning" (Anson 1989: 354).

How does the type of topic presented in a writing assignment contribute to student performance?

Chapter 12 provides a close look at the design of writing topics, one of the issues critical not only to course planning but to writing assessment (as discussed by Liz Hamp-Lyons in Chapter 5). Because students are often asked to produce text in response to a topic supplied by a teacher, writing teachers need to know more about how the presentation of a topic can affect student performance. To address this issue, Joy Reid uses computer-based programs to analyze several hundred essays, written by Arabic, Chinese, Spanish and native English-speaking students, responding to two types of topic task: comparison and contrast, and describing or interpreting a chart or graph. Based on a series of text-analysis programs which facilitated the comparison, Reid's study describes the quantitative differences found in and across topic types. In addition, she compares performances of writers from specific language backgrounds, a focus that derives from work in the field of contrastive rhetoric.

In what ways do writers incorporate required outside readings in their academic assignments?

Chapter 13 by Cherry Campbell focuses on one aspect of the reading–writing connection: input – one of the labels Joan Carson Eisterhold, in Chapter 6, discusses as typical of how writing teachers view reading matter. Although using one or more texts as the stimulus for a writing assignment is a frequent task in the academic environment (Horowitz 1986), this can serve as a constraining factor on the output of student writing. For example, essays based on readings must exhibit, in ways that other assignments do not require, the student's ability to understand and interpret the text. In her study, Campbell looks at both native and nonnative writers who were given a reading about some basic concepts in anthropology and were asked to utilize some of those concepts in writing an essay about fraternities and/or sororities. She compares native and nonnative uses of such strategies as quoting, summarizing, and paraphrasing, as well as the students' abilities to document the source of the information utilized. Campbell concludes with a number of teaching suggestions for improving student performance in this area of academic writing.

References

Anson, C. M. (1989). Response styles and ways of knowing. In C. M. Anson (Ed.), *Writing and response: Theory, practice, and research* (pp. 332–366). Urbana, Ill.: National Council of Teachers of English.

Horowitz, D. M. (1986). What professors actually require: Academic tasks for the ESL classroom. *TESOL Quarterly, 20,* 445–462.

Lautamatti, L. (1978). Observations on the development of the topic in simplified discourse. In V. Kohohen and N. E. Enkvist (Eds.), *Text linguistics, cognitive learning, and language teaching* (pp. 71–104). Turku, Finland: Afinla. Reprinted in U. Connor and R. B. Kaplan (Eds.), *Writing across languages: Analysis of L2 text* (pp. 87–113). Reading, Mass.: Addison-Wesley, 1987.

McKay, S. L. (1989). Topic development and written discourse accent. In D. M. Johnson and D. H. Roen (Eds.), *Richness in writing: Empowering ESL students* (pp. 253–262). New York: Longman.

Yorio, C. (1989). The other side of the looking glass. *Journal of Basic Writing, 8,* 32–45.

7 Composing in English: effects of a first language on writing in English as a second language

Alexander Friedlander

Traditionally, ESL teachers have emphasized the need for ESL writers to think and write as completely as possible in English. The belief is that if ESL writers do any of their work in their first language, this will inhibit acquisition of the second language (L2) and will interfere with the generation of L2 structures, due to transfer of structures and vocabulary from the first language in an incorrect way. For instance, Arapoff (1967) suggested that students should avoid topics related to firsthand experience because they may then translate from their first language into English.

However, a number of studies have indicated that, regardless of a language prescription, writers will transfer writing abilities and strategies, whether good or deficient, from their first language to their second language. Mohan and Lo (1985), for instance, cite a study by Das which indicated that students had similarly deficient rhetorical strategies in their first language and in English. In other words, students who lacked first language strategies displayed a similar lack of strategies for writing in their second language. Mohan and Lo suggest that this deficiency may be developmental – students who have not developed good strategies for writing in their first language will not have appropriate strategies to transfer to their second language. Edelsky's study (1982) of the writing of first, second, and third graders in a bilingual program also indicates that writing knowledge transfers across languages. Her results show that writers use first language strategies and knowledge to aid their second language writing. She concludes that writers apply their knowledge about writing from their first language to writing in their second language, in order to form hypotheses about writing in the second language.

In another study, Jones and Tetroe (1987) looked at ESL writers generating texts in their first and second languages; they found that these ESL writers transferred both good and weak writing skills from their first language to English. This transfer was independent of language proficiency, which affected only quantity of planning. They noted that weaker writers' failure to use writing strategies in English was based on

This article is based on part of the author's doctoral dissertation (Friedlander 1987).

their failure to use these strategies in their first language. In other words, strategies that were never acquired in their first language could not be transferred to the second language. In contrast, Moragne e Silva's (1986) subject had effective L1 strategies to transfer to the L2 writing context; her subject's first language and second language composing processes displayed similar high-level goal structures and problem representations. In an analysis of Japanese and Chinese students writing essays in their respective first languages and in ESL, Carson et al. (1990) conclude that the acquisition of L2 literacy skills by adults already literate in their first language is a complex phenomenon involving multiple variables.

As Flower and Hayes (1981) have indicated with writers of English as a first language, writing processes are ongoing throughout a writing task, and writing does not begin and end with one draft. Traditional approaches to writing, such as modes of discourse or grammar-based approaches, falter because they do not help students to see writing as an evolving process.[1] Rather, they place constraints in the path of writers. Such constraints can hinder the development of writing skills, particularly for those writers whose first language is not English. For example, Edelsky (1982) found that bilingual children who were unable to juggle constraints on their composing had greater difficulty in text production than those who were able to master composing constraints.

One constraint on composing processes faced by all ESL writers is language. If ESL writers retrieve information about a writing topic from memory in their first language and then have to translate into English before writing anything down, this act of translation can lead to an overload of their short-term memory and a diminishment in the quality of the content of their writing. Given these studies indicating that first language writing strategies can positively affect second language composing, I want to identify under what circumstances the first language could be of greater help to adult ESL writers than their second language in retrieving from memory knowledge about a particular subject.

Evidence of a first language assisting writers can be found in some studies of ESL adults. Chelala (1981), Lay (1982), Johnson (1985), and Jones and Tetroe (1987) found that switches to the first language aided ESL writers in retrieval of topic information. While the first two studies report these findings peripherally, Lay's study directly addresses the issue of first language use while composing. Her study, limited to four Chinese subjects and their composing in English, investigated, among other questions, how much the first language is used and whether there are any patterns in the use of the first language. She found that her Chinese subjects tended to switch to using their first language when writing about

---

1 See Krapels (this volume) for a review of several studies examining the writing process of L2 students and offering insights into teaching writing as a process.

a topic studied or acquired in their first language background. She also reports that their first language served as an aid and not a hindrance to writing, since her subjects used Chinese when they were stuck in English – to find a key word, for instance. Lay notes that the greater the number of switches into the first language, the better the quality of the essays in terms of organization and ideas.

Lay discusses situations that give rise to the use of the first language. First, she argues that the first language is more likely and useful at certain stages of language development. As writers acquire more English, such first language use would lessen. Second, she claims that use of the first language is more likely with certain topics, particularly topics related to Chinese experience. Third, she indicates that the first language helps topic search on unfamiliar topics. Lay's results suggest that foreign students will be able to plan more easily and will have one less constraint on composing in English if they write about topics acquired in an English-language setting. My hypothesis suggests that, like Lay's indications, the first language will assist retrieval of information on certain topics.

Other evidence comes from a study by Cumming (1987). He reports that inexpert French ESL writers use their first language to generate content, regardless of the language of the topic. Expert writers, in contrast, use translation, not just to generate content but also to generate and verify appropriate word choice. In this situation, these writers seem to be using a strategy of first language reference, where they know that their first language will enhance their writing in English.

These studies point to the potential for a positive effect resulting from second language writers using their first language while generating texts in English. By extension, if ESL writers are retrieving topic knowledge in their first language, and if we force them to translate into English either before they write down any text or notes or while they are planning their texts, we may be imposing additional and unnecessary constraints on their composing; they may be using up too much of their short-term or working memory store. Since the amount of information we can retain in short-term memory is quite limited and decay of information is quite rapid (Peterson and Peterson 1959), the translation can constrain text production by limiting what writers are able to retain. Rather, we may want to encourage ESL writers to think about their knowledge of a topic and produce a written plan in their native language and then translate into English. The plan, which could consist of enumerated or itemized points, phrases, or even sentences, would then include information retrieved from memory on the subject of the essay, but retrieved and written in the writer's first language.

In such cases we may argue that, whereas beginning learners of English need to operate in their second language as much as possible to develop their acquisition of English, more advanced users of English have developed their proficiency to such a level that their native language does not interfere with their writing in English; such writers should be able to improve aspects of their writing if they use their first language to retrieve and write down topic-area information and then translate their first language notes into English. Teachers would need to understand when the first language can most advantageously be used; they would thus be able to help writers avoid situations where being forced to operate entirely in English would constrain ESL text production, such as when writers have to produce text under time restrictions (e.g., in examinations).

The hypothesis I advance, thus, is that positive transfer of first language-related content will be enhanced when writers write using the language in which the information was acquired. To restate this, L2 writers will plan for their writing more effectively, write better texts containing more content, and create more effective texts when they are able to plan in the language related to the acquisition of knowledge of the topic area. By planning, I mean the process of coming up with and organizing ideas to be included in the final essay. Such ideas retrieved from the writer's memory will be drawn from the writer's topic-area knowledge – that is, what the writer knows about the topic of the essay.

A simple example will explain this hypothesis. Let us consider Chinese students writing about their home. Since they would have learned or acquired knowledge about this topic area in Chinese, the hypothesis claims that they will be able to retrieve more content knowledge for their text if they first operate and plan the essay in their native language, Chinese, and then translate this plan into English. Similarly, since their knowledge of North America may have been learned while at a North American university, they will presumably be able to retrieve that information more easily when thinking in English. Even if they have learned the knowledge from a Chinese roommate, their experience has occurred in an English language environment; they may also have had opportunities to discuss the issue with non-Chinese individuals.

However, we can pose a rival hypothesis: ESL students may have encoded information in the language of acquisition, but now that they are in an English environment, they will more easily retrieve material when thinking in English, because English is the language of prominence for them. In other words, even though writers have learned about their homes in Chinese, or about North America from Chinese friends, they have acquired English terms for similar situations; as a result, the prominent language (English) will aid more in the retrieval of information. Of course these are simple situations. We may find that more complex situations, which would be culture- or language-specific and not easily translatable or experienced in the other setting, would remain encoded in the language of acquisition and would be retrieved best in that language. If writers have to devote too much of their limited short-term memory capacity to language and thus have to translate before writing anything down, language may be constraining their text production. Conversely, if we know that writers work best if they are able to retrieve information in the language of storage, and then translate, we can use that as a pedagogical tool, since appropriate retrieval of information from memory to generate ideas can enhance writing.

My study provides evidence to enable us to make a more sensitive statement about the function of the first language while ESL writers are composing English texts. Such evidence will point to how ESL writers can effectively use their first language to aid their text development in English and will also suggest conditions where the first language can enhance generation of topic-area knowledge.

The study

Overview

The study tests the hypothesis that ESL writers will be able to plan more effectively and produce texts with better content when they are able to plan in the language related to the acquisition of topic-area knowledge.

In this study, 28 Chinese-speaking subjects at Carnegie Mellon University (CMU) responded to two letters, personally addressed to them. For their response to one letter, they were asked to generate a written plan in their native language; for the other they were asked to plan in English, before writing their texts in English and then revising the drafts. In developing the plans, subjects were instructed to brainstorm, or generate ideas on the topic, and then to organize these ideas for their essays. They were advised to generate the ideas in the plan in point form, rather than in complete sentences. The final plan, then, was intended to be a list of points (single words, short phrases) and not a rough draft. Once they had completed the plan, the subjects could then start to write the essay. In addition, a subgroup of subjects provided verbal think-aloud protocols as they worked through the two tasks.

Design

In order to assess which language is preferable for planning and whether it is preferable to plan in the language of topic knowledge, subjects either planned in the language of topic knowledge and then wrote their texts in English (match condition), or planned in the language not related to topic knowledge before writing the texts in English (mismatch condition). Thus, writers in the match condition planned in Chinese, their

TABLE I. EXPERIMENTAL DESIGN BY CONDITION

	Topic	
Condition	CMU	*Qingming*
Match	English	Chinese
Mismatch	Chinese	English

first language, on a Chinese festival, *Qingming,* and in English, their second language, on a subject related to life at an American university. Writers in the mismatch condition planned in English on the Chinese festival, *Qingming,* and in Chinese on the English topic subject. In all cases, after completing their plan, they wrote the final text in English (Table 1). Subjects were randomly assigned to the first language and topic; this assignment then determined the language and topic for their second task.

Materials

In order to arrive at topics that had almost certainly been acquired in a particular language background, I sought possibilities from the subjects' experience. For the Chinese topic, I selected a Chinese festival, *Qingming,* as this topic-area knowledge would certainly have been acquired by these subjects in their youth, before they had been exposed to English. *Qingming* is an annual, traditional, and well-known festival that is held in the rainy season and honors ancestors.

For the English topic, I selected a situation they had all experienced: the difficulties in adapting to a new cultural environment and a different educational system at an American university (Carnegie Mellon University). Knowledge of this topic was closely identified with their English language experience.

To provide tasks that were as realistic as possible, the topics were presented in the form of letters written by directors of international student programs to the subjects; the subjects were asked to respond to these letters. In the case of the *Qingming* topic, subjects were asked to give a director of an international studies program information about this festival and others so that the director could help prepare a group of American students for a visit to China. The essay prompt asked subjects to compare *Qingming* to American festivals. The English topic asked them to help a director of a foreign student office plan an orientation program for new foreign students at Carnegie Mellon University. In particular, subjects were asked for advice about issues and subject areas to include in the orientation program.

Data analysis

After subjects completed the tasks, all materials were translated into English. The resulting data analysis focused on the time each subject took to complete each task, and how much time they spent on the plan, the draft, and the revision; the number of details in each plan and essay; the length, in numbers of words, of the plans and the essay; and separate holistic ratings of the plans and the essays. The holistic ratings were performed by trained raters using a six-point scale, with 1 = weak and 6 = strong. For consistency, I chose to work with English translations of all materials. The data were analyzed using the SAS General Linear Models Procedure.

Results

As the effects of the experimental manipulation are seen in the variable entitled match (see Table 1), I will first present the results for this variable, before examining effects for other grouping variables.

Match

There was clear evidence of enhanced performance when subjects generated their plans using the language in which they had acquired the knowledge. They produced more details and wrote longer and better plans and essays in the match condition. First, the plans were more detailed, averaging 15.46 main ideas and subtopics in the match condition versus 10.33 in the mismatch condition (ANOVA, $p = 0.05$; see Table 2). This result indicates that writers retrieved more details about their topic areas when they used Chinese for the plans on *Qingming* and English for the plans on Carnegie Mellon. In contrast, when subjects produced plans for the *Qingming* topic in English and the Carnegie Mellon topic in Chinese, their texts did not have the same level of detail.

Second, when they used the language of acquisition to generate their plans, the resulting plans were significantly longer, by 25 words (75.45 in the match condition, 51.98 in the mismatch condition). While length itself is not necessarily an indicator of quality, the result for the quality rating does indicate that the plans produced when writers were able to use the language of topic knowledge acquisition were richer in information. When they had the advantage of the match condition, writers scored a little less than one point higher on the holistic quality rating (4.27 vs. 3.44 on the six-point scale). This means that these plans were more complete and contained a greater amount of information that

TABLE 2. MEANS FOR CONDITION

Variable	Match	Mismatch	p
Details[a]	15.46	10.33	0.05
Plan length	75.45 words	51.98 words	0.05
Plan quality[b]	4.27	3.44	0.03
Essay length	484.96 words	365.77 words	0.03
Essay quality[b]	4.67	3.61	0.001
Time	70.71 min.	60.98 min.	NS

$N = 28$.
[a]Number of specific details.
[b]Scale = 1–6, with 6 high.

would serve as valuable guidelines for the writers as they wrote their essays.

The essays resulting from the plans in the match condition were longer and of superior quality than those produced in the mismatch condition. The essays from the match condition were over 100 words longer (484.96 vs. 365.77 words), suggesting a greater amount of content. This is confirmed in the ratings: The raters considered these essays superior in quality (4.67 vs. 3.61). These ratings confirm that the essays produced in the match conditions did a better task of meeting the needs of their reader and contained more valuable advice for the directors of the two programs.

In contrast, the time factors – time taken to plan the response, to write the text, to revise, and total time spent by subjects on the task – do not indicate any main effects or significant interactions. Although writers did spend nearly 10 minutes longer on their writing task in the match conditions (70.17 vs. 60.98 minutes), the log transformations of the raw data indicate that this time difference is not significant.

Topic

When I examined the data from the perspective of topic, looking at performance on the *Qingming* topic versus the Carnegie Mellon topic, I found that the writers produced shorter plans on *Qingming*. However, these plans and their resulting essays were rated as superior to those produced on the CMU topic. First, they wrote shorter plans on the *Qingming* topic (53.42 vs. 74.01 words; see Table 3). Second, despite being shorter, these plans were rated as superior to those on Carnegie Mellon. The ratings were 4.25 versus 3.47 on the six-point scale. An analysis of these plans indicates that they contained a richer source of material that the writers could use to generate their texts. As one might

TABLE 3. MEANS FOR TOPIC

Variable	Qingming	CMU	p
Plan length	53.42 words	74.01 words	0.05
Plan quality[a]	4.25	3.47	0.003
Essay length	430.30 words	420.40 words	NS
Essay quality[a]	4.49	3.89	0.01

$N = 28$.
[a]Scale = 1–6, with 6 high.

expect, based on the plan results, the essays written using these plans proved to be superior for the *Qingming* topic (4.49 vs. 3.89), although these essays are of similar length for the two topics (430.3 words on *Qingming*; 420.4 on CMU). In other words, writing about the topic related to their first language resulted in superior texts.

Language

When I analyzed the data from the perspective of language alone, comparing operating in English to operating in Chinese (independent of topic), I found few significant differences. When planning in Chinese, writers produced 14.55 details compared with 11.07 when planning in English (ANOVA – $p = 0.05$). In other words, using a first language appears to allow better retrieval of ideas, irrespective of the language of the topic knowledge. However, whether planning in Chinese or in English, writers wrote plans of similar length (60.14 words in Chinese, 61.86 in English).

No significant differences were noted in the quality of the plans produced in English and in Chinese, nor in the resulting essays. In fact, the plans and the essays received almost identical ratings whether the subjects planned in Chinese or English.

Summary

These results indicate that writers benefit when they match the language to the topic – in this case, Chinese when writing on a topic related to that language background and English on a topic related to their English experience. Writers are able to produce longer texts and plans, as well as more detailed plans; the resulting products are rated as better than products produced when they write based on plans created in mismatched conditions (using Chinese for the topic related to their English experience and English for the topic related to their Chinese experience).

Thus, language appears to constrain writers only in certain ways while they are writing. When ESL writers use their second language to write on a topic related to their first language, and when they plan in their second language, they are constrained in terms of amount of material retrieved; in contrast, translation does not appear to hinder writers in their text production by causing them to take more time over their texts.

Discussion

The hypothesis stated that ESL writers would be able to plan more effectively and write better texts when they planned in Chinese for the Chinese topic, *Qingming,* and in English for the English topic, Carnegie Mellon (CMU). The results of the analyses support the hypothesis. These ESL writers were able to plan more effectively and write texts with better content when they used the language of the topic knowledge to plan their responses. Further confirmation comes from the analyses of the other dependent measures, with more details in the texts and longer plans and essays in the language-match conditions.

The rating data also indicate that retrieval of topic-area information is enhanced and texts resulting from this retrieval are qualitatively better when writers plan in the language of the topic knowledge; when these writers planned in Chinese for *Qingming* and English for CMU, they produced superior plans and essays. In this respect, language is serving to assist and benefit information retrieval; these subjects benefited from planning in the language related to the topic. This result echoes Lay's finding (1982) that use of the native language for certain topic areas led to improved essay quality.

Regardless of the language used, however, writers did a better job of planning and text production on the Chinese topic than on the English topic. This difference is indicated in the ratings of the plan and text, where these subjects scored significantly higher. This result can partially be explained by the subjects' greater familiarity with the *Qingming* topic. They had experienced the festival annually as they grew up and had participated to a greater or lesser extent in the ceremonies. In contrast to this lifetime experience, they had been at CMU for one to two years, in most cases. Consequently, the CMU experiences were not as ingrained, and they did not have as much knowledge to activate on this topic. Some studies indicate that when students write on topics for which their knowledge is "well-integrated" (Langer 1984: 28), and in which they are highly involved (Bridgeman and Carlson 1984), organization of their writing is likely to be superior to essays produced on topics for which their knowledge is less secure. With Chinese-speaking writers, consequently, using Chinese to generate topic-area material makes a difference when they write on topics related to their Chinese background.

TABLE 4. SHORT PLAN GENERATED IN ENGLISH FOR THE QINGMING TOPIC

April 4
grave ground
fruits, flowers
raining
ancestor worship
respect
pay visit tomb

Another indication from this study emerges from plan length – the plans for the *Qingming* topic were much shorter than those produced for the CMU topic (whether composed in Chinese or in English), 53.42 versus 74.01 words. A close examination shows that the *Qingming* plans tend to consist of short phrases, one to three words long, with relatively few chunks longer than this.

Table 4 shows the short phrases typical of the *Qingming* plans. The words set down here are all cues to specific elements of the festival, phrases found in all of the *Qingming* plans: four cues relating to the ancestor-honoring nature of the festival; two relating to the season; and one relating to a custom. While these are not the only details found in plans on *Qingming,* these are found in almost all the plans. Additionally, we find a similar brevity of expression in setting down these phrases on *Qingming.* These cues, brief as they are, then enabled the writers to produce their texts, in which they expanded upon and explained these details.

In contrast, in the plans on the CMU topic, writers often wrote complete sentences and even paragraphs rather than shorter word or phrase cues. Table 5 includes only half of a very long plan on CMU. Such long plans were typical for the CMU topic.

Unlike the short cues of the *Qingming* plans, the English topic plans are much longer and fuller. While both plans contain much useful information, the English plan becomes the text. In other words, the writers tended to turn their long phrases into sentences without adding new material. The *Qingming* plans, in contrast, served as pointers which the writers expanded by adding details to flesh out the ideas.

An explanation for this difference in plan length and detail may lie in chunk size. Certain topic-area information, particularly culturally based information, seems to be more easily accessed through a very brief cue. The activation of this cue allows the subject to access a wealth of associated details, perhaps because the topic-area knowledge is ingrained. These very brief cues for the *Qingming* topic often result in quite lengthy amounts of text. Indeed, these subjects appear to have *Qingming* schema, and all of the pointers in the short plans are thus

TABLE 5. SECTION OF LONG PLAN GENERATED IN ENGLISH FOR THE CMU TOPIC

My advice:
meeting with the professors in each dept.;
to take workshop-class in CMU, like self in class;
to watch video tapes of the CMU model classes;
to show the new students the blue-book and papers which the senior students
    have done;
to teach them in the classroom languages by ESL stuff, the most important;
to introduce the students who came before them in the same dept.;
to provide English writing, speaking classes for the new students;
to help, if necessary, the new comers who have big problem in English by
    tutors;
to regulate a exam of English after the orientation, if passed, able to get into
    classroom; if not, have to take language classes first;
and the English classes not free, should have a couple of units, let's say about
    4 or 6 per semester.

attributes of this schema. The interviews with the subjects after the writing confirm that they have related information about *Qingming* stored in memory.

In contrast, these writers do not have a wealth of associated detail stored with their CMU knowledge. The material they set down in long-phrase or sentence form in the plans, resulting in longer plans, represents all the knowledge they have on the topic. This may mean that the knowledge stored is quite shallow — they have not had the time or the repeated exposure necessary to develop a complex and rich network of associations in their memory structure. Consequently, when they retrieve such topic-area information, they are retrieving all they know; they do not have any other activated knowledge.

Although language is dependent on topic (i.e., matching language to topic for planning is advantageous), language alone (i.e., using Chinese versus English) is not a factor, except in terms of the number of details: Subjects retrieved more information when using their first language. That is, when we ignore the effect of the topic and focus exclusively on operating in a particular language, we find no significant difference in plan or essay length or quality. We do find some language switching, though — use of Chinese in the English plan and English in the Chinese plan. Such switching is primarily linked to culture-specific terms and concepts. When writers planned in Chinese, they used English words only for names of holidays, like Halloween and Thanksgiving.

In contrast, when planning in English, these writers used Chinese either because of vocabulary difficulties or for terms that are clearly culture-based. The vocabulary items, words like *cemetery* and *tomb,* are words that writers may not have had cause to use in their sojourn in the United States and for which, consequently, they do not have the English vocabulary easily available. The cultural items include terms for which there are no easy English equivalents, like *moon-cakes* (a type of cake eaten during *Qingming*), names of historical figures related to the festival, and, in a number of cases, extracts from poems about *Qingming*. In the interviews, some subjects indicated that they found it easier to retrieve information in Chinese because they had not thought previously about this topic in English. This evidence suggests that such information is encoded in memory in Chinese. Indeed, the results favoring the matching condition of using Chinese for the Chinese topic support this interpretation.

These findings suggest some interpretations about language storage in memory and indicate interesting directions for future studies. In terms of level of detail in the plans, writers produced fewer details on *Qingming* when they planned in English than when they planned in Chinese (7.18 vs. 15.65). This difference suggests that language may be constraining retrieval of information on a topic area, since writers are able to retrieve more information about *Qingming* in Chinese. However, the similarity in amounts of detail for the English topic for both planning languages (English, 14.89; Chinese, 13.26) suggests that topic-area knowledge acquired by subjects after they become bilingual may be accessible in either language without much difficulty. In other words, knowledge about topics like CMU, which these Chinese speakers acquired as bilinguals, is retrieved whether operating in Chinese or in English with similar ease. The differences between the level of detail in the *Qingming* plans in Chinese and English would extend this idea, suggesting that certain information may be stored in memory in a monolingual storage pool (cf. Berrueta-Clement 1973). In this case, such topic-area knowledge is tagged in memory to the first language and is more readily retrieved in that language.

Indeed, bilinguals may have a variety of experiential storage pools in memory, as well as first and second language monolingual storage pools, which are most easily accessed when operating in that language. Such experiential pools may be common – accessible from either language – or language-dependent. (See McLaughlin 1978; Paradis 1985; and Hakuta 1986 for a fuller discussion of independent and interdependent theories of language storage.)

Since the subjects generated similar amounts of detail on the English topic in both languages, the languages must have some degree of interdependence in memory. Similarly, in order to generate the plans on the *Qingming* topic in English, these writers must be able to access a common store that enables them to express in English information about a topic that was experienced in a Chinese cultural setting (cf. Hakuta 1986). If the languages were completely independent, I should have found differences in the amount of detail retrieved on the English topic in both languages. Because these amounts are similar, subjects were apparently accessing a common store for the CMU topic. Of course, because the use of Chinese in the plans and the texts indicates that subjects were translating at least to some extent, they appear to have been retrieving some topic-area information from a Chinese store, suggesting that some knowledge is stored in language-specific form.

Additionally, when I consider that they were able to retrieve fewer details on *Qingming* when they planned in English and that even when planning in English they used Chinese for some culture-specific concepts, the indication is that some topic-area information is retrieved from a monolingual language store. If I may speculate for a moment, experiences like *Qingming*, which were acquired during a pre-bilingual stage of language development and are cultural in nature, appear to be tied to a monolingual pool and seem to be more easily retrieved when operating in that language. For instance, in addition to the differing amounts of detail, subjects produced plans almost twice as long on *Qingming* when working in Chinese than in English. To assess this conclusion, we would need further studies comparing culture-specific topics to more general topics.

At the same time, extending the notion of language-specific storage, we could also posit that some experiences related to second language acquisition may be stored in a second language topic-area store and be more easily retrieved in that language. In a related study (Friedlander and Huckin 1987), Chinese writers provided verbal protocols while writing in Chinese on an English topic to a Chinese reader. However, certain concepts and experiences were expressed in English despite the task requirements to work entirely in Chinese. The protocols indicate that one person spoke, and wrote, in English some text on the topic area of teaching assistants, while another wrote in English most of a paragraph on the subject of computers at Carnegie Mellon University. Interviews with the subjects afterward revealed that these experiences had been acquired at CMU in a completely English-language setting. These writers had not written about these topic areas to friends back home and had encountered and talked about these topic areas only in an English setting. Even when talking with Chinese friends, they used English for these topic areas. In the writing task, they expressed their ideas in English, because they found themselves retrieving the information in English; later, before sending the letter, they said that they would translate into Chinese. These findings, from a pilot study, suggest further evidence for storage pools in memory linked to different languages.

Conclusions

This study was based on the belief that certain writing situations will be improved if ESL writers are able to use their first language at certain points while they are generating their texts. According to this view, the first language would enable them to retrieve information about certain topics more easily with less constraint than if they had to translate the information before writing down any text. In particular, the study suggested that ESL writers would be able to produce better texts and their writing would be enhanced if they planned in the language related to acquisition of knowledge of a topic area. Thus, if writing in English about a Chinese topic, Chinese speakers would benefit if they produced a plan in Chinese and then used that plan to generate their English text. Similarly, if writing in English about an English topic, their writing would benefit if they produced their plan in English.

The analyses revealed that, when writers planned in Chinese on the Chinese topic (*Qingming*) and in English on the English topic (CMU), their plans and texts were rated significantly better than when they planned in Chinese on the English topic and in English on the Chinese topic. Subjects also wrote longer plans and essays in the matching conditions. These results suggest that these subjects did benefit from using the language of topic knowledge acquisition, although a genre difference (the *Qingming* topic asked subjects to compare and contrast) may account for some of the benefits; as Langer (1984) and Bridgeman and Carlson (1984) suggest, comparison/contrast is more likely to result in better-structured writing. In addition, subjects retrieved more details for *Qingming* when planning in Chinese than in English, but retrieved similar amounts of details for the CMU topic in both languages, suggesting that topics related to a Chinese experience in particular benefit from using the first language for a portion of the composing.

The data also revealed that essays and plans written on the Chinese topic, *Qingming*, were rated as superior to those on the Carnegie Mellon topic, while the plans for *Qingming* were much shorter than those for Carnegie Mellon. These results hold across languages, whether the plan was generated in Chinese or in English.

As I mentioned earlier, these rating differences may result from differences in topic requirements, since the *Qingming* topic required a comparison/contrast structure. However, particularly when we view these differences in relation to the plan length and the difference in details for *Qingming* in the two languages, they appear to offer some insights into how language is stored in and retrieved from memory.

This study also suggests some directions that can impact on classroom pedagogy (with the understanding that the subjects in this study were

Chinese speakers). First, planning on certain language topics seems to be enhanced when writers use the language of topic-area knowledge. In this case, if writers are writing on topics related to their first language experience, their writing should be assisted and they should be able to draw on a greater amount of topic area information if they create a portion of their plan or preliminary draft in their first language. Second, translation from the native language into English appears to help rather than hinder writers when the topic-area knowledge is in the first language. Writers would thus lose little by writing in their first language and then translating into English at the appropriate time for their emerging texts.

Third, the writers in this study were able to access more information when working in their first language on a first language topic. Newly arrived foreign students, typical in freshman writing courses, often write about topics related to their native language background; the evidence suggests that information on such topics is more readily retrieved in the first language. In such writing situations, ESL writers should be encouraged to use their first language while composing initial drafts. Looking at this idea from an opposite angle, if teachers want their students to avoid their first language and use English as much as possible, then they should try to avoid assigning topics related to their students' first language background. In this circumstance, with English-related topics, students should be using their second language, English, more readily.

In conclusion, this study suggests that planning and preliminary considerations of a topic can be enhanced if ESL writers understand that using the language of topic-area knowledge can have a positive effect on their planning and writing.

References

Arapoff, N. (1967). Writing: A thinking process. *TESOL Quarterly, 1*, 33–39.

Berrueta-Clement, J. (1973). Ethnic and intra-ethnic differentiation in cognitive characteristics: A study of bilinguals and monolinguals in Nebaj, Guatemala. Unpublished doctoral dissertation, University of California, Irvine.

Bridgeman, B., and Carlson, S. (1984). Survey of academic writing tasks. *Written Communication, 1*, 247–280.

Carson, J. E.; Carrell, P. L.; Silberstein, S.; Kroll, B.; and Kuehn, P. A. (1990). Reading-writing relationships in first and second language. *TESOL Quarterly, 24*, 245–266.

Chelala, S. (1981). The composing process of two Spanish-speakers and the coherence of their texts: A case study. Unpublished doctoral dissertation, New York University.

Cumming, A. (1987). Decision making and text representation in ESL writing performance. Paper presented at the 21st TESOL Convention, Miami Beach, Fla., April.

Edelsky, C. (1982). Writing in a bilingual program: The relation of L1 and L2 texts. *TESOL Quarterly, 16,* 211–228.

Flower, L., and Hayes, J. R. (1981). A cognitive process theory of writing. *College Composition and Communication, 32,* 365–387.

Friedlander, A. (1987). The writer stumbles: Constraints on composing in English as a second language. Unpublished doctoral dissertation, Carnegie Mellon University.

Friedlander, A., and Huckin, T. (1987). Composing in ESL: Language acquisition and the retrieval of topic knowledge. Paper presented at the Annual American Educational Research Association Conference, Washington, D.C., April.

Hakuta, K. (1986). *Mirror of language: The debate on bilingualism.* New York: Basic Books.

Johnson, C. (1985). The composing processes of six ESL students. Unpublished doctoral dissertation, Illinois State University.

Jones, C. S., and Tetroe, J. (1987). Composing in a second language. In A. Matsuhashi (Ed.), *Writing in real time* (pp. 34–57). New York: Addison-Wesley.

Langer, J. (1984). The effects of available information on responses to school writing tasks. *Research in the Teaching of English, 18,* 27–44.

Lay, N. (1982). Composing processes of adult ESL learners: A case study. *TESOL Quarterly, 16,* 406.

McLaughlin, B. (1978). *Second language acquisition in childhood.* Hillsdale, N.J.: Erlbaum.

Mohan, B., and Lo, W. (1985). Academic writing and Chinese students: Transfer and developmental factors. *TESOL Quarterly, 19,* 515–534.

Moragne e Silva, M. (1986). First and second language composing processes: A case study. Paper presented at the 20th Annual TESOL Convention, Anaheim, Cal., March.

Paradis, M. (1985). On the representation of two languages in one brain. *Language Sciences, 7,* 1–39.

Peterson, L., and Peterson, M. (1959). Short-term retention of individual verbal items. *Journal of Experimental Psychology, 58,* 193–198.

8 The teaching of topical structure analysis as a revision strategy for ESL writers

Ulla Connor
Mary Farmer

In the process-centered approach to composition, writing is viewed as a recursive process in which students are encouraged to revise as they write and to produce multiple drafts of their essays. This approach toward writing instruction is based on an accumulating body of empirical support that suggests that this is the process successful and experienced writers typically follow when they write. Sommers (1978) was one of the pioneers in researching how native English-speaking writers revise. She noted what others have since confirmed: that inexperienced writers tend to revise at the lexical level only, and that they tend to adhere to rigid rules of style and usage regardless of appropriateness (see also Beach 1976; Perl 1979; Bridwell 1980; Flower and Hayes 1981; Faigley and Witte 1984; Freedman 1985; Anson 1989). Experienced writers, however, tend to revise at all levels (lexical, phrasal, sentential, etc.) and are more likely to make efforts to "shape the argument" to fit the writer's purpose.

If native speakers experience problems during revision, then probably it can be safely assumed that these problems also occur and are even more acute for the nonnative speaker. It is important that we teach ESL students to consider the situational and contextual causes of revision in a piece of writing. This chapter describes a promising new linguistically based revision strategy, *topical structure analysis,* that helps students to consider the discourse level in conjunction with the surface level of their writing. We will explain the theory behind topical structure analysis, how topical structure analysis differs from some other text-based theories of coherence, how to perform a topical structure analysis, and how to make it work as a revision strategy and a check of coherence in process-centered ESL writing classrooms (see also Connor 1987; Cerniglia, Medsker, and Connor 1990). Our intent is *not* to suggest that this method would replace teacher and peer comments in writing instruction (reviewed by Leki, this volume). Rather we are proposing a

This is a revised and expanded version of a paper originally presented at the 38th Annual Conference on College Composition and Communication, Atlanta, Georgia, March 18–21, 1987.

supplementary procedure that would encourage students to consider and reconsider the text as a whole and to allow them to gauge for themselves the relative coherence of their writing.

Topical structure analysis

Topical structure analysis, originally developed by Lautamatti (1978) for the purpose of describing coherence in texts, focuses on the semantic relationships that exist between sentence topics and the discourse topic. Through topical structure analysis, these relationships can be studied by looking at sequences of sentences and examining how topics in the sentences work through the text to progressively build meaning. Lautamatti identifies three possible progressions of sentences: parallel, sequential, and extended parallel. Very briefly, in *parallel progression,* the sentence topics are semantically identical; in *sequential progression,* the sentence topics are always different, as the comment of the previous sentence becomes the topic of the next sentence, and so on; and, in *extended parallel progression,* a parallel progression may be temporarily interrupted by a sequential progression.

Topical structure analysis was used in a study on the textual causes and effects of revision by Witte (1983a), who felt that it would allow him to study the textual stimulus for revision. Copies of the expository paragraph originally used and analyzed by Lautamatti (1978), titled "Language and Community" (shown in Table 1), were distributed, and students were asked to revise the passage so that it would be "easier to read and understand." These revisions were first holistically rated and categorized according to whether they were low-scoring or high-scoring, and were then submitted to topical structure analysis. The analysis revealed that the low-scoring revisions exhibited a lack of clear focus (or coherence), indicating that the reviser was uncertain as to what the discourse topic was.

Topical structure analysis considers both global and local coherence of texts. For that reason, it is a more satisfying method of analyzing coherence than others put forth previously. For example, Christensen (1967) viewed coherence as related to structural unity of paragraphs. Paragraphs, according to him, are a sequence of structurally related sentences linked together through coordination and subordination. For example, if the first sentence of a paragraph is the topic sentence, the second will be a development of it, subordinated to it. The rest of the sentences may be coordinate to a previous or subordinate to the preceding sentence. Thus, Christensen focuses on the rhetorical roles of sentences, whereas topical structure analysis is concerned with the semantic meanings of sentences and their sequencing to develop the overall discourse topic.

Weissberg's (1984) work on information dynamics in scientific ESL texts is equally useful in explaining coherence at the local level. His research examined the placement of given and new information in sequential sentences and how new information becomes given. His analyses of paragraphs from scientific texts offer important information about the patterns of given and new information and suggest strategies for improved style and readability.

We believe that approaches such as Christensen's and Weissberg's are needed to understand full dimensions of local coherence of texts and student writing. However, we think that topical structure analysis has an added advantage in that by using it students are forced to assess both the global coherence (what the essay is about) and local coherence (how sentences build meaning in relation to each other and the overall discourse topic).

How to perform a topical structure analysis

Working closely with Lautamatti's and Witte's work, we isolated three principles that would be crucial for students to understand: (1) identification of sentence topics, (2) determining sentence progression, and (3) "charting" the progress of sentence topics.

In order to be able to identify sentence topics, students need to have some familiarity with the arrangement of information within a sentence according to what might best be termed its *topic* and *comment*. *Topic* can be explained as simply the main idea or topic of the sentence, which often but not always coincides with the grammatical subject of the sentence. In most essays and texts, one noun or noun phrase expresses this. The noun that expresses the sentence topic can occur in many places in a sentence – beginning, middle, or end, as the sample text in Table 1 shows. *Comment* can be explained as "what is being said about the topic," which is often the grammatical predicate. For example, in sentence 4 of the sample text (see Table 1), the sentence topic is "a child" and the comment is "is very unlikely to survive."

Students are reminded that the context determines the sentence topic in many cases; occasionally more than one word as a sentence topic may be correct. Students should not belabor the decision over the sentence topic, however, since a certain amount of intuitiveness is required.[1] Students are asked to identify sentence topics first in isolated sentences

---

1 Despite the fairly intuitive nature of topic identification, previous research has shown high interrater reliabilities: 86.5% in Witte's research (1983b) and 88.9% in Connor and Schneider's work (1988).

TABLE I. SAMPLE TEXT AND DIAGRAM

Language and Community

(1) When <u>a human infant</u>[a] is born into any community in any part of the world <u>it</u> has two things in common with any other infant, provided neither of them has been damaged in any way either before or during birth. (2) Firstly, and most obviously, <u>new born children</u> are completely helpless. (3) Apart from a powerful capacity to draw attention to their helplessness by using sound there is nothing <u>the new born child</u> can do to ensure his own survival. (4) Without care from some other human being or beings, be it mother, grandmother, sister, nurse, or human group, <u>a child</u> is very unlikely to survive. (5) <u>This helplessness of human infants</u> is in marked contrast with the capacity of many new born animals to get to their feet within minutes of birth and run with the herd within a few hours. (6) Although <u>young animals</u> are certainly at risk, sometimes for weeks or even months after birth, compared with the human infant <u>they</u> very quickly develop the capacity to fend for themselves. (7) It would seem that <u>this long period of vulnerability</u> is the price that the human species has to pay for the very long period which fits man for survival as species.

(8) It is during this very long period in which <u>the human infant</u> is totally dependent on others that <u>it</u> reveals the second feature which it shares with all other undamaged human infants, a capacity to learn language. (9) For this reason, biologists now suggest that <u>language</u> is 'species specific' to the human race, that is to say, they consider the human infant to be genetically programmed in such a way that it can acquire language. (10) This suggestion implies that just as <u>human beings</u> are designed to see three-dimensionally and in colour, and just as they are designed to stand upright rather than to move on all fours, so <u>they</u> are designed to learn and use language as part of their normal development as well-formed human beings.

 1. a human infant
 2. new born children
 3. the new born child
 4. a child
 5.   this helplessness of human infants
 6.   young animals
 7.   this long period of vulnerability
 8. the human infant
 9.   language
10. human beings

Source: Lautamatti (1978:78).
[a]Underlining indicates sentence topic.

and then in passages. When reading passages, students are asked to read the whole passage and tell what it is about in order to link the sentence topics with the discourse topic.

In order to be able to determine sentence progression, students would need to know how topics can build meaning through either parallel, sequential, or extended parallel progression. As briefly explained earlier, in parallel progression, sentence topics are semantically identical, as in sentence 1 (S1) through S4 in Table 1. This kind of progression – repetition of topic – is meant to reinforce the idea for the reader. In sequential progression the sentence topics, which are always different, are typically derived from the content of the comment in the previous sentence (S5, S6, S7, and S9 in Table 1). This helps to develop individual topics by adding details to an idea – a requirement for good prose. Too much development for a sentence topic (if it is not the main idea of the essay) may distract the reader from the main idea. In extended parallel progression, the writer returns to a topic mentioned earlier in the essay (S8, S10 in Table 1).

Drawing a diagram and interpreting it

After students have identified and underlined the sentence topics in their essays, they are ready to draw diagrams corresponding to the structure of their essays. As the sample text in Table 1 shows, sentence topics with parallel progression are placed exactly below each other. Sequential topics are indented progressively, and extended parallel progression is aligned under the parallel topic to which it refers.

After students have drawn the diagrams, they should study them carefully to check for coherence of ideas and make changes accordingly. This is the most challenging part, and student writers need a lot of practice. Table 2 shows short sample passages that we use to show students parallel, sequential, and extended parallel progression. Sequential progression is especially difficult to master because it can be found in a text that is completely incoherent, as Sample 4 shows (Table 2). This is an example of a sequential progression where the topics of each sentence are unrelated, whereas the topics in Samples 2 and 3 are related to the overall theme of the passage. Samples 2 and 3 – although both coherent – are different from each other in the distribution of given/new information: Sample 3 shows a "classic" case of sequential development, where a comment of a sentence becomes the topic of the next sentence, whereas Sample 2 depicts a text with less "classic" information dynamics. Both of these are characteristic of many real texts.

In order to practice identifying coherence problems, we also use sample student essays with varying levels of coherence. A sample essay with a low level of coherence is shown in Table 3 with its accompanying dia-

Parallel progression

SAMPLE 1

(1) <u>Chocolates</u> are a national craving. (2) Records show that <u>they</u> are sold in huge quantities – 11.2 pounds per capita per year. (3) <u>Designer chocolates</u> often sell for nearly $30/lb. (4) It is obvious that <u>these candies</u> are America's number one choice.

1. Chocolates
2. they
3. Designer chocolates
4. these candies

Sequential progression

SAMPLE 2

(1) <u>Computer interviews</u> are used by market researchers to assess product demand. (2) Using these, many different <u>products</u> are analyzed. (3) For example, people may be asked about <u>detergents</u>.

1. Computer interviews
2.   products
3.   detergents.

SAMPLE 3

(1) <u>I</u> saw a strange man in the street. (2) <u>He</u> was wearing a large badge. (3) The <u>badge</u> was multicolored and gaudy.

1. I
2.   He
3.   badge

SAMPLE 4

(1) <u>School</u> is boring. (2) Many of my <u>friends</u> have motor cycles. (3) As you all know, most <u>teenagers</u> have part-time jobs.

1. School
2.   friends
3.   teenagers

Extended parallel progression

SAMPLE 5

(1) <u>Body language</u> varies from culture to culture. (2) To say yes, <u>Americans</u> nod their heads up and down. (3) <u>Japanese and Italians</u> use the same nod to say no. (4) <u>Body language</u> is an important skill for international managers.

1. Body language
2.   Americans
3.   Japanese and Italians
4. Body language

TABLE 3. SAMPLE STUDENT ESSAY WITH DIAGRAM

Janie and Dorm Life

(1) There were many <u>changes</u> coming to Purdue from such a small town like Danville, Indiana. (2) The massive <u>number</u> of new faces, huge, unfamiliar buildings, but I have also learned a lot about myself, the faculty of Purdue, and getting to know the friendly girls living on the same dorm floor as myself.

(3) <u>Dorm life</u> is not as drab as I had first imagined. (4) My <u>room</u> is fairly large enough for two girls. (5) My <u>roommate</u> and I can also decorate our "home" to our satisfaction. (6) The <u>food</u> is a step above high school cafeteria-style lunches I was accustomed to in the past. (7) The <u>bathroom facilities</u> accommodate to all of the girls needs at various time intervals. (8) Getting along with most of the <u>girls</u> in our south west wing at Robert Owen Hall is the name of the game. (9) My <u>roommate and I</u> have to live together for the next nine months, so why not get along with each other now and save any trouble occurring later, which may cause an unhappy freshman year at Purdue. (10) This type of <u>experience</u> may discourage most people from returning back for another semester.

(11) Moving in to a <u>dorm</u> is like driving a car for the first time in which you are the only one behind the wheel. (12) Though mom and dad are only a phone call away and are paying most of the bills, <u>I</u> am the final one deciding where my college career will lead. (13) <u>College,</u> as well as dorm life, in general, is only going to be as pleasurable as I make it. (14) <u>I</u> learn and grow in many ways everyday.

(15) Though Purdue and Owen Hall are wonderful places to be, at times, they also have their <u>disadvantages</u>. (16) There is a never ending <u>circle</u> of

gram. The sample essay was written by a native English-speaking, freshman-level student to describe a place. Based upon the diagram, "Janie and Dorm Life" is unsuccessful because it does not have any extended parallel progression to refer back to "changes" in becoming a college student, the main topic. There are also too many different sentence topics, resulting in too much sequential progression (S2–S9) to allow for adequate development. The writer needs to make changes to develop the subtopics better and to adhere to the focus more consistently.

Topical structure analysis in the ESL writing classroom

For several years we have taught topical structure analysis as a revision tool for ESL students in intermediate- and advanced-level writing classes

TABLE 3 *(continued)*

figuring out who what and when, privacy invasion, and quiet hours noise ordinance. (17) I hope that I may help some <u>younger friends</u> of mine make wise decisions on how to conduct themselves while away at the college of their choice. (18) I want to remind <u>them</u> of what their first priority while attending school, studying first, social life second.

1.	changes
2.	number
3.	dorm life
4.	room
5.	roommate
6.	food
7.	bathroom facilities
8.	girls
9.	roommate and I
10.	experience
11.	dorm
12.	I
13.	college
14.	I
15.	disadvantages
16.	circle
17.	younger friends
18.	them

at Indiana University in Indianapolis. When presenting this procedure, we explain to students the steps in topical structure analysis in the same sequence and manner as we did in this chapter. Several sample texts are analyzed, including paragraph- and essay-length texts of varying coherence. Then students draw their own diagrams, and we go over them with the students individually to help interpret what they mean. Students quickly become comfortable, and coherence diagrams – even if not required – become part of many students' writing folders or portfolios along with prewriting, drafts, peer comments, and other facilitative procedures. Cerniglia et al. (1990) have developed a computer-assisted instructional lesson to teach topical structure analysis, for use in the classroom or in a tutorial session.

We think that students will benefit most by using this method after their first draft. At that point in the writing process, students are still prepared to make substantive changes. For many students, this coherence check becomes a heuristic that helps them sort out their ideas.

Student response has been positive; many have remarked that the procedure helps them examine the meanings of their sentences and forces them to relate these meanings to the main topic and purpose of their writing. When we teach the analysis as a revision tool, we note improvement in student writing, specifically in regard to clearer focus (thanks to added extended parallel progression) and better development of subtopics (thanks to an improved ratio of parallel and sequential progressions). In an example of improved coherence in ESL revisions after the use of topical structure analysis, the appendix includes a fourth draft of an ESL essay on child abuse, a student-generated coherence diagram, and a subsequent revision – the fifth draft of the same essay – accompanied by a new student-generated diagram.

The most significant improvement in the essay is the increased clarity of focus stemming from a transitional sentence (S4): "Most of them, though, are highly dependent on the emotional background of one or both parents." This helps keep the focus on the reasons for child abuse. The student's own written comments after the exercise speak for the value of the activity in forcing the student to evaluate the function of each sentence in light of the main discourse topic. The student mentioned that the exercise helped her reorganize the essay and focus on reasons of child abuse rather than on unrelated examples of child abuse. She also mentioned the new concluding paragraph, which includes the word *reasons*, referring back to the introduction.

We are not claiming that topical structure analysis is a panacea for all writing problems. But we feel that because topical structure analysis illustrates graphically the development of an essay using students' own written words, it is a useful check of coherence in writing, which should be used in conjunction with teacher and peer comments. In addition, although we have yet to research and document this particular aspect, the analysis appears to be easily internalized, with carryover benefit to subsequent writings.

Appendix: Draft and revised essay with coherence diagrams

1. Draft

(1) <u>Violence</u> toward children is no more a new phenomenon, it continues today as it existed in the past. (2) <u>A child abuse or neglect</u> is a child that is humiliated, beaten or sexually abused. (3) <u>The causes</u> that lead parents to torture, neglect or abuse their children are very complex.

(4) Many <u>people</u> with varying degrees of emotional disorder, inadequate skills or distaste for marriage find themselves trying to copy a role that is a constant irritant to them. (5) As a consequence <u>they</u> explode their rage on their children, without knowledge that this must be a negative factor in the development of their children.

(6) One important reason that the <u>interaction</u> between parent and child does not always go well is that parents try to follow a specific rule about how the child should be raised rather than looking to the particular baby for clues about how the child best be handled. (7) Sometimes the <u>relation</u> between parent and child is restricted because the parents underestimate the child's potential. (8) Some parents think that their children do not listen or that they can't communicate, <u>they</u> tend to forget that children have limitations, and that they can't behave in the way parents like. (9) <u>Children</u> can be abused or neglected because of who they are rather than what they do. (10) <u>Babies</u> who are unwanted, or who are the wrong sex, or who have some physical problems, victims of the parent's disappointment. (11) The baby's appearance, as in the case of the <u>little boy</u> who looks just like the father, who left the mother when she was pregnant, or the little girl who reminds her father of his mother's abused.

(12) <u>Parents of abused children</u> are subect to a behavior role that they felt when they were children. (13) <u>They</u> were themselves abused and have a difficult time responding to their babies with love. (14) <u>A women</u> is often forced by social pressures to ignore her desires and feelings. (15) She has to assume the <u>role</u> of wife and mother and sometimes marriage is seen as a terrible mistake. (16) Also, the constant <u>demands</u> of the child for his mother's attention is another way that feelings of isolation develop because she has to interpret her own social activities. (17) Few parents understand the limitations of the child and this causes them to become frustrated or angry when their own <u>demands</u> are not satisfied.

(18) <u>Other parents</u> see the persistent crying of the baby as accusatory and of their inability to stop the baby's so they become frustrated. (19) <u>They</u> might interpret the baby's cry as "if you were a good parent the baby wouldn't be crying like this." (20) <u>Feelings</u> of rejection and stress appear and lead parents to abuse their children.

(21) <u>Parents</u> who have no friends, family or neighbors during the bad periods are more likely to take out their problems on their children. (22) Their <u>social group</u> is so small that nobody is able to help the abused child or report the parents until the damage has been done.

(23) <u>Parents</u> are crucial to a child's learning, because they reinforce and punish

their behavior; also, because they are the most important people in the child's life. (24) As long as people do not accept the idea that physical or emotional <u>punishment</u> is not a method of controlling a child. (25) This <u>situation</u> will continue. (26) A <u>child</u> is a human being with the same rights and privileges of an adult. (27) <u>Parents</u> must understand that children are not pieces of property belong to them. Instead, they are human beings whose welfare should be protected.

1. Violence
2.   A child abuse or neglect
3.   The causes
4.   people
5.   they
6.   interaction
7.   relation
8.   they
9.   Children
10.   Babies
11.   little boy
12.   Parents of abused children
13.   They
14.   A women
15.   role
16.   demands
17.   demands
18.   Other parents
19.   They
20.   Feelings
21.   Parents
22.   social group
23.   Parents
24.   punishment
25.   situation
26.   child
27.   Parents

2. Revision after diagram

(1) <u>Child abuse</u> or neglect continues today as it existed in the past. (2) A <u>child</u> is abused or neglected when he or she is humiliated, beaten or sexually abused. (3) The <u>reasons</u> behind it are very complex and difficult to determine. (4) <u>Most of them</u>, though, are highly dependent on the emotional background of one or both parents.

(5) The most common <u>reasons</u>, result from either an emotional disorder, inadequate skills or a distaste for marriage found in one or both parents. (6) <u>Any one of these reasons</u> forces the parent to copy a role that is a constant irritant.

(7) <u>Parents</u> who were abused as children may develop emotional disorders and are subject to a behavior role that they learned from their parents. (8)

Since they were themselves abused, <u>they</u> have a difficult time responding to their children with love. (9) On the other hand, <u>inadequate skills</u> may lead parents to interpret the persistent crying of the baby as an accusatory finger of their failure as parents. (10) <u>They</u> believe that a good parent will know how to stop the baby from crying. (11) <u>The distaste for marriages</u> commonly reflected in the woman forced by social pressures to ignore her own desires and feelings.

(12) <u>She</u> has had to assume the role of wife and mother, forcing her to interrupt her own social activities. (13) <u>This constant pressure</u> may lead sometimes to the belief that marriage is a terrible mistake. (14) When one or more of these <u>forces</u> interact, they result in the parent exploding his or her rage on the child.

(15) <u>The interaction between parents and children</u> is an important factor in the development of their children. (16) <u>It</u> is also a potential source for child abuse. (17) When <u>parents</u> follow inflexible rules about how the child should be raised, without any consideration for his feelings or when parent failed to properly estimate the child's potential and limitations; they may begin to cross the line between sensitive to abusive parents.

(18) <u>Children</u> can also be abused, because of who they are rather than what they do. (19) <u>This group</u> will include those babies who are unwanted, have the wrong sex, or have some physical problems. (20) <u>They</u> are the victims of their parents' frustrations, and disappointments. (21) <u>It</u> will also include the unfortunate case of a baby that because of the way he looks, reminds the mother of the father that abandoned them.

(22) Finally, <u>parents</u> who have no friends, family or neighbors during the bad periods are more likely to take their frustrations on their children. (23) <u>Their social group</u> is so small that nobody is able to help the abused child or report the parents until the damage has been done.

(24) In conclusion, <u>these reasons</u> are not self-evident by themselves and few parents will admit to abusing their child. (25) <u>They</u> are fed by strong feelings of love and fear from the child and on the misunderstanding that children are property of the parents. (26) <u>Parents</u> are crucial to a child's learning because they reinforce and punish their behavior; also because <u>they</u> are the most important people in the child's life.

(Appendix continues on next page.)

1. Child abuse
2.   child
3.   reasons
4.   most of them
5.   reasons
6.   Any one of these reasons
7.   Parents
8.   they
9.   inadequate skills
10.   They
11.   The distaste for marriages
12.   She
13.   This constant measure
14.   forces
15.   The interaction between parents and children
16.   It
17.   parents
18.   Children
19.   This group
20.   They
21.   It
22.   parents
23.   Their social group
24.   these reasons
25.   They
26.   Parents
             they

References

Anson, C. M. (Ed.) (1989). *Writing and response: Theory, practice, and research*. Urbana, Ill.: National Council of Teachers of English.

Beach, R. (1976). Self-evaluation strategies of extensive revisers and nonrevisers. *College Composition and Communication, 27,* 160–164.

Bridwell, L. S. (1980). Revising strategies in twelfth grade students' transactional writing. *Research in the Teaching of English, 14,* 197–222.

Cerniglia, C. S.; Medsker, K. L.; and Connor, U. (1990). Improving coherence by using computer-assisted instruction. In U. Connor and A. M. Johns (Eds.), *Coherence: Research and pedagogical perspectives,* pp. 227–241. Washington, D.C.: TESOL.

Christensen, F. (1967). *Notes toward a new rhetoric*. New York: Harper & Row.

Connor, U. (1987). Research frontiers in writing analysis. *TESOL Quarterly, 21,* 677–695.

Connor, U., and Schneider, M. (1988). Topical structure and writing quality:

Results of an ESL study. Paper presented at the 22nd Annual TESOL Convention, Chicago, Ill., March.

Faigley, L., and Witte, S. P. (1984). Measuring the effects of revision on text structure. In R. Beach and S. Bridwell (Eds.), *New directions in composition research* (pp. 95–108). New York: Guilford Press.

Flower, L., and Hayes, J. (1981). A cognitive process theory of writing. *College Composition and Communication, 32,* 365–387.

Freedman, S. W. (Ed.) (1985). *The acquisition of written language: Response and revision.* Norwood, N.J.: Ablex.

Lautamatti, L. (1978). Observations on the development of the topic in simplified discourse. In V. Kohonen and N. E. Enkvist (Eds.), *Text linguistics, cognitive learning, and language teaching,* (pp. 71–104). Turku, Finland: Afinla. Reprinted in U. Connor and R. B. Kaplan (Eds.), *Writing across languages: Analysis of L2 text* (pp. 87–113). Reading, Mass.: Addison-Wesley, 1987.

Perl, S. (1979) The composing process of unskilled college writers. *Research in the Teaching of English, 13,* 317–336.

Sommers, N. I. (1978). Revision in the composing process: A case study of experimental writers and student writers. Unpublished doctoral dissertation, Boston University.

Weissberg, R. C. (1984). Given and new: Paragraph development models for scientific English. *TESOL Quarterly, 18,* 485–500.

Witte, S. P. (1983a). Topical structure and revision: An exploratory study. *College Composition and Communication, 34,* 313–341.

(1983b). Topical structure and writing quality: Some possible text-based explanations of readers' judgments of students' writing. *Visible Language, 17,* 177–205.

9 What does time buy? ESL student performance on home versus class compositions

Barbara Kroll

Writing is frequently a difficult skill for *any* language user, which is to say that writing presents a fairly challenging task for both native and nonnative speakers. For English as a second language (ESL) students, it seems fair to say that writing academic papers is particularly difficult. ESL students must learn to create written products that demonstrate mastery over contextually appropriate formats for the rhetorical presentation of ideas as well as mastery in all areas of language, a Herculean task given the possibilities for error. It is partially the multiplicity of skills involved which contributes to the overall difficulty of writing. Collins and Gentner (1980) make the following observation about native-speaker writing:

> Much of the difficulty of writing stems from the large number of constraints that must be satisfied at the same time. In expressing an idea the writer must consider at least four structural levels: overall text structure, paragraph structure, sentence structure (syntax), and word structure.... Clearly the attempt to coordinate all these requirements is a staggering job. (p. 67).

If various aspects of writing are seen as "structural levels" that must be coordinated, it is reasonable to hypothesize that success may vary from level to level. For example, one particular student might exhibit greater mastery over sentence structure while another might exhibit greater mastery over overall text structure. Further, because of the particular difficulty that ESL students may have with the code of English (as partially predicted by principles of cognitive theory; McLaughlin 1987: 133–142), extending the amount of time allotted to producing an essay might affect the level of mastery exhibited on any or all of the levels identified by Collins and Gentner.[1]

A relationship between the element of time and the level of grammatical accuracy was originally suggested by Krashen (1977, 1981, 1982) in his monitor model. The model predicts that given certain conditions, the learner can apply consciously learned grammar rules to alter

---

1 The TOEFL program, for example, is currently conducting research into the possible effect on a candidate's score of extending the amount of time available for the Test of Written English (*TOEFL Test of Written English Guide* 1989: 20).

and improve the accuracy of his or her written or spoken utterances. One of the conditions that Krashen originally posited for the use of the monitor was *time* (Krashen 1981: 3), though in later work he did not list time as a key variable (1985: 3).

Time may also be a key factor in other aspects of writing, such as the ability to produce a text with control over such discourse features as organization and coherence. In addition, many students and teachers feel that writing under pressure is a very unnatural situation and perhaps cannot lead to work that is truly representative of anyone's best capabilities. This philosophy is advanced in a report by Sanders and Littlefield (1975): "Unfortunately, the rigidly controlled essay test situation surely represents the ultimate in an artificial writing situation; as such, it is exactly the kind of situation shunned in many modern composition courses" (p. 147). Recently, many school writing programs have abandoned the traditional timed examination in favor of a portfolio system to assess student writing (Burnham 1986; Elbow and Belanoff 1986; Lucas, Carlson, and Bridwell-Bowles 1989; Belanoff and Dickson, in press); and Ruth and Murphy (1988: 153) call for additional research to explore the effects of time on writing performance in testing situations.

In order to help teachers to structure courses that will facilitate progress in the writing development of their ESL students, we should explore both issues raised so far: differential abilities in various aspects of writing and the role of time. Understanding both contributes to goal setting in teaching, and we want to have specific goals rather than simply having the abstract goal of wanting students to write like competent native speakers.

One of the difficulties in establishing clear goals for L2 writing students is the fact that native-speaker (NS) proficiency is hardly a simple issue. There is no single written standard that can be said to represent the "ideal" written product in English. Therefore, we cannot easily establish procedures for evaluating ESL writing in terms of adherence to some model of native-speaker writing. Even narrowing the discussion to a focus on academic writing is fraught with complexity. While Spack (1988: 30) sees the role of the writing teacher as initiating students into the "academic discourse community," Johns (this volume) points out that there are competing interpretations of what a teacher's role should be and even of what modes or types of prose should be produced in the composition classroom.

The question of error is also of major concern in any examination of NS or L2 writing. The output of a type of nonsuccessful native speaker often referred to as a "basic writer" was first examined in depth in a classic study by Shaughnessy (1977). She indicated that mistakes learners make are often neither attempts to deliberately sabotage language in reckless disregard of its rules nor necessarily careless inattention to details. Rather, the mistakes of learners are often the result of internally consistent and carefully worked out but misguided interpretations of language. Error analysis itself is a complex field (reviewed by Brown 1987: 168–195), but it offers the insight that many errors on the part of ESL students, like the errors of Shaughnessy's basic writers, stem from intralingual errors within English.

Despite the more recent concern for process over product in ESL composition classrooms (discussed by Krapels, this volume), many teachers remain troubled by persistent student error, and researchers continue to explore audience reactions to written errors by ESL students (Vann, Meyer, and Lorenz 1984; Santos 1988).

This study examines whether or not there is a connection between the level of syntactic accuracy (including morphology and word choice) and the overall organizational success of a student essay by measuring both of these features independently. In short, it investigates whether it is possible to write a good essay in bad English or a bad essay in good English. The focus of this investigation, however, is time: Does time buy a reduction of error and an improvement in rhetorical competency? To what extent does the amount of time allowed for the preparation of an essay affect its success both on the syntactic and the discourse levels?

Research design and methodology

This chapter presents a descriptive analysis of 100 essays written by 25 advanced ESL students at the freshman composition level. The subjects in this study were all undergraduate foreign students (i.e., not immigrants) enrolled in special sections of freshman composition for international students at the University of Southern California (USC). Twenty-five students were selected – in a stratified random sample – to represent the five largest foreign language groups at USC at the time: Arabic, Chinese, Japanese, Persian, and Spanish.

In contrast to much previous research on writing, which analyzed compositions produced under strictly controlled conditions with specified time limitations, the compositions analyzed here were divided into two major groups: those produced in class and under pressure of time, and those produced at home with 10–14 days of preparation time. Each subject contributed four essays to the data base: two written in a 60-minute time frame that was a controlled test/pressure situation, and two written over a 10- to 14-day period. It should be emphasized that during the 10- to 14-day interval, no class time was spent on any activity that directly related to the preparation of the "home" essays. Further, unlike Friedlander's study (this volume), which focuses on analyzing the *planning process* of essay preparation, or Connor and Farmer's study (this volume), which focuses on a technique for improving the *revision process,* this study focuses on the written *products* of student writers.

The findings reported here stem from two ways in which the data were coded, a sentence-level syntactic analysis and a global-level essay analysis. In the first procedure, each composition was examined in detail; every syntactic, morphological, and lexical error was identified and labeled, except for spelling, which was overlooked (a procedure similar to procedures followed by Neilson 1979, and Bardovi-Harlig and Bofman 1989).

In closely examining each sentence in the corpus of essays, the criterion for deciding whether or not an error had been committed and, if so, what type of error, was to determine what "syntactic reconstruction" could most easily and economically render the sentence into acceptable English given the context. For example, a singular subject with a plural verb was labeled a "subject-verb agreement" violation, while a correctly formed past tense had to be labeled "incorrect tense" if the context clearly showed a present-tense orientation. Following this procedure, a total of 33 different categories of error were identified for coding. In all, a total of 2,307 errors were identified and labeled in the corpus of 100 compositions (1,599 sentences; 28,444 words); each was assigned to one of the 33 categories.

The second measure that was used to code the data was to assign a kind of "specialized" holistic score to represent each essay's adherence to principles of organization and coherence, or what might be termed "pure discourse features" of an essay. A set of written scoring guidelines (also referred to as a "rubric") was developed following procedures detailed by Myers (1980) and White (1985).[2] The key to the rubric developed for this study was that readers had to overlook and ignore all errors not related to the features directly under examination, and had to focus solely on the "larger" issues of discourse. This procedure necessitated reading through the errors of syntax and attending only to the level of organization, coherence, and discourse fluency. In other words, the essays were being scored as if they had no grammatical errors; readers focused beyond the level of syntax (similar in intent to work done by Freedman 1977).

For the rubric used in this study, many of the features mentioned were identified as attributes of rhetorical control in such widely used guidelines as the rubrics used for scoring the TOEFL Test of Written English and the City University of New York (CUNY) placement exam. Features

---

2 Lloyd-Jones (1987) provides a full review of the literature on holistic assessment.

that most contributed to a high holistic score included (but were not limited to):

1. focused limitation of the topic
2. remaining on the focused topic throughout the essay
3. effective use of paragraphing
4. consistency in point of view
5. logical sequencing of ideas
6. artful use of transitions.

Identifiable features that lowered the score of a paper included (but were not limited to):

1. noticeable introduction of irrelevancies
2. failure to provide a clear sense of purpose
3. shifting point of view
4. infelicitous, inappropriate, or nonexistent transitions
5. assumption of an argument's validity with no development of the argument.

Two ESL teachers experienced in the reading of compositions and with previous practice in holistic grading were trained as graders for the essays; they achieved an interrater reliability coefficient of .85, showing a high degree of agreement on the scores.

Finally, the holistic score was compared to a score representing the syntactic accuracy of the same composition in order to determine whether or not there was a correlation between the level of success in each skill area.

Syntactic analysis results

Errors were tabulated to assess their frequency and distribution as well as to determine the accuracy level of each individual paper. Table 1 shows the percentage of each of the 33 tabulated errors found in class and home essays.

To focus on the level of class versus home performance, the Spearman rho correlation of the distribution of the 33 errors in class and at home was run. The correlation between class and home for all 33 errors was .904, with a significance level of $p < .05$. As this correlation shows, there was a very similar distribution of the error categories in class and home compositions, which is to say that the pattern of errors committed seems unaffected by the time factor.

TABLE I. ERROR CATEGORIES AND PERCENTAGES

		Percentage error in corpus	
Error	Name	Class	Home
Sentence structure errors			
1	Whole sentence or clause aberrant	1.5	1.0
2	Subject formation	1.0	1.3
3	Verb missing	.8	.3
4	Verb complement/object complement	2.1	1.7
5	Prep. phrase/infinitive mixup	1.0	.5
6	Dangling/misplaced modifier	.4	.4
7	Sentence fragment	1.3	2.2
8	Run-on sentence	3.1	2.1
9	Parallel structure	1.0	.9
10	Relative clause formation	.5	.4
11	Word order	3.0	1.8
12	Gapping error	2.0	1.8
13	Extraneous words	1.8	.9
14	Awkward phrasing	1.8	2.7
	Section totals	21.3	18.0
Verb-centered errors			
15	Tense	7.1	4.5
16	Voice	.9	.9
17	Verb formation	3.6	2.9
18	Subject-verb agreement	3.8	3.6
19	Two-word verb	1.4	.4
	Section totals	16.8	12.3
Reference errors			
20	Noun-pronoun agreement	2.3	1.7
21	Quantifier-noun agreement	.4	.5
22	Epenthetic pronoun	.4	.2
23	Ambiguous/unlocatable referent	2.6	3.1
24	Voice shift	1.2	.4
	Section totals	6.9	5.9
Word-level choice			
25	Lexical/phrase choice	11.1	11.7
26	Idiom	.6	1.3
27	Word form	6.0	7.9
28	Singular for plural (except verbs)	5.0	5.5
29	Plural for singular (except verbs)	2.5	1.8
30	Quantity words	1.2	.9
31	Preposition	6.2	7.5
	Section totals	32.6	36.6

TABLE I (*continued*)

Error	Name	Percentage error in corpus	
		Class	Home
Article errors			
32	Missing/extra/wrong article	10.8	14.0
Punctuation			
33	Missing/extra/wrong mark	11.8	13.5
	Total number of errors	1,142	1,165

Accuracy ratio

Apart from tabulating the total number of errors and categorizing their distribution, the occurrence of error within the framework of each composition was also calculated, because the number of syntactic errors becomes meaningful only within a consideration of the range of opportunity for error. For example, suppose Student A made 10 errors in a composition of 10 pages totaling 2,500 words, and Student B made 10 errors of a similar nature in a composition totaling 150 words. We could not call their performances similar. Using the total number of words in a composition and tabulating the number of errors is one of the standard measures used in forming the basis for a kind of accuracy ratio (Brière 1966; Brodkey and Young 1981; Haswell 1988).

In Table 2, a general or overall accuracy ratio is shown for each language group. These figures were derived from a two-step procedure. First, the total number of words in each composition was divided by the number of errors in each composition. Then the resulting individual accuracy scores for the subjects in each language group were averaged for class and home compositions.

The numbers in Table 2 can be read, for example, as follows. There are an average of 19.4 words between each error in class compositions written by Arabic speakers. The higher the number, the fewer errors are found proportionately; conversely, the lower the number, the greater the proportion of errors. Further, since these numbers are ratios, they can be compared. We can say, for example, that Japanese writing in class had nearly three times as many errors as the Arabs writing at home.

TABLE 2. MEAN INDIVIDUAL ACCURACY RATIOS BY LANGUAGE GROUP

Language group	Class	Home
Arabic	19.4	22.7
Chinese	15.9	20.7
Japanese	7.8	12.0
Persian	16.8	19.3
Spanish	14.0	15.5
Group mean:	14.8	18.0

The highest accuracy ratio here is 22.7, by the Arabic speakers in the home corpus; in contrast, the lowest is 7.8, for the Japanese class corpus. The means show that the Arabic essays were the most accurate (in both the class and home conditions) while the Japanese essays were the most flawed. Table 2 also shows that all five language groups show a proportionately better performance (at least minimally) at home.

In addition to expressing the accuracy scores of the essays as the average ratio of words per error in the class and home conditions, it is also possible to determine a percentage of error by dividing the number of errors by the total number of words. This is the converse of the procedure used to arrive at the accuracy ratio; it yields a decimal which translates into a percentage. For example, in a composition of 176 words with 12 errors, we can derive an accuracy ratio of 14.7, or we can derive an error percentage of .068, meaning that 6.8% of the total output contains errors. This latter procedure allowed for a t-test to be conducted to measure the difference between the class and home percentages. The resulting value was $t = 1.78$. This is not significant at the $p = < .05$ level ($p = .088$). In other words, despite the fact that the average accuracy ratios in the class and home conditions differed, the differences observed were not statistically significant.

Holistic evaluation results

In order for a paper to merit an upper-half grade (4, 5, or 6), it had to demonstrate control over both the structure of the essay and the structure of individual paragraphs. With this in mind, a score of 4 or higher demonstrates at least a fair degree of rhetorical competency. Table 3 summarizes both the percentages of upper-half and lower-half scores for each language group in class and at home, and also the mean score.

As seen in Table 3, for class compositions, the Chinese, Persian, and Spanish subjects had the same distribution of scores (40% upper vs.

TABLE 3. HOLISTIC SCORE PERFORMANCE

	Class			Home		
Language group	Upper half (%)	Lower half (%)	Mean score	Upper half (%)	Lower half (%)	Mean score
Arabic	50	50	3.8	80	20	4.2
Chinese	40	60	3.4	60	40	3.7
Japanese	20	80	2.4	10	90	2.8
Persian	40	60	3.2	30	70	3.3
Spanish	40	60	3.3	60	40	4.1
Group mean	38	62	3.2	48	52	3.6

60% lower), with the Arab breakdown for the scores fairly similar at 50% and 50%. Only the Japanese subjects had a noticeable difference in upper-half and lower-half scores. The preponderance of lower-half scores for the Japanese both at home and in class ranked the Japanese essays as the worst in terms of rhetorical competency. At the opposite extreme, the Arabs showed the largest percentage of scores in the upper half and emerged as the group with the best rhetorical competency.

The actual mean scores of all language groups is also shown in Table 3. In terms of home versus class essays, it appears that there was a slight tendency for subjects to write higher-rated essays at home, based on the group mean scores of 3.2 for class versus 3.6 for home. All five language groups averaged slightly higher scores for the home compositions (including the Japanese), but *t*-tests for significance indicate that none of the differences was statistically significant. However, as there are so few subjects in this study, the lack of statistical significance, despite the apparent differences, is not surprising.

Distribution of holistic scores

We can also consider the distribution of the scores in the corpus irrespective of the subjects' language background. This is done by tabulating the total number of essays that received each of the possible scores. Such a breakdown is shown in Table 4 (as computed in percentages). Not surprisingly, the majority of the scores clustered around the mid-range of possible scores. We see that 56% of class compositions and 52% of home compositions received scores ranging from 3 to 4.5, indicating that just over half of the papers were neither very poorly organized nor very well organized. The percentage of scores at the very bottom of the scale decreased by half from class to home (from 16% to 8%), whereas the percentage of highest scores tripled (from 2% to 6%).

TABLE 4. DISTRIBUTION OF HOLISTIC SCORES

Score	Class (%)	Home (%)
1, 1.5	16	8
2, 2.5	14	18
3	32	26
4, 4.5	24	26
5, 5.5	12	16
6	2	6
Total lower half	62	52
Total upper half	38	48

While lower-half scores clearly outnumbered upper-half scores in class compositions (62% vs. 38%), the gap was considerably narrower in home compositions (52% vs. 48%). In other words, there was a shift of 10 percentage points in the movement from class to home in the direction of more upper-half scores. Thus even though the differences were not statistically significant, the subjects wrote better-organized compositions at home. With increased time, they were able to reduce somewhat the incidence of the poorest level of performance and noticeably increase the incidence of above-par performance.

The interface of syntactic and rhetorical assessments

Once scores assessing (1) the syntactic accuracy and (2) the discourse/rhetorical effectiveness of each composition have been obtained, it is possible to consider the connection between syntactic proficiency on the one hand and fluency at the level of organization and coherence on the other. However, results of the Spearman correlation test for these scores show that the two scores for the compositions were not statistically correlated. The value of rho (the correlation coefficient) in each case is low: rho = .083 for syntactic accuracy and holistic score compared for class essays; and rho = .043 for the two scores compared for home essays. Neither of these values is significant at the $p < .05$ level. Consequently, there is no necessary relationship between syntactic accuracy and rhetorical competency in the 100 student essays.

The lack of relationship between the syntactic accuracy level and the holistic scores was also revealed by tabulating the ranges of accuracy ratios that co-occurred with each possible holistic score. That is, one

TABLE 5. RANGE OF WORDS/ERROR RATIOS[a] FOUND FOR EACH HOLISTIC SCORE

Holistic score	Range of words/error ratios		
	Class	Home	Class & home
1, 1.5	5.3–35.0	7.0–21.4	5.3–35.0
2, 2.5	9.3–32.2	7.4–54.0	7.4–54.0
3	5.0–17.6	6.0–18.5	5.0–18.5
4, 4.5	5.4–33.4	6.7–86.3	5.4–86.3
5, 5.5	8.8–66.4	10.0–37.8	8.8–66.4
6	22.3[b]	9.1–28.4	9.1–28.4

[a] Also referred to as "accuracy ratio."
[b] There was only one class paper that received a score of 6 from both readers. Therefore, there is no real upper or lower range of words/error ratio at this score level.

can look at each holistic score level (e.g., a score of 1, a score of 2, etc.) and then tabulate the accuracy ratios (or words/error scores) found at each score level. This calculation is shown in Table 5.

For example, for class compositions the same essays that received holistic scores of either 1 or 1.5 (the very bottom of the scale) also exhibited accuracy ratios (words/error) ranging from a low of 5.3, which is a very poor score, to a high of 35.0, a very high score. Conversely, the highest holistic scores of 5, 5.5, and 6 co-occurred with relatively low words/error ratios. In other words, the writers were able to show control over the level of either syntax or rhetoric while simultaneously showing poor control at the other level. If there had been a correlation to the scores, we would have found low scores on the holistic scale corresponding to low scores in the range of accuracy ratios and high scores corresponding to high scores. The data show that we cannot predict students' ability to perform in one area on the basis of their performance in the other area.

Discussion

These findings have shown that while the time allowed for the preparation of an essay can contribute to some improvement for the writer both on the syntactic level and the rhetorical level, it does not appear that additional time *in and of itself* leads to a sufficiently improved essay such that there is a statistical significance to the differences between class and home performance.

First, we examined the type and distribution of errors exhibited in the 100 essays in the data base to determine the subjects' control over the linguistic code. In fact, the distribution of the specific language errors was remarkably similar in essays written in class and at home. Therefore, it seems fair to say that in-class writing samples may be as representative of a student's grammatical abilities as out-of-class samples. Then the relationship between error (what is wrong) and accuracy (what is right) was measured. Such a measure showed that all five language groups performed better at home than in class, though not dramatically. The fact that the syntactic level improved only slightly in moving from class to home may attest to the fact that subjects did not spend much, if any, time on grammatical revision. Without a specific injunction to focus on form, perhaps few students do. However, Fathman and Whalley (this volume) show that grammatical form does improve when students *revise* papers on which they receive form-based feedback.

In comparison to the other groups, the Spanish group performed only marginally better at home than in class. A closer examination of their specific errors indicates that the lack of marked improvement in the Spanish group's home performance mostly derived from problems with only 2 of the 33 error categories: word choice and word form. Whereas 15.2% ($N = 46$) of all Spanish class errors fell into these two categories, 23.8% ($N = 87$) of their home errors were in the categories of word choice and word form.

In addition, although the Spanish-speaking subjects produced by far the most lengthy corpus of all the groups, their high incidence of error, particularly in word choice and word form, gives them the second lowest accuracy ratios after the Japanese subjects, who collectively produced the shortest corpus. This underscores the poor performance of the Japanese, who had a reduced opportunity for error given their shorter papers but who made proportionately more errors than any other group.

Turning to rhetorically oriented assessment, we looked first at upper- and lower-half holistic scores. Only the Japanese subjects had a noticeable difference in upper-half and lower-half scores. The preponderance of lower-half scores for the Japanese both at home and in class ranked the Japanese essays as the worst in terms of rhetorical competency. They also ranked lowest in syntactic accuracy. At the opposite extreme, the Arabs showed the largest percentage of scores in the upper half and emerged as the group with the best rhetorical competency as well as having the highest scores for syntactic accuracy.

On an individual basis, 52% of the subjects ($N = 13$) averaged higher scores for their two home essays over their two class essays, while only 32% of the subjects ($N = 8$) averaged lower scores. In his dissertation, Hartvigsen (1981) found a similar distribution of holistic scores for in-class versus out-of-class essays written by native speakers. In his sample, approximately 50% of the subjects had higher mean scores for their out-of-class essays, while only 14% had higher means for in-class essays (with 36% of his subjects having the same means).

In this study, we have seen that individual differences in performance on class and home essays were not statistically significant, though the measures used to assess syntactic accuracy and rhetorical competency did indicate at least a marginal level of improvement for home essays. In fact, 64% of the subjects averaged higher syntactic accuracy ratios when writing at home, and 52% of the subjects averaged higher holistic scores for their home compositions.

Last, we examined the relationship between performance at the syntactic level and performance at the rhetorical level. If the holistic scores on the individual compositions correlated with the accuracy ratios, that would have indicated that performance at one skill level was connected to performance at the other skill level. In other words, such a correlation would have shown that there was a relationship between rhetorical competency and syntactic accuracy. However, such was not the case, and differential levels of control seem to be the norm.

In fact, there are many possible areas where writing might exhibit varying degrees of control. McKay (1989: 253) claims that a "written discourse accent" might be found due to "a lack of native fluency in one or more areas of proficiency, which in the case of writing, includes grammar, word choice, cohesion, rhetorical organization, and topic development."

Implications

It might be suggested that perhaps the students who wrote the essays analyzed here did not know enough about what constitutes good writing or about the writing process. Such students would attack every task with the same lack of skill regardless of the conditions they were writing under. In fact, as noted previously, no class instruction was directed toward assisting the subjects in this study to maximize the extra time available to them for preparing the essays written outside of class. Under such conditions, their performance might have been accidental rather than calculated, haphazard rather than planned. In fact, they might have spent less time on their out-of-class papers. Without any mental formulation of what constitutes good writing or an awareness of the steps involved in producing it, students cannot know how to proceed in the task of writing and time could not buy them anything. To remedy this type of situation, teachers need to train students in a repertoire of strategies for composing as well as to recognize the attributes of effective writing. As Bizzell (1986: 52) points out, students need "a better understanding of the whole process of working on a piece of writing [and] to give adequate time to the task *and to make the time spent more productive*" (italics mine).

Finally, if performance at the level of syntax and the level of rhetoric differs so widely, it might be pedagogically appropriate to offer different types of classes to students who exhibit different types of problems in writing (Kroll 1990). For, unfortunately, "even when an ESL writer produces an error-free composition in English, a hidden agenda leads the evaluator to find fault with other formal features" (Land and Whitley 1989: 285), and we can only help our students improve if we address *all* aspects of writing performance.

References

Bardovi-Harlig, K., and Bofman, T. (1989). Attainment of syntactic and morphological accuracy by advanced language learners. *Studies in Second Language Acquisition, 11,* 17–34.

Belanoff, P., and Dickson, M. (Eds.) (In press.) *Portfolio grading: Process and product.* Upper Montclair, N.J.: Boynton/Cook Heinemann.

Bizzell, P. (1986). Composing processes: An overview. In A. R. Petrosky and D. Bartholomae (Eds.), *The teaching of writing: Eighty-fifth yearbook of the National Society for the Study of Education* (pp. 49–70). Chicago: National Society for the Study of Education.

Brière, E. J. (1966). Quantity before quality in second language composition. *Language Learning, 16,* 141–151.

Brodkey, D., and Young, R. (1981). Composition correctness scores. *TESOL Quarterly, 15,* 159–168.

Brown, H. D. (1987). *Principles of language learning and teaching,* 2nd ed. Englewood Cliffs, N.J.: Prentice-Hall.

Burnham, C. C. (1986). Portfolio evaluation: Room to breathe and grow. In C. Bridges (Ed.), *Training the new teacher of college composition* (pp. 125–138). Urbana, Ill.: National Council of Teachers of English.

Collins, A., and Gentner, D. (1980). A framework for a cognitive theory of writing. In L. W. Gregg and E. R. Steinberg (Eds.), *Cognitive processes in writing* (pp. 51–72). Hillsdale, N.J.: Erlbaum.

Elbow, P., and Belanoff, P. (1986). Portfolios as a substitute for proficiency examinations. *College Composition and Communication, 37,* 336–339.

Freedman, S. W. (1977). Influences on the evaluators of student writing. Unpublished doctoral dissertation, Stanford University.

Hartvigsen, M. K. (1981). A comparative study of quality and syntactic maturity between in-class and out-of-class writing samples of freshmen at Washington State University. Unpublished doctoral dissertation, Washington State University.

Haswell, R. (1988). Error and change in college student writing. *Written Communication, 5,* 479–499.

Krashen, S. D. (1977). The monitor model for adult second language performance. In M. Burt, H. Dulay, and M. Finnocchiaro (Eds.), *Viewpoints on*

English as a second language (pp. 152–161). New York: Regents.

(1981). *Second language acquisition and second language learning.* Oxford: Pergamon Press.

(1982). *Principles and practice in second language acquisition.* Oxford: Pergamon Press.

(1985). *The input hypothesis: Issues and implications.* London: Longman.

Kroll, B. (1990). The rhetoric/syntax split: Designing a curriculum for ESL students. *Journal of Basic Writing, 9,* 40–55.

Land, R., Jr., and Whitley, C. (1989). Evaluating second language essays in regular composition classes: Toward a pluralistic U.S. rhetoric. In D. M. Johnson and D. H. Roen (Eds.), *Richness in writing: Empowering ESL students* (pp. 284–293). New York: Longman.

Lloyd-Jones, R. (1987). Tests of writing ability. In G. Tate (Ed.), *Teaching composition: 12 bibliographical essays* (pp. 155–176), Ft. Worth: Texas Christian University Press.

Lucas, C.; Carlson, S. B.; and Bridwell-Bowles, L. (1989). The writing portfolio in assessment reform. Panel presented at the 40th Annual Conference on College Composition and Communication, Seattle, Wash., March.

McKay, S. L. (1989). Topic development and written discourse accent. In D. M. Johnson and D. H. Roen (Eds.), *Richness in writing: Empowering ESL students* (pp. 253–262). New York: Longman.

McLaughlin, B. (1987). *Theories of second-language learning.* London: Edward Arnold.

Myers, M. (1980). *A procedure for writing assessment and holistic scoring.* Urbana, Ill.: National Council of Teachers of English.

Neilson, B. (1979). Writing as a second language: Psycholinguistic processes in composition. Unpublished doctoral dissertation, University of California at San Diego.

Ruth, L., and Murphy, S. (1988). *Designing writing tasks for the assessment of writing.* Norwood, N.J.: Ablex.

Sanders, S. E., and Littlefield, J. H. (1975). Perhaps test essays can reflect significant improvement in freshman composition. *Research in the Teaching of English, 9,* 45–153.

Santos, T. (1988). Professors' reactions to the academic writing of nonnative-speaking students. *TESOL Quarterly, 22,* 69–90.

Shaughnessy, M. P. (1977). *Errors and expectations.* New York: Oxford University Press.

Spack, R. (1988). Initiating ESL students into the academic discourse community: How far should we go? *TESOL Quarterly, 22,* 29–51.

TOEFL Test of Written English guide. (1989). Princeton, N.J.: Educational Testing Service.

Vann, R. J.; Meyer, D. E.; and Lorenz, F. O. (1984). Error gravity: A study of faculty opinion of ESL errors. *TESOL Quarterly, 18,* 427–440.

White, E. M. (1985). *Teaching and assessing writing.* San Francisco: Jossey-Bass.

10 Feedback on compositions: teacher and student verbal reports

Andrew D. Cohen
Marilda C. Cavalcanti

Recent survey work has suggested that there may be a misfit between written feedback teachers provide on compositions and the learners' interests – that is, between what the teachers give and what the students would like to get. Part of the problem lies in the nature of the teacher's feedback, which is unclear, inaccurate, and unbalanced – because it focuses only on certain elements in written output (e.g., grammar and mechanics) and because it overemphasizes negative points (see Marzano and Arthur 1977; Cardelle and Corno 1981; Semke 1984; Zamel 1985; Pica 1986). Furthermore, comments are often not structured enough to help writers to develop their ideas (Butturff and Sommers 1980). Leki (this volume) reviews several of the issues involved in teacher response.

Even in a process approach to L1 (first language) writing with conferencing, peer response groups, and multiple drafts, case study research has found that learner and teacher do not necessarily share common information, skills, and values when they come to the interaction situation (Sperling and Freedman 1987). For example, a teacher's oral clarification of feedback may consist simply of deciphering his or her handwritten responses, which may not be the student's problem. It is further suggested that learners may make changes according to what they think the teacher's values are, out of a belief that the teacher knows best.

In addition, there may be disagreement as to when such feedback should be given. In a large-scale survey of feedback in L1 writing, teachers were seen to favor giving feedback during the writing process, whereas the students preferred their teacher to respond to the final version (Freedman 1987). A review of L1 writing research found that teacher feedback was most effective if it was both focused and followed by subsequent student revision (Hillocks 1986). A review of the research

This chapter is a revised version of a paper presented at the 1988 TESOL Convention in Chicago. We are grateful to Ann Raimes, Vivian Zamel, and to participants at the TESOL talk for their helpful comments. We also wish to acknowledge Eladyr Maria N. Salina and Lisete A. G. Marcondes for their assistance in collecting and analyzing the data for this study.

155

literature on the process of revision would suggest that currently, teacher feedback is not seen to have much effect on subsequent student writing (Fitzgerald 1987).

Regardless of the nature of teacher feedback, both L1 and foreign language (FL) students seem to be limited in their repertoire of strategies for revising their compositions (Cohen 1987), even when they understand the teacher's comments (see Pringle and Freedman 1985). Furthermore, recent surveys of English as a second language (ESL) writers found learners to vary greatly in their response to feedback (see Radecki and Swales 1988; Belcher 1989). Perhaps the main concern that learners have in common is the grade they receive on their compositions (Freedman 1987).

To date the bulk of the research seems to have dealt with teacher feedback on L1 writing. For this reason, our research has concerned teacher feedback on both L1 and FL (foreign language) writing. This chapter reports on three small-scale studies aimed at investigating the relationship between what teachers provide as feedback on compositions and what students think of and do with this feedback. The first study served as a preliminary or pilot study, and was conducted at a Brazilian English as a foreign language (EFL) institute because it provided one of the few nonuniversity contexts in which to study advanced EFL writing.[1] The second and third studies were conducted at two Brazilian universities, with Portuguese L1 and EFL students, respectively.

The following research questions were asked:

1. What do language teachers focus on in giving feedback on written compositions in an advanced L1 or FL writing course?
2. What feedback do students report that they usually get from the teacher? What are students' attitudes toward this feedback and what preferences might they have?
3. How do students handle the feedback they receive? What are the strategies they use?

Research design

Subjects

There were two sets of subjects for these studies: three experienced women teachers of writing and nine students. The teacher in the EFL institute study was not a native English speaker but had re-

---

1 The local Brazilian universities were at the time involved in a series of strikes, which prompted us to find a suitable alternative.

ceived her schooling in England before immigrating to Brazil. For the university studies, both teachers were native Portuguese speakers; one taught an advanced undergraduate course in EFL composition and the other taught a freshman course for advanced composition in Portuguese L1.[2]

Three students were selected by each teacher to provide in-depth verbal reports as to how they handled teacher feedback on a case study basis. Those selected were intended to represent high, intermediate, and low performers in EFL and Portuguese L1 writing, as determined by their respective teachers.

In the EFL institute study, two students were male, 16 and 27 years of age respectively, and the third was female, 17 years of age. The university EFL students were all female, 21–22 years of age. Of the L1 students, two were female and one was male, all 17–18 years of age. In addition, the class group that the case study students were part of served as subjects for questionnaire data (described later). There were 11 students in the EFL institute study, 13 university EFL students, and 19 L1 students filling out the questionnaires.

Instrumentation

COMPOSITION

The EFL institute writing sample was on the topic "Good Fences Make Good Neighbors." The composition was intended as practice for the composition portion of an English language proficiency examination.[3] According to the teacher's understanding of the test specifications, this portion was to be marked for the range and appropriateness of vocabulary, sentence and paragraph structure, correctness of grammar, and spelling and punctuation. The compositions were not to be marked for content (i.e., opinions, logic of argumentation, creativity in selecting and developing detail).[4] The compositions ranged in length from 380 words in the case of the high performer to 270–280 words for the intermediate and the low performers.

In the university EFL course, the students had to read a story by Carlos Drummond de Andrade (a contemporary Brazilian writer) and write a composition discussing either (1) whether the story could be understood or not or (2) whether life itself could be understood or not. The inter-

---

2 The course also involved instruction in reading skills.
3 Respondents are expected to write two essays for this particular exam, each to be comprised of some 350 words.
4 According to one of the students, she and her peers were unaware that the compositions were *not* to be assessed for content, regardless of whether the teacher had announced this point.

mediate and low performers opted for the former topic, the high performer for the latter. The compositions ranged from 200 to 230 words in length. The university L1 writing sample was a composition on the topic "Suicide." The composition was intended to be assessed primarily for its merits as an example of argumentative discourse. The three students wrote compositions of differing lengths: The high performer wrote 550 words, the intermediate performer 350 words, and the low performer 180 words.

TEACHER VERBAL PROTOCOL

The procedure consisted of having the teachers think aloud while interacting with each composition and providing written feedback. These think-aloud protocols were tape-recorded.

TEACHER QUESTIONNAIRE

A questionnaire was designed to ask the teacher about the nature of the course, the purpose of the particular writing assignment, the categories of feedback offered (grammar, mechanics, vocabulary, organization, content, and other), and plans for follow-up.[5]

STUDENT VERBAL PROTOCOL

After the teacher handed back the compositions, the students were asked to react to the feedback by indicating their first impressions, their general understanding, and their attitudes. They were also asked to provide comments of a more general nature concerning their experience in the course. These activities were intended to guide the students' self-observations. All verbal reports were recorded in Portuguese L1.

STUDENT CHECKLIST

A checklist was designed to enable the nine case study students to indicate their understanding of each of the teacher's comments and their intended plan of action with respect to any points they did not understand. The categories for the checklist were based on those obtained from a prior survey of students' repertoire of strategies for handling feedback (Cohen 1987). For each of the teacher's comments, students were asked whether they understood the problem and whether they knew how to resolve it (on a scale of 5 to 1, "totally" to "not at all"). They were also to indicate which of the following strategies they would use if they did not under-

---

5 The questionnaire included a query about follow-up work because revision is atypical in the Brazilian context. Students generally add words above the text that they have already produced. Rewriting is viewed as artificial — an activity without any genuine purpose.

stand the comment: request an additional explanation from the teacher, consult a grammar book, consult a dictionary, ask a peer, or look back at previous essays.

STUDENT QUESTIONNAIRE

A questionnaire was constructed to inquire about the type of feedback (i.e., mechanics, grammar, vocabulary, organization, or content) all the students in the L1 and EFL classes perceived themselves to be receiving and the type they would prefer to receive. Learners also indicated the strategies they used for handling feedback: making a mental note, writing down points, identifying points in need of further explanation, requesting an explanation, consulting previous compositions, consulting a grammar book, or rewriting the essay incorporating the teacher's comments. Finally, the questionnaire requested self-ratings of the respondents' writing ability.[6]

Data collection

In the EFL institute study, the learners wrote their compositions in class, whereas the learners in the university studies wrote their compositions out of class.[7] The three teachers then corrected the compositions, and in the case of the nine selected students, tape-recorded their comments alone and at their own pace (the EFL institute teacher in English, the other two in Portuguese), as they provided written feedback. Once the taping was completed, they filled out the Teacher Questionnaire. After the compositions were returned to the learners, interviews were conducted with the nine students to ascertain students' self-observation (introspection and retrospection) and students' interactive response to the checklist relating to their teacher's comments. All students in the three classes were given the Student Questionnaire to fill out. In the L1 study, the three selected students all had individual interviews with the teacher. In the university EFL study, there were no such interviews due to a university strike, but the high performer discussed her composition with the teacher by telephone. In the EFL institute study, such interviews were apparently not part of the course.

6 Copies of the instruments are available from the authors.
7 In the EFL institute study, the compositions were written in class because at that phase of the course, the essays were practice for an upcoming overseas proficiency exam. However, Kroll (this volume) finds that individual differences in performance on essays written in class vs. at home are not statistically significant.

Results

Focus of teacher feedback

EFL INSTITUTE STUDY

In the EFL institute study, the teacher's self-report on the questionnaire showed that she concerned herself with mechanics, grammar, vocabulary, and organization, but purposely not with content, because content was not assessed on the English language proficiency examination. She expressed the view that the students benefited most from comments about mechanics, grammar, and organization. She felt that her comments were of "great benefit" to the students. She reported using a marking system whereby she indicated the type of error but did not actually correct it.[8]

The comments that the teacher actually made on the essays mostly pointed out problems rather than praised strengths. The high performer received 4 teacher comments on grammar, 3 on mechanics, and 5 on vocabulary (see Table 1). The intermediate performer received 4 comments on grammar, 3 comments on mechanics, 8 on vocabulary, and 1 on organization. The low performer had 6 on grammar, 6 on mechanics, 2 on vocabulary, and 2 on organization.

Emerging from the analysis of the teacher's verbal protocol were a few instances of undelivered praise and correction. For example, in appraising the high performer's composition, the teacher taped a comment about how impressed she was with the way a certain sentence was constructed and another one about the impressive choice of vocabulary. Yet in neither case did she write these comments on the composition itself. She also expressed pleasure at the use of advanced vocabulary by the intermediate performer, again without indicating it to the student himself. By the same token, the teacher also refrained from correcting the choice of vocabulary when the form that the intermediate performer chose was wrong but in her opinion reflected an effort to use advanced vocabulary.[9]

In their separate assessment of the three compositions, the investigators found that the teacher only dealt with approximately half of the issues that could have been dealt with (see Table 1).[10] As content was not dealt with by the teacher, no attempt was made by the investigators

8 At the beginning of the term, the students received a copy of the marking code.
9 In this instance, the idea was one of "distancing yourself from your neighbor" and the student used "evicting your neighbor."
10 These teacher comments were generally clear and comprehensible to the researchers, given the added protocol data which provided the teacher's reasoning for each comment. Often the teacher did not indicate the type of comment called for, which left such interpretations to be made by the researchers.

to add comments in this category. In the other categories, the investigators found many more comments on vocabulary for the low performer and a fair number of organizational issues for the intermediate and low performers (see Table 1).

UNIVERSITY EFL STUDY

In the university EFL study, the teacher reported focusing on all five categories, with the emphasis being on content – that is, developing logical reasoning. She felt that students benefit most from comments about organization. She noted that she frequently indicated the existence of a problem, sometimes indicated the type of problem, and sometimes gave the correct form. She did not give follow-up tasks to deal with the problems she commented on in the student's compositions, and only occasionally requested that students rewrite their papers if she felt that they would benefit from the rewriting. She thought that rewriting could be helpful, especially for dealing with problems of grammar and spelling that had not been commented on in her feedback. Furthermore, she stressed the importance of conferences with her students. Finally, she doubted the usefulness of her feedback in cases where the student was not interested in it.

As for the comments that the EFL teacher actually made, the high performer received only 4 comments, 2 of them dealing with organization; the intermediate performer received 19, mostly on mechanics (7) and grammar (4); and the low performer received 17, mostly on content (7) and organization (6). Thus, the teacher varied her comments according to the writer and the particular composition. All were comments pointing out deficiencies except for one written on the high performer's paper: "Very good organization of ideas." The vast majority of teacher comments simply signaled the existence of a problem without pointing out its nature. As in the EFL institute study, there was some indication that the teacher refrained from making all the comments that she could have. A case in point occurred near the end of her taped protocol concerning the low performer, when the teacher made the following comment that she did not write on the paper: "A certain naivete in her line of reasoning."

The investigators' assessment showed that for the high performer, the teacher avoided or overlooked over twice as many problems as she commented on; there were 12 more for the intermediate one, and 8 more for the low performer (see Table 1).

UNIVERSITY L1 STUDY

In the university L1 study, the teacher reported that she focused on accuracy of vocabulary and organization. She felt, as did the teacher in

TABLE 1. TEACHERS' COMMENTS, INVESTIGATORS' ADDITIONAL COMMENTS, AND STUDENTS' HANDLING OF TEACHERS' COMMENTS

	Gram.	Mech.	Vocab.	Org.	Cont.	Total	N.U. (%)[a]	N.H. (%)[b]
EFL institute study								
High performer								
Teacher comments	4	3	5	—	—	12	0	25
Invest. comments	4	3	5	—	—	12		
Intermediate performer								
Teacher comments	4	3	8	1	—	16	0	31
Invest. comments	5	3	9	3	—	20		
Low performer								
Teacher comments	6	6	2	2	—	16	6	21
Invest. comments	2	4	7	3	—	16		
University EFL study								
High performer								
Teacher comments	1	—	1	2	—	4	50	50
Invest. comments	3	1	5	—	—	9		
Intermediate performer								
Teacher comments	4	7	3	2	3	19	26	37
Invest. comments	6	1	4	1	—	12		
Low performer								
Teacher comments	3	—	1	6	7	17	62	81
Invest. comments	5	—	1	2	—	8		

University L1 study

High performer						
Teacher comments	—	—	2	—	2	100
Invest. comments	3	4	6	4	20	100
Intermediate performer						
Teacher comments	—	—	4	3	7	28
Invest. comments	4	—	5	6	17	28
Low performer						
Teacher comments	—	1	1	5	8	12
Invest. comments	3	—	2	1	8	37

Note: Number of comments are given for the areas of grammar, mechanics, vocabulary, and content. A dash means that no comment was given.

[a] N.U. = comment not understood.
[b] N.H. = not clear how to handle comment.

the university EFL study, that students benefited most from comments dealing with organization. With regard to format for comments, she indicated that she never supplied the appropriate form, but would frequently indicate the cause without giving the answer and would sometimes just indicate that there was a problem without indicating its nature. She reported that she usually designed follow-up exercises based on problem areas in the compositions, and she had her students revise their work. She indicated that she had doubts about the usefulness of some of her comments – those that were imprecise.

As to the classification of comments that the L1 teacher actually made on the three selected students' compositions, the high performer received 2 comments altogether, on organization; the intermediate performer received 7, 4 on organization and 3 on content, and the low performer received 8, 5 of them on content (see Table 1).

As in the two EFL studies, the teacher also made a number of comments in the verbal report protocol that were not communicated to the students on their compositions. For example, at one point in the protocol the teacher asked herself whether or not she should comment on a grammar point. Her reluctance to do this could be interpreted as a desire to focus only on certain categories of problems (e.g., organization – type of text). At other times, the teacher indicated a problem only through her intonation, but did not express it in the protocol and also did not write any comments about it on the student's composition.

The researchers' assessment of the three compositions yielded ten times more comments for the high performer, about twice as many more for the intermediate performer, and the same amount for the low performer (see Table 1).

Students' attitudes toward teacher feedback

EFL INSTITUTE STUDY

According to the eleven students in the EFL institute study, most of the teacher's comments concerned mechanics and grammar, some dealt with vocabulary, few dealt with organization, and little or no attention was given to content (see Table 2). When asked the extent to which they felt their teacher was assuming the role of *judge* of their work and the extent to which they saw her as an adult reader *interested in their ideas,* all but one always saw her as a judge and fewer than half felt she was always an interested reader (see Table 3).[11] The three students in this case study reported that their teacher usually gave much attention to

11 These questionnaire items were inspired by a study of English native-language writing that found considerable benefit in the teacher's assuming the role of interested reader (Ziv 1984).

TABLE 2. STUDENT QUESTIONNAIRE DATA ON TEACHER FEEDBACK PATTERNS

Frequency of comments	Gram.	Mech.	Vocab.	Org.	Cont.
EFL institute study (N = 11)					
Many	11	11	8	4	5
Some	—	—	2	—	4
Few	—	—	1	6	2
None	—	—	—	1	—
University EFL study (N = 13)[a]					
Many	8	5	5	10	10
Some	4	5	7	2	1
Few	—	1	—	—	1
None	—	1	—	—	—
University L1 study (N = 19)					
Many	7	8	3	12	16
Some	12	11	13	5	2
Few	—	—	3	2	1
None	—	—	—	—	—

[a]Although there were 13 students in the study, one of them did not provide data for Table 2.

mechanics, grammar, and vocabulary on their compositions, some attention to organization, and little to content.

When asked in another item on the questionnaire what their preferences for feedback were, 5 of the 11 students said that they preferred more feedback about content, 3 preferred more on organization, 2 on grammar and mechanics, and 1 on vocabulary use. With regard to the three selected students, the writer rated "high" preferred more feedback on content and organization, and the low performer indicated a desire for more feedback on the content of the essay. The intermediate performer did not respond to that questionnaire item.

The high performer was rather surprised and pleased about the teacher's feedback on this particular piece of writing because he had not regarded it as a good one when he handed it in. As to the teacher's actual comments, the student said he did not know whether they included "content" in that he was not sure he understood what this category meant. On the Student Checklist, he indicated understanding all of the teachers' comments and yet noted that he did not know how to handle 25% of them (Table 1).

The intermediate performer expected positive feedback from the teacher, mainly because he felt the introduction to his essay was particularly well written. His expectations were confirmed. The student men-

TABLE 3. STUDENT PERCEPTIONS OF TEACHER'S ROLE

Teacher's role	Always	Usually	Sometimes	Almost never
EFL institute (N = 11)				
Judge	10	—	1	—
Interested reader	4	4	1	2
University EFL (N = 13)				
Judge	8	3	2	—
Interested reader	9	2	2	—
University L1 (N = 19)				
Judge	11	7	1	—
Interested reader	2	7	8	1

tioned that he appreciated his teacher's paying attention to his ideas in the essay, since she was focusing less on content in the scoring of essays in the course. He indicated understanding of all of the teacher's comments but did not know how to handle 31% of them.

The low performer acknowledged the need to make thorough revision after writing an essay, although she herself had not done so in this case. She complained that the teacher did not make even one positive comment either about her essay as a whole or about any of its ideas. She indicated that she understood all but one of the teacher's comments, but was unclear as to how to handle 21% of them.

UNIVERSITY EFL STUDY

As for the student report in the university EFL study (N = 13), 10 students described their teacher as providing many comments about organization and content, 8 students indicated that she also provided them many comments about grammar, and fewer reported that she gave many comments about vocabulary and mechanics (see Table 2). The students perceived the teacher's role almost equally as judge and as interested adult reader (Table 3). There was a clear indication by all but two of the students that the teacher always/usually assumes the role of interested reader. Only two of the students questioned the usefulness of teacher comments.

When asked in another item on the questionnaire what their preferences for feedback were, 6 of the 13 learners reported that they would like more emphasis on content and vocabulary, 5 preferred more emphasis on organization, and 2 wanted more on mechanics and grammar. As for the three students in the case study, the high and intermediate performers felt that the current emphasis was fine, whereas the low performer wanted more emphasis on content, especially on issues of creativity.

The high performer received four comments, two of which she did not understand fully and did not know how to handle (see Table 1). She noted that she was purposely writing concisely because she feared being too repetitive. As it turned out, the teacher felt she needed to expand her essay by providing examples. This learner displayed a most positive attitude toward her teacher's feedback, resulting largely from the regular interaction sessions she reported having with her teacher. As she put it: "We talk. She presents her ideas and I present mine. From the ideas I present, she then tries to improve upon them."

The intermediate performer received 19 comments, 26% of which she did not understand fully and 37% of which she did not know how to handle. All the same, she spoke positively about the feedback she received; she appreciated getting immediate feedback from the teacher on comments that were not clear to her. She did note that she would welcome positive comments about the content of her essay: "I would have liked it if the teacher had commented on the content of my composition and on whether she liked it or not."

As for the low performer, she received 17 comments, 62% of which she did not understand fully and 81% of which she did not know how to handle (Table 1). She expressed disillusionment regarding her grade on the composition. She felt that her essay was deserving of merit for its creative element. She noted that the previous semester, the teacher had given separate grades for content and for grammar, and she preferred that arrangement.[12] The student expressed the concern that the teacher might not perceive the delivery of her ideas in the same way that she did. For example, the student might feel that she was making a point effectively, being careful not to be redundant, while her teacher would comment that the idea was in need of elaboration. She did note that to add to her difficulties, she had problems writing argumentative texts in Portuguese as well. She added a further point of misfit between her intentions and the teacher's assessment, namely, that in several instances the teacher did not share her schemata for a given point and therefore did not appreciate the depth of the argument involved: "She didn't analyze the story correctly. She didn't get my meaning at a deep level, even if it was trivial."

---

12 In reality, the instructional objectives for third-year composition at that university called for an emphasis on logical thinking through the writing of argumentative discourse, whereas second-year instruction focused on creativity through the writing of narratives.

UNIVERSITY L1 STUDY

According to the 19 students in the university L1 study, many of the teacher's comments concerned content, somewhat fewer concerned organization, fewer dealt with grammar and mechanics, and fewer still with vocabulary (see Table 2). The students saw their teacher always/ usually as a judge and only usually/sometimes as an adult reader interested in their ideas (see Table 3). In addition, half of the students expressed doubts as to the usefulness of teacher comments. One student said she had doubts because "the comments pile up in my mind, making the act of writing somewhat complex and tiring, and they produce unfavorable results in subsequent compositions."

In the L1 study, most of the students indicated a preference for more teacher comments on content and organization, and one-third wanted more comments on grammar. As for the three students in the case study, the low performer reported that the teacher gave a lot of emphasis to grammar and mechanics, whereas the student preferred emphasis on organization and content. The intermediate performer felt the current emphasis was fine. Although acknowledging the teacher's emphasis on organization and content, the high performer expressed a concern for still more emphasis on these two aspects.

The high performer received two comments, neither of which he understood fully or had a clear idea of how to handle (Table 1). Although his initial reaction upon getting his composition back was that any kind of teacher comment would be valid, in actuality he did not accept any of the teacher's comments and pointed out that he would not change anything in his text. As he put it, "It's difficult to write an essay following one line of reasoning and then to have to change details after the teacher's comments. I can't change details because then I would have to change the whole thing. I think it's better to leave the essay as is."

The intermediate performer received seven teacher comments, more than a quarter of which she indicated she did not understand fully and lacked a clear idea of how to handle. In her verbal report protocol, she said that she was looking forward to the teacher's comments. On the other hand, while going through the Student Checklist, she was reluctant to accept the teacher's comments. She eventually accepted two out of the seven comments, although begrudgingly. She did mention that she was willing to rewrite the essay.

The low performer received eight comments from her teacher, one of which she did not understand fully and three of which she did not know how to handle. She indicated in her verbal report that she was already expecting a negative reaction to her composition from the teacher. For example, she expected that her teacher would not find the text argumentative. She accepted all comments without discussion.

TABLE 4. STUDENT STRATEGIES FOR HANDLING FEEDBACK

Strategy	EFL institute (N = 11)			University EFL (N = 13)			University L1 (N = 19)		
	F*a*	S	R	F	S	R	F	S	R
1. Making a mental note	8	3	—	7	4	1	12	6	1
2. Writing down points by type	—	2	8	1	2	8	1	4	14
3. Identifying points to be explained	8	2	—	9	3	1	15	4	—
4. Asking for teacher explanation	7	4	—	10	3	—	10	6	1
5. Referring back to previous compositions	3	4	4	1	7	5	4	6	9
6. Consulting a grammar book	2	3	5	—	4	8	2	4	12
7. Rewriting a. only incorporating teacher's comments	6	2	2	2	1	8	—	9	7
b. revising and expanding	—	1	8	1	3	5	5	5	6
8. Not doing anything	—	2	1	2	3	7	1	4	11

*a*F = frequently, S = sometimes, R = rarely.

Student strategies in handling feedback

The results for the three studies were rather similar in terms of the strategies that students reported using.

EFL INSTITUTE

The majority of the students in the EFL institute study reported that they frequently made a mental note of the teacher's comments, identified the points they needed to discuss with the teacher, and asked the teacher about these points. As for the reported use of strategies such as "consulting previous compositions" and "consulting a grammar book," there was more of a spread from "frequently" to "rarely" (see Table 4). The three case study students also indicated that they frequently made a mental note of the teacher's comments. All other strategies were reportedly used to varying degrees (see Table 4). Only the low performer, for example, reportedly seldom used the strategy of identifying points for teacher explanation. Also, the high performer was more likely than the other two to rewrite incorporating the teacher's comments and to consult a grammar book. All three students expressed concern about their grade on this essay, as it was practice for a standardized language proficiency test that they wished to pass.

The three subjects were also asked to specify the strategy that they would use for each of the teacher's comments that they indicated not understanding. The high performer indicated that in one case he would ask the teacher directly and in another he would consult a grammar book. The intermediate performer indicated in two instances that he would talk with the teacher, in two other instances ask a peer, and in one instance consult a grammar book. The low performer noted that with one unclear comment she would consult her previous compositions and with another she would look in a dictionary.

UNIVERSITY EFL STUDY

In the university EFL study, as in the other EFL study, the students reported that they would make a mental note of the teacher's comments, would identify the points to be explained, and would ask the teacher for an explanation. They rarely made written lists of such points and rarely rewrote their essays. Also, they reported that only sometimes or rarely would they refer to a previous essay they had written or consult a grammar book (see Table 4). The strategies reported by the three selected students on the Student Checklist followed the same pattern as that just described for the whole group. In their protocols, the selected students described the role of the grade in their handling of the feedback. For example, the high performer noted, "I first try to see what errors I have made, and then I look at the grade." The other said that they first checked their grade before looking at the teacher's comments.

The three students indicated during the checklist task that in almost all the cases where they did not understand the teacher's comments, their strategy would be to go to her for additional assistance, as opposed to consulting a grammar book, dictionary, peer, or previous composition. In the interview session, the low performer indicated that she did not engage in extended feedback sessions but had only brief interactions with the teacher. As she put it, "I guess that only rarely do I actually sit down with the teacher."

UNIVERSITY L1 STUDY

In the university L1 study, the 19 students answering the Student Questionnaire tended to favor the same strategies for dealing with teacher feedback as in the other two studies: They would make a mental note of the teacher's comments, identify the points in doubt, and ask the teacher for an explanation. They would sometimes rewrite the composition, incorporating the teacher's comments, and only rarely would they make written lists of points or consult a grammar book (see Table 4). As noted earlier, the high performer in the case study refused to consider rewriting the essay incorporating the teacher's comments. He felt that having to do a rewrite meant having to conform to the teacher's line of reasoning, and that changing details meant changing the whole essay.

As in the university EFL study, the feedback-handling strategy that the three selected students favored was to ask the teacher for additional assistance. They indicated that they did not understand some of her comments on their essays. The high performer said he "partly understood" the two comments on his essay. What he was really saying, however, was that he did not accept either of the two comments. The intermediate performer noted that she would consult other people about one of the unclear comments.

Discussion and conclusions

The fit between the teacher's reported feedback and actual feedback varied from study to study. It was best in the university EFL study and weakest in the EFL institute study. In the university EFL study this fit was actually quite good. The teacher stated that she emphasized all five categories, and her students also reported that she did this, with emphasis on organization and content. The intermediate and low performers did, in fact, receive a spread of comments across the categories. In the L1 study, there was a relatively good fit between the feedback the teacher reported giving and what she gave. Regarding comments on organization, her students said the same, and the comments on the three selected compositions also featured comments on organization.

We do note, however, that there were certain discrepancies in the L1 study. While the teacher reported an emphasis on vocabulary accuracy, her students saw this as the least emphasized category in her feedback, and none of her comments on the three essays dealt specifically with vocabulary. Furthermore, although the teacher did not mention a focus on content, her students reported her giving many comments on this aspect of their writing, and on the intermediate and low performers' compositions she made numerous such comments.

In the EFL institute study, the fit between what the teacher said she gave feedback on and her actual feedback was only moderately good. Whereas the teacher indicated that her students benefited from feedback on organization of writing, she was reported by her students to provide only some feedback of this nature, and analysis of the essays revealed few comments in this category. The independent assessment of the compositions by the investigators suggested that there were perhaps six instances where such feedback would have assisted either the intermediate or the low-performing students. There was, however, a relatively good fit between student preferences for feedback and what they actually got.

These three studies also revealed instances of teacher bias. For example, the imbalance between the number of comments the teachers made in a category and those added subsequently by the investigators might suggest that the teachers were focusing *more* on certain categories than on others, perhaps according to whether they perceived the student to be at one proficiency level or another. For example, in the case of the low EFL institute student receiving only two comments on vocabulary from the teacher and seven more from the investigators, the teacher seems to have made a conscious choice to concentrate her comments on grammar and mechanics (see Table 1).

Another example of discrepancy can be seen with the low performer in the university EFL study; the teacher's expressed emphasis on content and organization conflicts with the student's *perception* that the comments emphasized grammar and mechanics. Although in this case the teacher's feedback did not support the student's perception regarding typical comments, the teacher may indeed have felt compelled to deal with grammar and mechanics, because the student was a low performer, even though the expressed emphasis was on content and organization. Most likely the student's perception was based on the teacher's feedback patterns over various compositions, for which the behavior of focusing primarily on grammar and mechanics would conform to the pattern reported in the literature – namely, extensive attention to these matters over others.

These instances may reflect a form of teacher bias in writing comments – i.e., a mindset that certain students have certain types of problems that need to be commented on. It may be valuable to investigate this sort of bias in order to determine whether a teacher might be depriving low performers of types of feedback that could be beneficial to them – for example, support in the use of vocabulary or organization for a low performer. It may also be that low performers, such as those in the university EFL study, would benefit from more extensive interactive sessions with the teacher. Future research could investigate the nature of the teacher's relationship to the lower performers in the writing classroom, including such issues as teachers' accessibility to all the students in their class and their willingness not to prejudge what type of feedback is appropriate for a given student.

Besides the matter of teacher bias, these studies uncovered a further concern: whether the teachers were aware of points they did not comment on that were nonetheless worthy of comment, as determined by the researchers. Besides the several instances where the teacher made a comment in the taped protocol without writing it on the paper, there were numerous instances where the teacher not only failed to comment on an incorrect form but did not acknowledge any awareness of it. A Teacher's Checklist could be added to the current research design so that the teacher could indicate for each identified omission of a comment whether that omission was a conscious choice (e.g., not to include comments on aspects that were not emphasized in a particular task, not to overwhelm the student with comments, not to give a comment beyond the student's level of proficiency, not to give the learner a sense of being favored or prejudiced against, not to spend too much time on any one essay), an oversight,[13] or the result of a lack of knowledge about that issue. Such research would need to be conducted with diplomacy since it would indicate the teacher's skill in the target language, and thus could offend the teacher, particularly a nonnative.

Furthermore, the EFL institute study called attention to an apparent mismatch between the choice on the teacher's part *not* to deal with content and a clear desire on the students' part to have such feedback. It would appear that even in situations where it is irrelevant to the marking system to be used, such feedback may be expected by students and may well motivate them to write more and better compositions. This appears to be a case of the teacher teaching to the test, which in this case may somewhat lessen her students' enthusiasm for the writing process. Perhaps the teacher could indicate comments about content separately if such comments were not part of the perceived task.

It is not the intention of the authors to be prescriptive and to suggest that a category of feedback, such as content or organization, should receive equal treatment or even priority. The preference for one or another category depends on the cultural background of the students and the teacher, on the needs at hand, on the given writing assignment, and so forth. The real issue stressed in this chapter is that of fit between what the teacher provides and what the students want, rather than what either group *should* be dealing with. Of course, we need to bear in mind that learners' expectations and preferences may derive from previous instructional experiences, experiences that may not necessarily be beneficial for the development of writing. Hence, if the focus was on grammar in the students' courses, they may feel that focus should be on grammar in the teacher's feedback (Vivian Zamel, personal communication). In such cases, it may be vital for teachers not to cater to the

---

13 Cohen carefully examined over ten weeks' time his own comments on written work in an EFL class that he taught. He found numerous oversights in his comments to students – sometimes giving feedback on an erroneous form, for example, and at other times neglecting to mention it (Cohen and Robbins 1976).

students' expectations but to shift those expectations according to what contributes most to the development of writing skills.[14]

With regard to positive reinforcement, research has shown that a balance between criticism and praise may be the best means of encouraging quality writing (see Cardelle and Corno 1981). The teachers in all three studies may be missing an opportunity to motivate writing by increasing the extent of praise contained in the ongoing comments within the composition. These case studies revealed almost no use of praise – just an occasional positive comment at the end of the essays in the EFL institute study and one positive comment at the end of the high performer's essay in the university EFL study. Yet the data in this set of studies would suggest that students – especially the weak ones – are quite anxious to receive at least some feedback as to what they are doing right.

On a methodological issue regarding teacher data, it may be that the process whereby the teachers taped their rationale for each comment produced an unnatural situation that perhaps influenced the nature of the comments. The teachers may have been more guarded in their comments about their feedback because they were called upon not only to discuss these comments but to record them. The Portuguese L1 teacher at first had a negative reaction to the tape recorder. She turned it off, but then she turned it on again, left it on, and forgot about it. The teachers were not given any special training in how to use the tape recorder. The fact that they were left to do the recording on their own may have had a positive effect, but some reactive effects also resulted from the research technique, as is inevitable (see Cavalcanti 1983).

In future work, it may be useful within the Teacher Questionnaire to have teachers describe the strategies that they use when they do not understand a student's point on a composition. Furthermore, teachers could be asked to indicate whether they noted improvements in student writing from paper to paper, and if so, in what areas these improvements occurred.

As to the students' repertoire of strategies, the finding that the students in all three studies usually simply made a mental note of the teacher's feedback – rather than recording the feedback systematically – is consistent with findings from previous research (e.g., Cohen 1987), and would suggest the advisability of training students at all proficiency levels in the use of alternative strategies. One such strategy would be the judicious use of revision, incorporating the teacher's comments, since

14 See Fathman and Whalley (this volume) for a more positive view than that presented in this chapter regarding the benefits of feedback on grammar, especially when coupled with feedback on content.

the teachers in the EFL studies indicated that as a rule the students did not rewrite their compositions.

The teacher in the university EFL study, for example, indicated that the students did not usually rewrite their compositions for her because she "was lucky enough to get a composition once!" Thus, she would simply have the students write the corrected form on the line above the erroneous form. Furthermore, the teacher believed that if students were asked to revise their compositions, incorporating the feedback, they would then make mistakes elsewhere.[15] She felt that her students were not interested in learning how to write in English – or in their native language, for that matter. This situation could be interpreted as showing a conflict between sound educational practice and the perceptions of students who see compositions as isolated, required tasks instead of as learning experiences. The teacher may not share their limited view of writing but feels compelled to abide by it. The insistence upon rewriting would be consistent with recommendations growing out of research in first language composition, which generally favor both focused teacher comments and subsequent revision by the student (see Hillocks 1986: 166–168).

These studies have shown that there are striking similarities between the ways in which teacher feedback on student compositions function in both the native language and the foreign language. We did note one difference, namely, that the L1 students were more likely than EFL students to disagree with the teacher's comments and even reject such comments out of hand, perhaps due to their native control of the language. It would be useful in future studies to explore sources of resistance to teacher comments on the part of native students, and to probe issues of overload, exemplified by the student who said that teachers' comments "tend to pile up" in his mind.

The feedback situation as reflected by this set of case studies is probably not atypical of situations in many classrooms where writing is taught around the world. In other words, despite the apparent benefits to be accrued from the typical approaches to feedback, there appear to be a number of missing ingredients. One such ingredient is a clear agreement between teacher and student as to what will be commented on and how such comments might be categorized. It is possible that the teachers and students in these studies had different perceptions as to what the five categories (grammar, mechanics, etc.) in their respective questionnaires

---

15 The process-oriented approach to writing, discussed by Silva, by Johns, and by Krapels in this volume, would suggest that learners be encouraged to write and rewrite extensively – that in writing more, learners have more opportunity for practicing their skills, gain confidence in their writing ability, and come to write more error-free prose.

referred to, and it would be beneficial in future research to determine what these perceptions actually are. Another such ingredient would be the discussion of possible repertoires of strategies students could use in order to derive maximum benefit from the feedback provided by the teacher. Clear teacher-student agreements on feedback procedures and student training in strategies for handling feedback could lead to more productive and enjoyable composition writing in the classroom.

We contend that if effective interactive feedback procedures are in operation, teachers are then able to observe the effects of their feedback through improvement in students' writing, in their attitudes toward writing, and in their language acquisition in general. In turn, the students welcome the feedback because of the benefits that they receive from it.

References

Belcher, D. D. (1989). How professors initiate NNS students into their disciplinary discourse communities. *Texas Papers in Foreign Language Education 1*, 207–225.

Butturff, D. R., and Sommer, N. I. (1980). Placing revision in a reinvented rhetorical tradition. In A. Freedman and I. Pringle (Eds.), *Reinventing the rhetorical tradition* (pp. 99–104). Conway, Ark.: L & S Books/Canadian Council of Teachers of English.

Cardelle, M., and Corno, L. (1981). Effects on second language learning of variations in written feedback on homework assignments. *TESOL Quarterly, 15*, 251–261.

Cavalcanti, M. C. (1983). The pragmatics of FL reader-text interaction: Key lexical items as source of potential reading problems. Unpublished doctoral dissertation, University of Lancaster.

Cohen, A. D. (1987). Student processing of feedback on their compositions. In A. L. Wenden and J. Rubin (Eds.), *Learner strategies in language learning* (pp. 57–69). Englewood Cliffs, N.J.: Prentice-Hall.

Cohen, A. D., and Robbins, M. (1976). Toward assessing interlanguage performance: The relationship between selected errors, learners' characteristics, and learners' explanations. *Language Learning, 26*, 45–66.

Fitzgerald, J. (1987). Research on revision in writing. *Review of Educational Research, 57*, 481–506.

Freedman, S.W. (1987). *Response to student writing*. Urbana, Ill.: National Council of Teachers of English.

Hillocks, G., Jr. (1986). *Research on written composition: New directions for teaching*. Urbana, Ill.: ERIC Clearinghouse on Reading and Communication Skills and the National Conference on Research in English.

Marzano, R. J., and Arthur, S. (1977). Teacher comments on student essays: It doesn't matter what you say. ERIC ED 147 864. Denver: University of Colorado.

Pica, T. (1986). An interactional approach to the teaching of writing. *English Teaching Forum, 24* (3), 6–10.

Pringle, I., and Freedman, A. (1985). *A comparative study of writing abilities in two modes at the grade 5, 8 and 12 levels.* Toronto: Ontario Ministry of Education.

Radecki, P. M., and Swales, J. M. (1988). ESL student reaction to written comments on their written work. *System, 16,* 355–365.

Semke, H. D. (1984). Effects of the red pen. *Foreign Language Annals, 17,* 195–202.

Sperling, M., and Freedman, S. W. (1987). A good girl writes like a good girl. *Written Communication, 4,* 343–369.

Zamel, V. (1985). Responding to student writing. *TESOL Quarterly, 19,* 79–101.

Ziv, N. D. (1984). The effect of teacher comments on the writing of four college freshmen. In R. Beach and L. S. Bridwell (Eds.), *New directions in composition research* (pp. 362–380). New York: Guilford Press.

11 Teacher response to student writing: focus on form versus content

Ann K. Fathman
Elizabeth Whalley

While reading student papers, teachers often ask themselves, "How can I give the best feedback to help my students improve their compositions?" The question is difficult because there is little agreement among teachers or researchers about how teachers should respond to student writing. Much of the conflict over teacher response to written work has been whether teacher feedback should focus on form (e.g., grammar, mechanics) or on content (e.g., organization, amount of detail). Griffin (1982) has noted, "the major question confronting any theory of responding to student writing is where we should focus our attention" (p. 299).

Changes in both the focus of composition teaching and the focus of feedback have occurred over time. Early in the nineteenth century, rhetoric was taught, and little or no attention was paid to grammatical correctness (Connors 1985). Toward the end of the nineteenth century and into the twentieth, interest in grammatical correctness grew. Textbooks focused on exercises that required students to find and correct errors. In recent years, there has been emphasis placed on the writing process (see Krapels, this volume). Many process writing textbooks have been published which focus on content through several drafts of a paper and leave scrutiny of form to the final draft. However, many teachers maintain a strong interest in correctness in spite of this recent focus on process (Applebee 1981).

Should classroom teachers' written feedback focus on form or content? Does the research in composition support the current trends in composition teaching to focus on content?

Early composition research studies looked at first language (L1) learners and examined the ways teachers treat form in the final drafts of students' papers. Arnold (1964), for example, did an experiment with tenth grade students to see whether focusing on all errors or on only one type of error per paper made any difference. No significant differences in writing ability were found at the end of the year.

Most L1 studies on feedback have not separated form and content as clearly because researchers were most interested in other effects: positive versus negative feedback (Gee 1970; Schroeder 1973; Hausner 1975); written versus tape-recorded feedback (Coleman 1972; Judd 1973); frequency of feedback (Sutton and Allen 1964; Clopper 1967). Interested in location of feedback, Stiff (1967) examined whether college freshmen profit most from comments made in the margins of a paper, comments made at the end of a paper, or a combination. He concluded that the location of comments had no effect. In a later study, Bata (1972) found similar results.

A small number of studies have focused on content alone, such as that done by Schroeder (1973); she found that students who received positive comments on their use of description increased their use of description in their writing. Noting the results of this study, Hillocks (1986) concluded that "focused feedback can have an effect on certain aspects of writing" (p. 166).

In trying to address the issue of feedback, many L1 researchers determined that until they knew what students actually *did* as they wrote, in other words, what their writing process was, it would be useless to try and design an optimal feedback model (Emig 1967; Murray 1968). Thus much of the L1 writing research began to examine the writing process of students. At the same time, researchers wanted to learn how good writers differed from poor writers. Studies revealed that good writers revised more than poor writers (Stallard 1974) and that good writers revised content more than form (Perl 1979; Sommers 1980; Faigley and Witte 1981). In a study that examined the effect of between-draft comments, Beach (1979) found that comments on a single dimension of content (in Beach's study it was "support") were effective and that such comments may be more helpful than ones that are verbose or scattered throughout the paper. These findings led to the suggestion that teachers should focus on content more than form and provide content feedback between initial and final drafts of papers. Freedman (1987) also has described how effective teachers provide feedback primarily *during* the writing process.

Researchers have also looked at the substance of teachers' comments. Sommers (1982), for example, found that most teacher comments are vague and do not provide specific reactions to what students have written. Because of this, she says students' revisions show mediocre improvement, and some revised essays even seem worse than the original.

Clearly more research is needed. Although Hillocks (1986), in his detailed summary of L1 research, found that in general feedback has little effect, he encourages researchers to continue to look at feedback because so many variables have not yet been investigated. Based on her review of L1 research, Herrington (1989) concurs.

The L2 (second language) research on composition has focused both on how teachers correct form and how they respond to content. Here the story is briefer and similarly inconclusive (see Leki, this volume; Cohen and Cavalcanti, this volume). Authors of research studies in this area draw different conclusions. Focus on form in some cases appears to be effective in helping students write better; in others it is not. Hendrickson (1978) found that providing the correct form, in addition to noting the errors, had no statistically significant effect on students' writing proficiency. Lalande (1982), however, found that his experimental group, which was given information on the kind of errors made, showed significant improvement over the control group, whose errors were simply corrected. In a study that also looked at direct methods of correcting student errors, Robb, Ross, and Shortreed (1986) found that location improved accuracy; anything but minimal feedback worked. Fathman and Whalley (1985) also found that students who received feedback on form do make more improvement on writing tasks than those who do not.

In the area of teacher feedback on content there are even fewer studies. In one, Zamel (1985) replicated the work of Sommers (1982) and examined the way teachers give feedback on content. She found that English as a second language (ESL) teachers are very much like L1 teachers. Their comments on content are vague and contradictory. In addition, she found that the students tended to respond to comments on form and ignored those on content. In another report, Cohen acknowledged that his own feedback to students was frequently unsystematic and inconsistent (see Cohen and Robbins 1976).

These findings make one wonder about the overall usefulness of teacher feedback. In a study that looked at the effects of no feedback, Graham (1983) found that those students who received feedback on every assignment did not make fewer errors than those students who received feedback on every third assignment. Thus more frequent feedback does not ensure greater improvement in writing. Even though research results lead to some questions about the usefulness of feedback on writing, teachers report that students want feedback. Consequently, teachers feel obliged to provide it. Because students want feedback and teachers feel obliged to give it, the question remains *when* during the writing process it should be provided.

The process/product debate continues: Should teachers focus on the writing process in the classroom or emphasize the importance of a correct final product in student writing? Related to this controversy is the debate over teacher feedback on content and form. While the debate continues over *where* the focus of feedback should be (Horowitz 1986; Silva 1988; Zamel 1988), nearly all researchers agree that attention must be paid to both content and form (Taylor 1981; Krashen 1984). Raimes (1983) suggests that teachers should look at content as well as errors in structure and focus on linguistic features after ideas have been fully developed. In keeping with these trends, many current textbooks lead teachers to focus first on content during the drafting stages and finally on form during the editing stage.

There remain many unanswered questions regarding form and content. Researchers continue to test new hypotheses while teachers try new ways of responding to student writing in the classroom. Disagreement continues over *how* and *when* teachers should correct errors and comment on content. In an attempt to address these issues, the following research questions were asked in this study:

1. How effective is teacher feedback that focuses on form (grammatical errors) in improving student writing?
2. How effective is teacher feedback that focuses on content in improving student writing?
3. When should teachers provide feedback that focuses on form versus content?

Research design

The 72 students in this study were enrolled in intermediate ESL college composition classes at two different colleges. Included in the study were students from mixed language backgrounds, primarily Asian and Hispanic. Students were at similar proficiency levels and had been placed in classes according to holistic ratings of a composition written on a specific topic. The general emphasis of classes focused on the process of writing.

The compositions and rewrites of these students were analyzed to determine how students' ability to rewrite compositions varied when they were focused on the form and/or the content of their writing. Written feedback from the teachers on grammar errors focused students on "form," while teachers' comments on content focused students on the "content" of their writing.

Each student in these classes was asked to write a composition telling a story about a sequence of eight pictures. The students were shown the pictures, given a short oral summary of the content by the teacher, and asked to write for 30 minutes about what was happening in the pictures. This method controlled content while encouraging fluency in writing.

Students in various classes were randomly assigned to one of four groups. The six classes included in the study were of different sizes, and students were not assigned to all four groups in all classes. The students in each group received a different kind of teacher feedback on their compositions: Group 1 received no feedback, Group 2 received grammar feedback only, Group 3 received content feedback only, Group 4 received grammar and content feedback. Grammar feedback consisted solely of underlining all grammar errors (e.g., verb forms, tenses, articles, agreement). Thus students were told the location of their errors only and were not given information on the kinds of errors or shown the correct forms. Content feedback consisted of general comments that were not text specific. The comments were written at the top of the paper and did not refer to any specific part of a composition. The feedback included positive comments such as "good description," "interesting narration," "imaginative story." General suggestions for improvement were also given, such as "add details," "improve transitions," "develop paragraphs." The comments were short, and they varied only slightly between compositions.

The original compositions written by students were returned a few days later. Each student received one of the four types of teacher feedback depending upon group assignment within classes. All students were asked to make revisions and rewrite their original compositions. They were given 30 minutes to complete their rewrites.

It was anticipated that students would focus on different aspects of their compositions depending upon the type of feedback the teacher provided. Those given no feedback could choose the focus of their revisions; those given grammar feedback would be more focused on form; those given content feedback would be more focused on content; and those with content and grammar feedback would focus on both form and content in their revisions.

The original compositions and revised rewrites were then read by two independent raters and assigned separate scores for grammar and for content. The grammar scores were based upon the number of grammar errors (e.g., tense, case, agreement) occurring in each composition. Thus the number of errors in each composition and rewrite was counted, and each paper was assigned a grammar score (e.g., a score of 14 indicated that 14 errors were made). Thus a small number of errors (a low numerical score) indicates good grammatical accuracy.

The content scores assigned to each composition and rewrite consisted of a holistic rating between 1 and 20. A holistic scoring guide (see Appendix to this chapter) was developed based on the "ESL Composition Profile" (Jacobs et al. 1981). The scores were based upon organization, description, coherence, and creativity. Thus the higher the numerical score, the better the content of the composition. The grammar and content scores on the original compositions and the rewrites were then analyzed to determine how teacher treatment of error affected form and content of student writing.

TABLE I. MEAN GRAMMAR AND CONTENT SCORES ON ORIGINAL COMPOSITIONS
AND REWRITES

Groups	Grammar: mean scores (no. of errors)			Content: mean scores (rating 1–20)[a]		
	Original	Rewrite	t	Original	Rewrite	t
No feedback (N = 14)	11.3	10.7	1.5	13.6	16.6	3.9*
Grammar feedback (N = 14)	11.0	4.2	7.8*	13.3	14.1	3.9*
Content feedback (N = 22)	18.1	18.5	−.4	9.5	12.1	5.7*
Grammar & content feedback (N = 22)	21.1	11.1	10.1*	10.0	12.0	4.8*

*p < .01
[a]See Appendix for complete scoring guide.

is this right? (handwritten annotation)

SDs are not reported! (handwritten annotation)

Results

The mean grammar and content scores on the compositions and rewrites were tabulated for each of the four student groups: (1) no feedback, (2) grammar feedback, (3) content feedback, and (4) grammar and content feedback. The changes in scores suggest possible effects of feedback on grammar and content in revisions, as shown in Table 1. Paired *t*-tests showed that students made significant improvement in grammatical accuracy in revisions only when teachers provided feedback on grammar errors. However, all groups significantly improved the content of their rewrites irrespective of the kind of feedback given by the teacher. Students improved the content of their revisions even when teachers gave them no comments on the content of their original essay, although more improvement was made when comments on content were given.

The percentage of students within each group receiving higher, the same, or lower scores on rewrites than on the original composition was then calculated (see Table 2). A majority of students receiving no feedback from the teacher increased their scores in grammar and content just by rewriting their compositions. When students were provided feedback on grammar errors only, all students improved their grammatical accuracy and 44% improved the content of their writing. Seventy-one percent of students receiving only content feedback improved their content scores, but 35% of these same students made more grammar errors in their revisions. When feedback on grammar and content were given,

TABLE 2. PERCENTAGE OF STUDENTS CHANGING SCORES IN COMPOSITION REWRITE

	No feedback		Grammar feedback		Content feedback		Grammar & content feedback	
	Grammar score	Content score	Grammar score	Content score	Grammar score	Content score	Grammar score	Content score
Higher score	66	71	100	44	24	71	100	77
Same score	13	29	0	44	21	29	0	23
Lower score	21	0	0	12	35	0	0	0

TABLE 3. MEAN NUMBER OF WORDS IN ORIGINAL COMPOSITIONS
AND REWRITES

| | Number of words | | |
Groups	Original	Rewrite	Increase
No feedback	241	292	51 (21%)
Grammar feedback	222	255	33 (15%)
Content feedback	220	255	35 (16%)
Grammar & content feedback	220	242	22 (10%)

all students improved grammatical accuracy, and 77% improved the content of their writing. The specific identification of grammar errors appears to have a greater effect on grammar revisions than general content comments have on revisions in content, since all students improved their grammatical accuracy when feedback on grammar was given (whereas all students did not improve the content of their writing when content feedback was given).

The effect of teacher feedback on how much students wrote was also examined, as some critics of error feedback have suggested that feedback inhibits writing fluency. Students did indeed write more on their rewrites when no feedback was given by the teacher, as indicated in Table 3. The increase in the number of words between the original and rewrite was least when feedback from the teacher was given on both grammar and content. This is not an indication of quality of writing, but does indicate that teacher treatment of errors does affect quantity of writing.

The effects of feedback given simultaneously on form and content were examined in this study because many current process proponents suggest that student focus should be directed first to content and later to structural errors (Chenoweth 1987). As Table 1 indicates, there was almost no difference between content scores on rewrites (mean scores = 12) when only content feedback was given as opposed to when grammar and content feedback were given at the same time. This suggests that focus on grammar in addition to content does not have a significant effect on the content of student rewrites.

Discussion and conclusions

The results of this study suggest that grammar and content feedback, whether given alone or simultaneously, positively affect rewriting. The identification of the location of errors by the teacher appears to be an effective means of helping students correct their grammar errors. These results substantiate earlier findings by Lalande (1982) and Robb et al. (1986) for L2 learners, which found that writing accuracy does increase with teacher feedback that gives the location of grammar errors. Further, grammar feedback by the teacher in this study had more effect on correction of grammatical errors than content feedback did on improvement of the content of student rewrites. This might well be due to the fact that the content feedback was not text specific and was more general than the grammar feedback that identified specific grammar errors.

Students made more improvement when feedback was given than when it was not; however, a majority of the students did receive higher scores on the grammar and content of their rewrites than on their original compositions without any intervention from the teacher. Students significantly improved the content and wrote longer compositions when they did revisions without any feedback, which suggests that rewriting is worthwhile and teacher intervention is not always necessary. As Graham (1983) noted, frequency of teacher feedback does not ensure better student writing. In the classroom, assignments like those suggested by Raimes (1983), which encourage revision without feedback and writing without teacher intervention (e.g., journal writing), should be valuable components of the curriculum. They require minimal teacher time, help the student write more fluently, and may result in student improvement.

Content feedback from the teacher did, however, help students, for the content scores of student rewrites improved more when teacher comments were given than when no content feedback was provided. It appears from this study that even general comments that do not refer to specifics within the text can be effective. While L1 and L2 research studies criticize teachers for "rubber stamping" student papers and not being specific (Sommers 1982; Zamel 1985), the results of this study show that general comments giving encouragement and suggesting revisions helped improve the content of composition rewrites. Although teacher intervention may not always be necessary for improvement to occur, general prescription by the teacher may be especially helpful for L2 learners if it gives encouragement, but allows the student flexibility in determining where and how revisions in content should be made. Both general comments by the teacher on first drafts and rewriting by students in the absence of many comments appear to be effective means of improving student writing.

The results of this study also suggest that when grammar and content feedback are presented at the same time, the content of rewrites improves approximately as much as when content feedback only is given. Focus on grammar does not negatively affect the content of writing. This would suggest that students can improve their writing in situations where content and form feedback are given simultaneously. The results of this study concur with Boiarsky's recommendation (1984) that teachers need not necessarily assign multiple drafts that separate revision and editing stages in order to improve student writing.

In summary, answers to the original research questions should provide insights into the value of teacher feedback on form and content in student writing.

1. *How effective is teacher feedback that focuses on form (grammatical errors) in improving student writing?* When teachers underline grammatical errors in the students' texts, students showed significant improvement in grammatical accuracy. All students made fewer grammar errors in rewriting their compositions.
2. *How effective is teacher feedback that focuses on content in improving student writing?* General comments giving encouragement and suggesting revisions helped improve the content of composition rewrites. However, all students, irrespective of the kind of feedback they received from the teacher, improved the content of their compositions when they rewrote them. This suggests that rewriting in itself is an important way to improve writing skills.
3. *When should teachers provide feedback that focuses on form versus content?* Grammar and content feedback can be provided separately or at the same time without overburdening the student. Students whose errors were underlined and who were given general comments on content improved significantly in both grammar *and* content when they rewrote their compositions.

The results of this study offer teachers a number of viable alternatives for responding to student writing. Teachers can decide how, when, and to what extent they will respond to student errors given the constraints of their curriculum, the objectives of their program, and the needs of their students.

Appendix: Content Feedback Scoring Guide

16–20
Superior paper in all aspects of content
Fully developed with outstanding to substantial use of specific details
Events unified by transitions
No unnecessary repetition
Language is fluent, only occasional inaccuracies in idiom and vocabulary mar the paper

11–15
Generally well-handled but may have one paragraph or several sentences that are not as focused as those in a 16–20 paper

Successful use of detail but not as developed as in a 16–20 paper
Narration told accurately, but with less imagination than for a 16–20 paper
Some transitions
May be a little repetitive
May have an unclear sentence or several words used inappropriately

6–10
A vague, general telling of the story
Few details
Few, if any, transitions
Likely to be repetitive
One or more sentences may be incomprehensible

1–5
Lack of understanding of the story
Little development
Few or no details
No transitions
Consistent misuse of vocabulary and/or idiom

References

Applebee, A. N. (1981). *Writing in the secondary school.* NCTE Research Rep. No. 21. Urbana, Ill.: National Council of Teachers of English.

Arnold, L. (1964). Writer's cramp and eyestrain – are they paying off? *English Journal, 53,* 10–15.

Bata, E. J. (1972). A study of the relative effectiveness of marking techniques on junior college freshman English composition. Unpublished doctoral dissertation, University of Maryland.

Beach, R. (1979). The effects of between-draft teacher evaluation versus student self-evaluation on high school students' revising of rough drafts. *Research in the Teaching of English, 13,* 111–119.

Boiarsky, C. (1984). What the authorities tell us about teaching writing. *Journal of Teaching Writing, 3,* 213–223.

Chenoweth, N. A. (1987). The need to teach rewriting. *ELT Journal, 41,* 25–29.

Clopper, R. R. (1967). A study of contract correcting as a means of significantly increasing writing and English skills. Unpublished doctoral dissertation, University of Maryland.

Cohen, A. D., and Robbins, M. (1976). Toward assessing interlanguage performance: The relationship between selected errors, learners' characteristics, and learners' explanations. *Language Learning, 26,* 45–66.

Coleman, V. B. (1972). A comparison between the relative effectiveness of marginal-interlinear-terminal commentary and of audiotaped commentary in responding to English compositions. Unpublished doctoral dissertation, University of Pittsburgh.

Connors, R. J. (1985). Mechanical correctness as a focus in composition instruction. *College Composition and Communication, 36,* 61–72.

Emig, J. (1967). On teaching composition: Some hypotheses and definitions. *Research in the Teaching of English, 1,* 127–135.

Faigley, L., and Witte, S. (1981). Analyzing revision. *College Composition and Communication, 32,* 400–414.

Fathman, A., and Whalley, E. (1985). Teacher treatment of error and student writing accuracy. Paper presented at the 19th Annual TESOL Convention, New York, March.

Freedman, S. W. (1987). *Response to student writing.* Urbana, Ill.: National Council of Teachers of English.

Gee, T.C. (1970). The effects of written comment on expository composition. Unpublished doctoral dissertation, North Texas State University.

Graham, M. (1983). The effect of teacher feedback on the reduction of usage errors in junior college freshman's writing. Unpublished doctoral dissertation, University of Southern Mississippi.

Griffin, C.W. (1982). Theory of responding to student writing: The state of the art. *College Composition and Communication, 33,* 296–310.

Hausner, R. M. (1975). Interaction of selected student personality factors and teachers' comments in a sequentially-developed composition curriculum. Unpublished doctoral dissertation, Fordham University.

Hendrickson, J. (1978). Error correction in foreign language teaching: Recent theory, research, and practice. *Modern Language Journal, 62,* 387–398.

Herrington, A. (1989). The first twenty years of research in the teaching of English and the growth of a research community in composition studies. *Research in the Teaching of English, 23,* 117–138.

Hillocks, G., Jr. (1986). *Research on written composition: New directions for teaching.* Urbana, Ill.: ERIC Clearinghouse on Reading and Communication Skills and the National Conference on Research in English.

Horowitz, D. (1986). Process, not product: Less than meets the eye. *TESOL Quarterly, 20,* 141–144.

Jacobs, H. L.; Zinkgraf, S. A.; Wormuth, D. R.; Hartfiel, V. F.; Hughey, J. B. (1981). *Testing English composition: A practical approach.* Rowley, Mass.: Newbury House.

Judd, K. E. (1973). The effectiveness of tape recorded evaluations of compositions written by seventh-grade and eighth-grade students. Unpublished doctoral dissertation, University of Connecticut.

Krashen, S. D. (1984). *Writing: Research, theory, and applications.* Oxford: Pergamon Institute of English.

Lalande, J., II. (1982). Reducing composition errors: An experiment. *Modern Language Journal, 66,* 140–149.

Murray, D. (1968). *A writer teaches writing: A practical method of teaching composition.* Boston: Houghton Mifflin.

Perl, S. (1979). The composing processes of unskilled college writers. *Research in the Teaching of English, 13,* 317–336.

Raimes, A. (1983). Anguish as a second language? Remedies for composition teachers. In A. Freedman, I. Pringle, and J. Yalden (Eds.), *Learning to write: First language/second language.* (pp. 258–272). London: Longman.

✓ Robb, T.; Ross, S., and Shortreed, I. (1986). Salience of feedback on error and its effect on EFL writing quality. *TESOL Quarterly, 20,* 83–93.

Schroeder, T. S. (1973). The effects of positive and corrective written teacher feedback on selected writing behaviors of fourth-grade children. Unpublished doctoral dissertation, University of Kansas.

Silva, T. (1988). Comments on Vivian Zamel's "Recent research on writing pedagogy." *TESOL Quarterly, 22,* 517–520.

Sommers, N. (1980). Revision strategies of student writers and experienced adult writers. *College Composition and Communication, 31,* 378–388.

　　(1982). Responding to student writing. *College Composition and Communication, 33,* 148–156.

Stallard, C. K. (1974). An analysis of the writing behavior of good student writers. *Research in the Teaching of English, 8,* 206–218.

✓ Stiff, R. (1967). The effect upon student composition of particular correction techniques. *Research in the Teaching of English, 1,* 54–75.

Sutton D. G., and Allen, E. D. (1964). The effect of practice and evaluation on improvement in written composition. ED 001 274. Washington, D.C.: U.S. Department of Health, Education and Welfare; Office of Education, Cooperative Research Program.

Taylor, B. (1981). Content and written form: A two-way street. *TESOL Quarterly, 15,* 5–13.

✓ Zamel, V. (1985). Responding to student writing. *TESOL Quarterly, 19,* 195–202.

　　(1988). The author responds to comments on Vivian Zamel's "Recent research on writing pedagogy." *TESOL Quarterly, 22,* 520–524.

12 Responding to different topic types: a quantitative analysis from a contrastive rhetoric perspective

Joy Reid

There are many reasons to assess writing: student placement in composition classes, program evaluation, instructional design needs, individual diagnosis and progress, evaluation of exit competencies, and mastery of course content. And, as Hamp-Lyons demonstrates in this volume, there are many factors involved in the design, implementation, and evaluation of writing tasks. This chapter is concerned with a limited area in writing assessment: the evaluation of second language writing skills through a 30-minute writing task. In particular, it examines what Ruth and Murphy (1988) call a "neglected variable" in writing assessment research: the impact of the topic task on the writers' responses in the assessment process. In addition, the study uses data from prior studies in contrastive rhetoric – the study of the hypothesis that different languages have different rhetorical preferences in textual organization, preferences reflected in syntactic and other textual differences (Grabe and Kaplan 1989) – to investigate and interpret differences between and among native speakers of four language backgrounds – Arabic, Chinese, Spanish, and English – writing in English. The present study uses a discourse analysis approach to identify the quantitative differences in the syntax and lexicon in a total of 768 responses to four writing assessment tasks, consisting of two topic types and two topic tasks of each type. Data from this study demonstrate that, at least quantitatively, different topic tasks administered to writers with different language and cultural backgrounds elicit responses that are linguistically measurable and measurably different.

Until recently, most discourse analysis studies with both native and nonnative speaker compositions involved laborious handcounts of discrete linguistic features in various types of discourse (see Poole and Field 1976; Kroll 1977; Tannen 1982, 1984; Beaman 1984; Gumperz et al. 1984; Chafe and Danielewicz 1985). This approach necessitated restriction of sample size and severe limitations of linguistic and cohesive

This research was supported by a Dean's Scholarship Grant from the College of Arts, Humanities and Social Sciences at Colorado State University. Funding for the original research came from the Exxon Education Foundation.

TABLE I. WWB STYLEFILES VARIABLES SELECTED FOR ANALYSIS

Fluency variable
1. Total number of words

Syntactic variables
2. Average sentence length
3. Percentage of short sentences
4. Percentage of complex sentences
5. Percentage of passive-voice verbs

Lexical variables
6. Average word length
7. Percentage of content words
8. Percentage of pronouns

factors. Although these studies revealed many provocative results, Biber (1986) points out that they were often contradictory because the global conclusions were based on restrictive methodology. With the advent of computer text analysis programs, however, large-scale studies of multiple linguistic features of written texts are now possible, and multidimensional statistical approaches now make comprehensive studies of textual variables feasible.

The present study was made possible by the Writer's Workbench (WWB) text-analysis programs. Software for this series of text-analysis programs was originally developed by AT&T/Bell Laboratories (MacDonald 1980; MacDonald et al. 1982; Cherry 1984; Cherry et al. 1983). The parser, which analyzes parts of speech, is the foundation of the WWB; it is approximately 90% accurate (Frase, Kiefer, and Smith 1985). Among the WWB text-analysis programs, one program, *Stylefiles,* numerically reports such factors as sentence and word length, sentence type, sentence openings, word class count, total number of words and sentences, and the percentage of word types in each prose sample. Table 1 lists the eight WWB fluency, syntactic, and lexical variables selected from *Stylefiles* for this study. Variables were selected on the basis of prior discourse analysis research with native and nonnative speakers; previous studies found that data in the analysis of these variables — among others – showed significant differences between spoken and written English (Biber 1985, 1986; Ostler 1987b), between and among styles of discourse (Grabe 1987), and between and among topic types (Carlson et al. 1985; Carlson 1988a,b).

The corpus[1]

In the process of determining whether or not the TOEFL examination, administered by the Educational Testing Service (ETS), should incorporate a direct measure of writing, Bridgeman and Carlson (1983)[2] surveyed faculty in 190 departments at 34 large universities in the United States and Canada in order to identify the types of writing tasks that best represented what prospective students would be expected to produce. Results of that survey formed the basis for the development and pretesting of the expository essay topic types used in the pilot project that preceded the TOEFL Test of Written English (TWE) and which are reported on in Carlson et al. (1985):

1. *Topic Type #1:* Comparison/Contrast and Take a Position (C/C)
2. *Topic Type #2:* Describe and Interpret a Chart or Graph (G)

Topic tasks for each of the two topic types were carefully designed and pretested by the researchers. The C/C topics used in the pilot project consisted of (a) the Space prompt, which directed students to write an essay comparing the advantages and disadvantages of the exploration of outer space, and to take a position on the topic, and (b) the Leisure prompt, which directed the students to compare the benefits and drawbacks either of active or of intellectual ways of spending leisure time, and to choose one preferred way of spending their leisure time.

The first task for the G topic type, the Farming topic, presented three bar graphs: (1) number of farms, (2) size of farm population, and (3) average farm size. The graphs depicted changes in farming in the United States from 1940 to 1980. The students were directed to write a report that described and interpreted the graphs and to explain the conclusions reached from information in the graphs, using the graphs to support their conclusions. The second G topic, the Continent topic, presented two pie charts: (1) the area of the world's continents and (2) the population of the continents. Students were asked to write a report that described and interpreted the charts, and to explain the relationships between the charts, using information from the charts to support their conclusions.

Carlson et al. (1985) obtained four 30-minute writing samples from

---

1 My thanks to Sybil Carlson, whose research provided the essays used in this study, and to the Educational Testing Service TOEFL program for its permission to use these essays.
2 For a complete explanation of the survey methods and the consequent selection, development, and pilot testing of the topics used in the Carlson et al. study, see Bridgeman and Carlson (1983), Carlson et al. (1985), and the *Test of Written English Guide* (1989).

TABLE 2. SCOPE OF THE STUDY

Language background	No. of essays	Topic types		Total
		Comparison/ Contrast	Chart/ Graph	
Arabic	95	45	50	95
Chinese	261	129	132	261
Spanish	184	92	92	184
English	228	116	112	228
Total	768	382	386	768

each of 638 applicants for admission to U.S. universities as undergraduate and graduate students. These prospective students, native speakers of Arabic, Chinese, and Spanish, wrote two C/C essays and two G essays (in English) in selected international test centers immediately following a regular TOEFL examination. Sample essays written by over 100 native speakers of English were also collected at several U.S. universities. All the essays were holistically scored by experienced, trained raters; in addition, a representative subsample was analyzed by the WWB at Colorado State University. Carlson concluded that "data obtained from the WWB, as a tool of investigating the features of writing samples that may be salient to readers, suggested that further investigation may provide useful information regarding relationship among features of the papers" (1988b: 78).

The present study uses a proportionally selected sample from the Educational Testing Service corpus initially developed and studied by Bridgeman and Carlson (1983), Carlson et al. (1985), and Carlson (1988a,b). It was the objective of this study to continue and expand Carlson's research, with emphasis on the significant linguistic differences between and among the two topic types and the four topic tasks used in her research. Table 2 shows the scope of the study.

Following the analysis of the relevant language features by the WWB *Stylefiles* program, two-tailed *t*-tests (separate variance) were run on the *Stylefiles* data for each of the 768 essays. In addition, an analysis of variance (ANOVA) was run on relevant *Stylefiles* data for each of the essay means. Because results of the ANOVA indicated that significant differences existed, a multiple comparison of means test, the Scheffé test, was run to identify significant differences between paired means.[3]

---

3 The Scheffé multiple comparison of means test was used because it is the most valid test for unequal sample sizes and because it is the only one of the seven SPSS[x] multiple comparison of means tests that uses paired comparison of means and maintains total experiment Type 1 error at $< .05$.

Results and discussion

Overview

Because, as Kaplan (1988: 279) states, text "is a complex multidimensional structure, and . . . the dimensions involved include at least syntactic, semantic, and discoursal features," text analysis provides only partial knowledge of the intricacies of rhetoric. In one innovative approach to determining the textual variations in English, Grabe and Biber (1988) discussed the relationship between the co-occurrence of various patterns in text rather than individual features. If, for example, one group of essays displays recurring structural patterns (e.g., a high percentage of passive-voice verbs and a low percentage of coordinate conjunctions) while another group of essays displays quite different recurring structural patterns, the two groups may differ because they are performing different functions, because they were written by different populations, and/or because they are responding to different tasks. The interpretation of these co-occurrence patterns in the light of situational, social, and cognitive functions may result in a definition of the overall linguistic similarities and differences among texts. It was, therefore, the goal of this study to identify the statistically significant differences between and among the topic types in this corpus, as well as the differences between and among the four native language backgrounds of the writers, to note the frequency of the co-occurrence of eight fluency, syntactic, and lexical variables, and to interpret the results of the WWB analysis.

In the initial analysis, a two-tailed *t*-test was run on the single fluency variable, total *number of words*.[4] Fluency, a complex concept, is defined in this study as language that produces stretches of connected discourse (Reid and Findlay 1986). While "fluent" writing may not routinely convey meaning that is grammatical and nativelike (Pawley and Syder 1983), it demonstrates an ease of writing, a "scribal fluency" of keeping pen to paper without the obvious "halting" (Galvan 1986) that can characterize breaks in thought and coherence on the part of the writer; often, then, fluency is demonstrated by overall length of essay. Of course, mere length does not necessarily ensure quality writing; an underdeveloped essay may be a collection of lengthy but empty sentences (or even nonsense words), while a specific and effective piece of writing may be relatively short (Hillocks 1986). But essay length is often indicative of development within paragraphs, structural completeness, and fluency. Indeed, in several studies with native and nonnative speaker writers, length of essay has correlated highly with quality writing (Nold and

---

4 In this paper, variables analyzed by WWB *Stylefiles* are italicized.

TABLE 3. WWB VARIABLE DIFFERENCES BETWEEN THE COMPARISON/CONTRAST
AND THE GRAPH TOPIC TYPES

Variables	C/C	G	Significance	F prob.
Fluency variable				
No. of words	208.0984	233.6859	G > C/C	.000
Syntactic variables				
Average sentence length	22.6194	22.2034	NS	
% Short sentences	29.0777	27.2749	NS	
% Complex sentences	38.4430	37.6021	NS	
% Passive-voice verbs	10.7979	9.6728	NS	
Lexical variables				
Average word length	4.5194	4.5851	G > C/C	.006
% Content words	57.6720	55.7335	C/C > G	.000
% Pronouns	4.8671	7.6542	G > C/C	.000

Freedman 1977; Faigley 1979; Wille 1982; Carlson et al. 1985; Reid 1986; Reid and Findlay 1986).

Other analyzed variables fall into two categories: syntactic and lexical. First, several syntactic variables for the C/C and G topic types were analyzed. The WWB determines *average sentence length* individually for each student essay; the *percentage of short sentences* measures sentences five words shorter than the individual average. The WWB classifies complex sentences as those that contain one independent clause, the modifying elements for that independent clause, and/or one or more dependent (subordinate) clauses; the *percentage of complex sentences* measures the number of such syntactic structures in each student essay and gives the individual percentage. Finally, *percentage of passive-voice verbs* in each student essay was quantified by the WWB.

Lexical, or word/vocabulary choice, variables included *average word length* and *percentage of pronouns,* both determined for each essay by the WWB. *Percentage of content words* is a measure of nouns, adjectives, nonauxiliary verbs, and adverbs in an essay. In other words, content words are those that provide meaning, not simply the structure of discourse. Table 3 gives the results of the two-tailed *t*-test analysis of these variables.

Differences between the Comparison/Contrast and Graph topics

The results of the WWB analysis of the selected language variables were not always consistent with the initial Bridgeman and Carlson (1983) research. The original study hypothesized that (a) the C/C and G topics would elicit different writing skills, (b) the C/C topics required somewhat more cognitive complexity than the more straightforward and impersonal G topics, and (c) because the G topics provided more information, they might impose more organization and, consequently, fewer cognitive demands than the C/C topics. If, as Bridgeman and Carlson (1983) suggested, the G topics were easier for writers to address, and the responses were expected to be less cognitively demanding, the essays might be predicted to be shorter. However, results in the present study showed that the student writers used significantly more words in the G essays than in the C/C essays.

Interpretation of such data is complex. It is not possible, for example, to determine that the writers wrote more fluently, or were more knowledgeable or comfortable, with the G topics. Other factors are almost certainly responsible, at least in part. For example, the G topics provided substantially more information for the writers; merely copying the information from the prompt would tend to make the G essays longer. In addition, the prompts instructed the writers to *describe* the graph; description and narration tasks have been found to be easier for native-speaker student writers to address successfully than other discourse modes, such as exposition or argumentation (Britton et al. 1975; Crowhurst and Piche 1979; Warantz and Keech 1982; Keech 1984; Applebee 1986) in elementary and secondary school as well as in the university. Wilkinson et al (1980: 90) found, for example, that narrative and expository tasks "tap different types of linguistic, stylistic, cognitive, moral, and affective considerations on the part of the writer." Further research is needed to identify the combination of factors involved, and to determine why the G topics elicited significantly more words than the C/C topics.

In the general area of syntactic variables, there were no significant differences between responses to the two topic types. These results also do not support the Bridgeman and Carlson (1983) research, which suggested that the G topics would elicit shorter, simpler sentence structures than the C/C topics. In addition, the results are not consistent with some previous research with native speakers of English that has shown significant syntactic differences when the mode of discourse changed (Crowhurst and Piche 1979; Freedman and Pringle 1980). Rushton and Young (1974: 186) found that the choice of topic appears to be a powerful influence upon syntactic selection and to have the "power to influence the level of linguistic performance of even linguistically 'deprived' groups." The results of the present research, however, indicate that, regardless of the topic task, student writers under the pressure of time, writing spontaneously without time for revision, used similar syntactic constructions in all four essays. The discrepancy may be due to the time constraints imposed on the writers; the limited sentence structure strategies and resources available to the majority of writers who were nonnative speakers of English; and/or the grouping of all the language groups together. As Faigley (1980) pointed out, more investigation is needed in the kinds of structures that make up sentences (or *t*-units); in this study, there may well be differences too discrete – or too complex – for the WWB analysis to quantify.

In contrast, the vocabulary chosen by student writers in their essays varied significantly with topic type. First, the essay writers used significantly longer words in the G task. In Biber's (1986) study of the co-occurrence of certain language features in the oral and written discourse of native speakers of English, he found that longer words convey more specialized meanings than shorter ones; high average word length indicates a "highly exact presentation of informational content in a text, conveying maximum content in the fewest words" (p. 394). Correspondingly, discourse with lower average word length has been described as less explicit and more interactional (Tannen 1984; Chafe and Danielewicz 1985). In other words, the high average word length in the G responses may indicate that the topics elicited more formal, informational responses than the more informal, interpersonal responses to the C/C topic type. Another possible reason for these results is that the G prompts provided the student writers with fairly sophisticated vocabulary; if the writers repeatedly used the given vocabulary, they may have increased their average word length.

The *percentage of content words* found in the essays also differed significantly: Writers used significantly more content words (e.g., nouns, adjectives, adverbs) in the C/C topics than in the G topics. Grabe and Biber (1988) point out that a high percentage of nouns is reflective of high "informational density" and exact informational contexts. In prior discourse analysis research (Halliday 1979; Biber 1986; Grabe and Biber 1988), a high percentage of content words usually co-occurs with a high average word length. Longer words, a higher percentage of content words, and a high percentage of nouns should therefore result in highly explicit, formal, and somewhat condensed meaning in English prose. However, this study did not support the co-occurrence of high average word length and high percentage of content words in the same topic type. Rather, writers in this corpus used longer words in the G topics and more content words in the C/C topics. One reason for this difference may be the differences in the availability of vocabulary in the two prompt types. Another might be that the discourse mode of the G prompts is essentially *descriptive;* the number of prepositions, articles, conjunctions, and auxiliary verbs (i.e., noncontent words) may increase in that discourse mode.

Student writers in the study also used significantly more pronouns in the G topics than in the C/C topics. Research by Grabe (1987) and Biber (1985, 1986) supports the notion that limited use of pronouns in discourse marks more informational, detached formal written discourse (Chafe 1982; Norment 1982). In contrast, the frequent use of pronouns in both written and oral English discourse is characteristic of the more personal, interactive, informal prose that is often identified with oral language features. The results in this study are not consistent with that previous research: While the G topics would seem to require more formal and more informational responses, the high percentage of pronoun use would characterize the responses as less formal and informational. This discrepancy may lie in the definition of pronouns. While the WWB classifies all pronouns – personal, possessive, and demonstrative – as pronouns, Biber (1986) and Grabe (1987) distinguish between personal and demonstrative pronouns, and even between the third-person pronouns *he/she* and *it*. One explanation, then, may concern the actual pronouns used by the student writers: Perhaps the more personal pronouns (I, you, he/she) were used more often in the C/C essay while more demonstrative pronouns (this, there) were used in the G topics. Since the WWB does not distinguish between the two types of pronouns, further, more discrete, research is needed. Another explanation might be that many of the writers in this study were creating prose that does not resemble the professional, experienced writing originally analyzed by Biber and Grabe. Rather, as Grabe and Biber (1988) point out in a more recent article, student essays represent neither real world writing nor real academic writing.

Generally, then, the linguistic data in this section of the study indicate that when student writers address two distinctly different topic types, their syntax does not necessarily change. However, there are significant differences in the lexical choices made by the student writers. The G topics elicited responses that contained frequent co-occurrences of some language features described as characteristic of highly abstract, formal academic prose (Chafe 1982; Biber 1986; Dantas 1987, 1989; Grabe 1987). The C/C topics, in contrast, elicited discourse that was more informal and more concrete, as indicated by more content words; the topics tended to require the writers to establish and maintain a closer relationship with the audience and to interact more with the readers.

Differences among the four language backgrounds

In addition to the analysis of the linguistic patterns of different topic types, this study investigated the differences between and among the four language backgrounds represented in the corpus: Arabic, Chinese, Spanish, and English. Information about such differences may contribute to contrastive rhetoric research, which maintains that written first lan-

TABLE 4. DIFFERENCES AMONG LANGUAGE BACKGROUNDS IN THE
COMPARISON/CONTRAST AND GRAPH TOPIC TASKS

Variables	Arabic		Chinese		Spanish		English	
	C/C (45)[a]	G (50)	C/C (129)	G (132)	C/C (92)	G (92)	C/C (116)	G (112)
Fluency variable								
No. of words	G > C/C		G > C/C		NS		G > C/C	
F prob.	.042		.036				.000	
Syntactic variables								
Average sentence length	NS		NS		NS		NS	
% Short sentences	NS		NS		NS		NS	
% Complex sentences	NS		NS		NS		NS	
% Passive-voice verbs	C/C > G		C/C > G		NS		NS	
F prob.	.002		.022					
Lexical variables								
Average word length	NS		NS		NS		G > C/C	
% Content words	C/C > G		C/C > G		C/C > G		C/C > G	
F prob.	.045		.000		.069		.000	
% Pronouns	G > C/C		G > C/C		G > C/C		G > C/C	
F prob.	.000		.000		.000		.000	

[a]Numbers in parentheses are the number of essays in each topic type.

guage texts by authors from different language groups vary because cultural conventions and need dictate the choice of linguistic and structural aspects of discourse (Purves 1988). If writers from different language and cultural backgrounds do indeed present written material in different ways, there may be differing co-occurrences of linguistic patterns to distinguish one from another. Because the progression of sentences in discourse represents a progression of ideas, the way ideas are ordered at the clausal level affects the hierarchical ordering of ideas at the paragraph level and beyond (Ricento 1985). In order to investigate the notion of contrastive rhetoric through sentence and word choice in the ETS essays, a second analysis of data was performed. Table 4 shows the results of the two-tailed t-test.

Students from three of the four language backgrounds wrote significantly more words about the G topic than they wrote about the C/C topics. Interestingly, the native speakers of Spanish wrote nearly the same number of words in their responses to each topic type. The reason for the similar number of words in the Spanish-speaker essays is unclear; most contrastive rhetoric studies assume that, of the three non-English languages in this study, Spanish most resembles English. However, recent research (Ostler 1987a,b; Reid 1988) suggests that significant differences between English and Spanish exist and that, in some ways, Spanish is more similar to Arabic than to English. For example, in Reid's research (1988), which examined the co-occurrence of language features in the corpus of the present study, native speakers of English used few coordinate conjunctions, a high percentage of passive voice verbs, and a high percentage of prepositions. However, both Arabic and Spanish writers (but not Chinese writers) used significantly more coordinate conjunctions, and significantly fewer prepositions and passive-voice verbs. Ostler (1987b) indicated that one reason for the similar linguistic co-occurrences in Arabic and Spanish may be the influence of 600 years of occupation by the Moors in Spain.

The syntactic variables in this section of the study do not change significantly between or among language backgrounds, except in the case of passive-voice verbs: The Arabic and Chinese writers used significantly more passive-voice verbs in their C/C essays than in their G essays. Previous research with native speakers of English has reported that the use of passive voice is indicative of the formal, "informational" character of U.S. academic prose (Biber 1986; Reid and Findlay 1986; Grabe 1987; Grabe and Biber 1988) as opposed to the more personal, interactional prose of narrative, for example (Chafe 1982). Such research would suggest that writers aware of the expectations of the "discourse community" – that is, the U.S. academic reader – would use a high percentage of passive voice in their essays, across topics and topic types.

The differences in passive voice use in this study may be due to different interpretations of the topic tasks and/or the topic types by student writers from different language/cultural backgrounds; by individual ability to use the passive voice; by differing levels of awareness of the expectations of the academic audience in the United States, or by differing cultural perceptions of quality writing (Carlson 1988b). As Soter (1988) indicates, ESL writers bring various cultural and educational experiences with them to their second language writing experiences: "They have been enculturated with regard to language in a variety of contexts and genres" (p. 201). Second language writers who are successful writers in their first languages often know what is socially and culturally appropriate in terms of the writer roles, audience expectations, rhetorical and stylistic conventions, and situational or contextual features of written text in their native languages. However, there is "no reason to assume that the nonnative English speaker will be aware of this set of conventions in English, or that the learner will be able to acquire these conventions for him- or herself" (Kaplan 1988: 294).

As in the first section of this analysis, the lexical variables in this section showed more significant differences than the syntactic variables. Interestingly, the native speakers of English accounted for the only significant difference in average word length, indicating that their writing was responsible for the overall significant difference in average word length in the previous section (see Table 3). The fact that native speakers of English used significantly longer words in the G essays suggests that the writers modified their vocabulary according to the topic type; perhaps they perceived the G topics as more technical and formal than the C/C topics. In contrast, native speakers of Arabic, Chinese, and Spanish did not use significantly longer words in the G topics, perhaps because they do not have comparable language resources or knowledge of audience expectations, and/or perhaps because of the dual constraints of second language writing and the 30-minute time limit.

In their use of content words, writers from all four language backgrounds used a significantly higher percentage of content words in the C/C topics than in the G topics. These results parallel the results in the first section of this analysis (see Table 3), indicating that the C/C topics elicited the use of more nouns, adjectives, adverbs, and nonauxiliary verbs than the G topics, which elicited sentence structures that contained proportionately more articles, prepositions, conjunctions, and auxiliary verbs. While some limited research with text types has labeled technical prose as having a high lexical load (Halliday 1979; Smith and Frawley 1983), this study does not support such results. Additional research is needed in order to determine whether, as researchers of native-speaker prose have pointed out, an extensive vocabulary and precise word choice improve the quality of native-speaker essays. What is known is that native-speaker raters give higher scores to native-speaker students who present their ideas concisely and use precise diction (Stewart and Grobe 1979; Grobe 1981; Pritchard 1981; Witte and Faigley 1981).

Finally, the percentage of pronouns used in the essays also differed between topic types for all four language backgrounds. In each case, the Arabic, Chinese, Spanish, and English writers used significantly more pronouns in the G topic tasks than in the C/C topic tasks. This result remains at odds with studies that associate pronoun use with personal, interactive prose (Biber 1986; Grabe 1987); Biber's study (1986: 396) showed that the "features associated with personal involvement and those features associated with high abstraction of detachment belong to separate textual dimensions." However, Biber (1986) also found that abstract, detached content is not always directly opposed to a high amount of personal involvement; in some text types (e.g., professional letters), the two dimensions correlated positively. In this study, the substantial use of pronouns by writers of all language backgrounds in the G topics may reflect the descriptive nature of the task, and/or the perception of the writers that the audience for – and the purpose of – the task were relatively informal. The findings indicate that, for whatever reasons – first language transfer, cultural and educational experiences, or avoidance of more complex syntactic structures, for example – the ESL writers' frequent use of pronouns may make their essays less "academic," and therefore less acceptable to the U.S. discourse community.

Generally speaking, the variable means in this section of the analysis parallel the previous section. Moreover, the mean differences between and among the four language backgrounds differed in the same direction. That is, in each case of significant difference, the Arabic, Chinese, Spanish, and English writers used significantly more (or fewer) language elements in the same topic type – for example, more words in C/C than in G, more content words in C/C than in G, and a lower percentage of pronouns in C/C than in G. These results suggest that contrastive rhetoric influences constitute one factor among several that shape second language writing (Grabe and Kaplan 1989).

Conclusions

Data from the present research suggest that quantitative differences do exist between the two topic types in the ETS corpus and among the responses of the four language backgrounds studied. It does not, however, answer the question of qualitative differences between topic types, nor does it take into consideration the complex interactions between writer and task, or between reader and product (Hamp-Lyons 1987, this volume; Steinhaus et al. 1989; Hughey, in press). At present, research results concerning the question of qualitative differences are contradictory. Several studies with native-speaker prose indicate that some topics elicit better writing than others, and that some topics are more difficult than others (Evans 1979; Warantz and Keech 1982; Freedman 1983; Keech 1984). Langer (1984: 144) indicated that "different assignments, given for different purposes, tap different aspects of a writer's knowledge of a topic." Other researchers, however, have found that different topic types do not necessarily result in qualitatively different responses from native speakers (Greenberg 1981; Brossell 1983).

In the Carlson et al. (1985) original study with the ETS corpus, the trained holistic scorers exhibited high agreement across topics and topic types; that is, the mean writing sample scores for the different topics were "approximately equivalent" (p. 74). In an intercorrelation study among the holistic scores on the four topic tasks, Carlson et al. (1985) indicated that, for the nonnative writers, "at least for these topics, there [were] not systematic differences in the way each topic type ranks students" (p. 57). These findings suggested that the different topics did not elicit qualitatively different writing performance and/or that the readers maintained a comparable scale for evaluating the writing sample despite possible performance fluctuations from topic to topic and/or from one mode of discourse to another. However, Carlson et al. (1985:58) pointed out that

> this evidence does not indicate whether different readers are evaluating the same features of writing or whether they are attending to different features when making decisions to assign a specific score to writing samples that address different topics (content) and require different approaches to the tasks.... Although we have no means by which to establish that the readers adjusted their standards with respect to specific features, depending on the specific topic and its task demands, the possibility cannot be rejected.

Other composition researchers are also concerned with the qualitative comparability of topic types. In an evaluative review of the Carlson et al. study, Greenberg (1986) used the domain-referenced classification for analyzing cross-cultural writing tasks developed by Purves et al. (1984). She found that the two topic types used in the Carlson et al. study differed in their instructions, stimuli, cognitive cues, purpose, and content. "In other words, while each task may be tapping an important aspect of functional writing competence...they are different types of tasks" (p. 539). She stated that "the lack of variation in the scores across the topic types may be due to the scorers or the scoring procedures rather than to the performance of the examinees" (p. 549). Park (1988), using a small subsample of the ETS corpus, found that, indeed, the Chinese and English hard science majors received significantly higher scores on the Farm topic (G) than on the Space topic (C/C), whereas the holistic scores of the social-science major group were not significantly different in the two writing tasks. Hoetker (1982), for example, and Hamp-Lyons (this volume) posit the possibility that holistic scoring may have only limited usefulness as a research tool for examining topic effects.

Implications

According to McKay (1989: 260), "topic development is largely a factor of cultural experience as well as social and educational policy." Because "testing is educational power" (Bridwell-Bowles 1989), simply selecting a topic and accompanying it with clear instructions that fit the purpose of the test is necessary, but not sufficient, to assess students' writing competence. Hamp-Lyons's research (this volume) has demonstrated, for example, that rhetorically specific wording, the topic type, and the testing content all affect performance, and Carlman (1986), working with native speakers of English, found that a writer's performance can vary widely from task to task and context to context. It would therefore seem essential that in a testing environment, comparability of topic tasks be a primary objective. As Ruth and Murphy (1988: 105) indicate, "we can describe and evaluate our students' writing performance when we have defined what we mean by competence in writing, when we know what our purpose is in evaluating students' writing, and when we understand the *nature and limitations of existing procedures* for measuring writing ability" (italics mine).

If, as the topic tasks in this study have shown, the nature of the writing task affects such discrete structural variables as the syntactic complexity, the use of cohesive elements, or the percentage of abstract words, then, as Raimes (1983: 266) states, "choosing topics should be the teacher's [as well as the tester's] most responsible activity." Moreover, Johnson (1983) has pointed out that factors that influence reading comprehension and hence the quality of a rater's assessment include the appropriateness of the text and the task demands. It is therefore incumbent on the teacher of nonnative speakers of English not only to design fair and appropriate topics, but also to encourage the students to internalize the shapes of North American academic writing, to distinguish between spoken and written modes, and to appreciate the "processes of subordinating and conjoining clauses" (Buckingham 1979) in order to present written information in situationally appropriate ways.

Recommendations for future research

Clearly, additional research is necessary. There is a particular need for a multidimensional methodology to assess a broad range of linguistic and rhetorical features in order to adequately account for variation in writing quality among second language writers (Connor and Lauer 1985). Further empirical research is also needed to investigate "the set of underlying textual dimensions which define similarities and differences among text types in English," and to identify "groups of linguistic features [rather than individual features] which co-occur with a high frequency in texts, indicating a communication function shared by these features" (Biber 1986: 385). Text types can differ by subject matter, purpose, rhetorical structure, style, and situational parameters, yet the identity of salient text-type distinctions is only beginning to be resolved (Faigley and Meyer 1983; Grabe 1987).

The most convincing research will occur with carefully controlled, large-scale corpora (Carlson 1988a). A variety of descriptive and empirical approaches is needed to study rhetorical patterns and relationships in order to reveal distinctions between and among cultures, populations, and text types (Ostler 1987b). Finally, the continued use of computer text analyses to quantitatively examine underlying text and genre dimensions and variations (Biber 1986; Grabe 1987) will help to identify the co-occurrence of certain linguistic features in discourse to ascertain whether or not those features correlate with particular rhetorical patterns (Ricento 1987, 1989).

As experimental and ethnographic composition research and contrastive rhetoric studies have increased, there is recognition among composition teachers and researchers that "the field of written composition is large enough and vital enough to make good use of both qualitative and quantitative methodologies" (Witte 1987: 207). In the areas of genre identification and contrastive rhetoric, theoretical explanations have yet to converge on a single acceptable general theory; however, a combination of descriptive and empirical studies have begun to provide an adequate basis for the hypotheses that different topic types elicit different responses and that rhetorical influences from a first language are one of several factors that shape second language writing (Grabe and Kaplan 1989).

References

Applebee, A. N. (1986). Problems in process approaches: Toward a reconceptualization of process instruction. In A. R. Petrosky and D. Bartholomae (Eds.), *The teaching of writing* (pp. 95–113). Chicago: National Society for the Study of Education.

Beaman, K. (1984). Coordination and subordination revisited: Syntactic complexity in spoken and written narrative discourse. In D. Tannen (Ed.), *Coherence in spoken and written discourse* (pp. 45–80). Norwood, N.J.:Ablex.

Biber, D. (1985). Investigating macroscopic textual variation through multi-feature/multi-dimensional analyses. *Linguistics, 23,* 155–178.

(1986). Spoken and written textual dimensions in English: Resolving the contradictory findings. *Language, 62,* 384–414.

Bridgeman, B., and Carlson, S. (1983). *Survey of academic writing tasks required of graduate and undergraduate foreign students.* TOEFL Research Report No. 15. Princeton, N.J.: Educational Testing Service.

Bridwell-Bowles, L. (1989). Assessment and reform: Composition gets political. Paper presented at the 40th Annual Conference on College Composition and Communication, Seattle, Wash., March.

Britton, J.; Burgess, T.; Martin, N.; McLeod, A.; and Rosen, H. (1975). *The development of writing abilities (11–18).* London: Macmillan.

Brossell, G. (1983). Rhetorical specifications in essay examination topics. *College English, 45,* 165–173.

Buckingham, T. (1979). The goals of advanced composition instruction. *TESOL Quarterly, 13,* 241–254.

Carlman, N. (1986). Topic differences on writing tests: How much do they matter? *English Quarterly, 19,* 39–49.

Carlson, S. (1988a). Cultural differences in writing and reasoning skills. In A.

Purves (Ed.), *Writing across languages and cultures: Issues in contrastive rhetoric* (pp. 227–260). Newbury Park, Cal.: Sage Publishers.

(1988b). *Relationships of reasoning and writing skills to GRE analytical ability scores.* ETS Research Report 88–13. Princeton, N.J.: Educational Testing Service.

Carlson, S.; Bridgeman, B.; Camp, R.; and Waanders, J. (1985). *Relationship of admission test scores to writing performance of native and nonnative speakers of English.* TOEFL Research Report No. 19. Princeton, N.J.: Educational Testing Service.

Chafe, W. L. (1982). Integration and involvement in speaking, writing, and oral literature. In D. Tannen (Ed.), *Spoken and written language: Exploring orality and literacy* (pp. 35–53). Norwood, N.J.: Ablex.

Chafe, W., and Danielewicz, J. (1985). Properties of spoken and written language. In R. Horowitz and S. J. Samuels (Eds.), *Comprehending oral and written language.* New York: Academic Press.

Cherry, L. (1984). A study of Part's and Style's performance on real student text. Unpublished manuscript, Bell Laboratories.

Cherry, L.; Fox, M.; Frase, L.; Keenan, S.; and MacDonald, N. (1983). Computer aids for text analysis. *Bell Laboratories Record,* May/June, 10–16.

Connor, U., and Lauer, J. (1985). Understanding persuasive essay writing: Linguistic/rhetorical approach. *Text, 5,* 309–326.

Crowhurst, M., and Piche, G. (1979). Audience and mode of discourse effects on syntactic complexity in writing at two grade levels. *Research in the Teaching of English, 13,* 101–109.

Dantas, M. (1987). Contrastive rhetoric and text-type research: A comparison of Portuguese and English newspaper editorials. Unpublished manuscript, Northern Arizona University.

(1989). Contrastive rhetoric and text-type research: A study of Portuguese and English. Paper presented at the 23rd Annual TESOL Convention, San Antonio, Texas, March.

Evans, P. (1979). Evaluation of writing in Ontario: Grades 8, 11, and 13. *Review and Evaluation Bulletins, 1* (2). Toronto: Ministry of Education.

Faigley, L. L. (1979). The influence of generative rhetoric on the syntactic maturity and writing effectiveness of college freshmen. *Research in the Teaching of English, 13,* 197–206.

(1980). Names in search of a concept: Maturity, fluency, complexity, and growth in written syntax. *College Composition and Communication, 31,* 291–300.

Faigley, L., and Meyer, P. (1983). Rhetorical theory and readers' classification of text types. *Text, 3,* 305–325.

Frase, L.; Kiefer, K.; and Smith, C. (1985). Theory and practice of computer aided composition. In S. W. Freedman (Ed.), *The acquisition of written language: Response and revision* (pp. 195–210). Norwood, N.J.: Ablex.

Freedman, S. W. (1983). Student characteristics and essay test writing performance. *Research in the Teaching of English, 17,* 313–325.

Freedman, A., and Pringle, I. (1980). Writing in the college years: Some indices of growth. *College Composition and Communication, 31,* 311–324.

Galvan, M. (1986). The writing processes of Spanish-speaking bilingual/bicultural graduate students. ERIC ED270744.

Grabe, W. (1987). Contrastive rhetoric: Text-type research. In U. Connor and

R. B. Kaplan (Eds.), *Writing across languages: Analysis of L2 text* (pp. 115–137). Reading, Mass.: Addison-Wesley.

Grabe, W., and Biber, D. (1988). Who are they writing for?: A linguistic comparison of freshmen argumentative essays and published English genres. Unpublished paper, Northern Arizona University.

Grabe, W., and Kaplan, R. B. (1989). Writing in a second language: Contrastive rhetoric. In D. M. Johnson and D. H. Roen (Eds.), *Richness in writing: Empowering ESL students* (pp. 263–283). New York: Longman.

Greenberg, K. (1981). *The effects of variations in essay questions on the writing performance of CUNY freshmen.* New York: City University of New York, Instructional Resource Center.

   (1986). The development and validation of the TOEFL writing test: A discussion of TOEFL Research Reports 15 and 19. *TESOL Quarterly, 20,* 531–544.

Grobe, C. (1981). Syntactic maturity, mechanics, and vocabulary as predictors of quality ratings. *Research in the Teaching of English, 15,* 75–85.

Gumperz, J. J.; Kaltman, H.; and O'Connor, M. C. (1984). Cohesions in spoken and written discourse: Ethnic style and the transition to literacy. In D. Tannen (Ed.), *Coherence in spoken and written discourse* (pp. 3–19). Norwood, N.J.: Ablex.

Halliday, M.A.K. (1979). Differences between spoken and written language: Some implications for literacy teaching. In G. Page et al. (Eds.), *Communication through reading: Proceedings of the 4th Australian Reading Conference,* Vol. 2 (pp. 37–52). Adelaide: Australia Reading Association.

Hamp-Lyons, L. (1987). Raters respond to rhetoric in writing. *TECFORS, 10* (3, 4), 16–27.

Hillocks, G., Jr. (1986) *Research on written composition: New directions for teaching.* Urbana, Ill.: ERIC Clearinghouse on Reading and Communication Skills and the National Conference on Research in English.

Hoetker, J. (1982). Essay exam topics and student writing. *College Composition and Communication, 33,* 377–391.

Hughey, J. (In press). Testing ESL composition. In D. Douglas (Ed.), *English language testing in colleges and universities.* Washington, D.C.: NAFSA.

Johnson, P. H. (1983). *Reading comprehension assessment: A cognitive basis.* Newark, Del.: International Reading Association.

Kaplan, R. B. (1988). Contrastive rhetoric and second language learning: Notes toward a theory of contrastive rhetoric. In A. Purves (Ed.), *Writing across languages and cultures: Issues in contrastive rhetoric* (pp. 275–304). Newbury Park, Cal.: Sage Publishers.

Keech, C. L. (1984). Apparent regression in student writing performance as a function of unrecognized changes in task complexity. Unpublished doctoral dissertation, University of California, Berkeley.

Kroll, B. (1977). Combining ideas in written and spoken English: A look at subordination and coordination. In E. O. Keenan and T. L. Bennett (Eds.), *Discourse across time and space* (pp. 69–108). Southern California Occasional Papers in Linguistics, Vol. 5. Los Angeles: University of Southern California.

Langer, J. (1984). Where problems start: The effects of available information on responses to school writing tasks. In A. N. Applebee (Ed.), *Contexts for learning to write: Studies of secondary school instruction* (pp. 135–148). Norwood, N.J.: Ablex.

MacDonald, N. H. (1980). Pattern, matching and language analysis as editing supports. In L. T. Frase (Chair), *Computer aids for text editing and design.* Symposium conducted at the American Educational Research Association meeting, Boston, Mass., April.

MacDonald, N.; Frase, L. T.; Gingrich, P.; and Keenan, S. (1982). The Writer's Workbench: Computer aids for text analysis. *Educational Psychologist, 17,* 172–179.

McKay, S. (1989). Topic development and written discourse accent. In D. Johnson and D. Roen (Eds.), *Richness in writing: Empowering ESL students* (pp. 253–262). New York: Longman.

Nold, E. W., and Freedman, S. W. (1977). An analysis of readers' responses to essays. *Research in the Teaching of English, 11,* 164–74.

Norment, N., Jr. (1982). Contrastive analyses of organizational structures and cohesive elements in English, Spanish (ESL) and Chinese (ESL) students' writing in narrative and expository modes. ERIC ED 269 764.

Ostler, S. (1987a). English in parallels: A comparison of English and Arabic prose. In U. Connor and R. B. Kaplan (Eds.), *Writing across languages: Analysis of L2 text* (pp. 169–185). Reading, Mass.: Addison-Wesley.

(1987b). A study in the contrastive rhetoric of Arabic, English, Japanese, and Spanish. Unpublished doctoral dissertation, University of Southern California.

Park, Y. M. (1988). Academic and ethnic background as factors affecting writing performance. In A. Purves (Ed.), *Writing across languages and cultures: Issues in contrastive rhetoric* (pp. 261–272). Newbury Park, Cal.: Sage Publishers.

Pawley, A., and Syder, F. (1983). Two puzzles for linguistics theory: Nativelike selection and nativelike fluency. In J. Richards and R. Schmidt (Eds.), *Language and communication* (pp. 191–227). New York: Longman.

Poole, M., and Field, T. W. (1976). A comparison of oral and written code elaboration. *Language and Speech, 19,* 305–311.

Pritchard, R. J. (1981). A study of cohesion devices in the good and poor composition of eleventh graders. Unpublished doctoral dissertation, University of Missouri, Columbia.

Purves, A. (Ed.) (1988). *Writing across languages and cultures: Issues in contrastive rhetoric.* Newbury Park, Cal.: Sage Publishers.

Purves, A.; Soter, A.; Takala, S.; and Vahapassi, A. (1984). Towards a domain-referenced system for classifying composition assignments. *Research in the Teaching of English, 18,* 383–416.

Raimes, A. (1983). Anguish as a second language? Remedies for composition teachers. In A. Freedman, I. Pringle, and J. Yalden (Eds.), *Learning to write: First language/second language* (pp. 258–272). London: Longman.

Reid, J. (1986). Using the Writer's Workbench in ESL composition teaching and testing. In A. Stansfield (Ed.), *Technology and language testing* (pp. 167–188). Washington, D.C.: TESOL.

(1988). Quantitative differences in English prose written by Arabic, Chinese, Spanish, and English writers. Unpublished doctoral dissertation, Colorado State University.

Reid, S., and Gilbert, F. (1986). Writer's Workbench analysis of holistically scored essays. *Computers and Composition, 3,* 6–32.

Ricento, T. (1985). A model for research in contrastive rhetoric. Unpublished manuscript, University of California, Los Angeles.

(1987). Aspects of coherence in English and Japanese expository prose. Unpublished doctoral dissertation, University of California, Los Angeles.

(1989). Contrastive rhetoric: Current research and pedagogical implications. Paper presented at the 23rd Annual TESOL Convention, San Antonio, Texas, March.

Rushton, J., and G. Young. (1974). Elements of elaboration in working class writing. *Educational Research, 16,* 181–188.

Ruth, L., and Murphy, S. (1988). *Designing writing tasks for the assessment of writing.* Norwood, N.J.: Ablex.

Smith, R., and Frawley, W. (1983). Conjunctive cohesion in four English genres. *Text, 3–4,* 347–373.

Soter, A. (1988). The second language learner and cultural transfer in narration. In A. Purves (Ed.), *Writing across languages and cultures: Issues in contrastive rhetoric* (pp. 177–205). Newbury Park, Cal.: Sage Publishers.

Steinhaus, K.; Reid, J.; Kroll, B.; and Kantor, R. (1989). Essay topic development: The TOEFL-TWE collaborative approach. Workshop presented at the 23rd Annual TESOL Convention, San Antonio, Texas, March.

Stewart, M., and Grobe, C. (1979). Syntactic maturity, mechanics of writing, and teachers' quality ratings. *Research in the Teaching of English, 13,* 207–215.

Tannen, D. (Ed.) (1982). *Spoken and written language: Exploring orality and literacy.* Norwood, N.J.: Ablex.

(Ed.) (1984). *Coherence in spoken and written discourse.* Norwood, N.J.: Ablex.

Test of Written English guide. (1989). Princeton, N.J.: Educational Testing Service.

Warantz, E., and Keech, C. L. (1982). Beyond holistic scoring: Rhetorical flaws that signal advance in developing writers. In J. R. Gray and L. P. Ruth (Eds.), *Properties of writing tasks: A study of alternative procedures for holistic writing assessment* (pp. 509–542). ERIC ED 230 576. Berkeley: University of California, Graduate School of Education, Bay Area Writing Project.

Wilkinson, A.; Barnsley, G.; Hanna, P.; and Swan, M. (1980). *Assessing language development.* Oxford: Oxford University Press.

Wille, S. C. (1982). The effects of pre-writing observational activities on syntactic structures. Unpublished master's thesis, University of Chicago.

Witte, S. (1987). Review of research on written composition: New directions for teaching. *College Composition and Communication, 38,* 202–207.

Witte, S., and Faigley, L. (1981). Coherence, cohesion, and writing ability. *College Composition and Communication, 32,* 189–204.

13 Writing with others' words: using background reading text in academic compositions

Cherry Campbell

Successful academic writing involves, among other things, the ability to integrate information from previous researchers in relevant areas of study. Even the most original academic paper integrates facts, ideas, concepts, and theories from other sources by means of quotations, paraphrases, summaries, and brief references. Yet this common feature of academic writing has rarely been directly studied either in the writing of native or nonnative speakers of English. Even rarer is documentation of the highly complex processes followed by academic writers using background sources – processes that involve reading, understanding, learning, relating, planning, writing, revising, editing, and orchestrating.

It has been suggested that the ability to use written sources appropriately may develop over time. In a report for the Schools Council of Great Britain on the written language of students 11 to 18 years of age, Britton et al. (1975) propose a theoretical scale of "degrees of copying." The scale begins with mechanical copying, and continues with copying for some purpose – for example, because the writer likes or agrees with the original, or because the writer is required to present information exactly. Actual composing begins further along the scale with summarization and expansion of written ideas, followed by imitation of style, and finally synthesis, which Britton et al. (1975) consider "rare in school work" (p. 46). They suggest that writers may have to pass through earlier stages before reaching the final stage of synthesis. Hence there is conceptual support for a multistage model of skill in using background information.

Most researchers studying the composing process have examined writing tasks that did not call for the use of information from a reading text. This is true of both first language (L1) studies (Emig 1971; Stallard 1974; Flower and Hayes 1977; Perl 1979; Pianko 1979; Peitzman 1981) and second language (L2) studies (Arthur 1979; Zamel

Preparation of this chapter was supported in part by the Center for Language Education and Research and by the National Council of Teachers of English. This work represents part of the research carried out for a doctoral dissertation in applied linguistics (Campbell 1987).

211

1982; Jones 1983; Scarcella 1984; Gaskill 1986; Friedlander, this volume). Subjects in these studies were given composition topics that did not involve background reading material but required them to provide ideas from their own experience. These studies of the composing process show that proficient writers plan before writing and work recursively with global issues, such as organization, content, and audience, along with revisions of syntactic and lexical problems. On the other hand, less proficient writers do less planning and show little concern for global problems; they spend more time on surface-level error correction, which often interferes with the flow of their writing (Stallard 1974; Flower and Hayes 1977; Perl 1979; Rose 1984).

A number of studies discuss both writing and reading in terms of summarization, which some scholars (Rumelhart 1977; Kintsch and van Dijk 1978) present as a highly structured model for language comprehension and production. Research has shown that summarization instruction is beneficial in working with expository text (Brown, Campione, and Day 1981; Taylor and Beach 1984), and that academic experience is beneficial in the planning and quality of summaries (Brown and Day 1983; Brown, Day, and Jones 1983; Taylor 1984). In a process study comparing professional with student writers, Taylor (1984) found that the professional writers studied the text more carefully, looked for structure and theme, planned more, checked back to the source text to verify the accuracy of their statements, took audience into consideration when determining the level of generality of their summary, and generally remained more objective. A possible developmental trend was observed by Winograd (1984), who looked at difficulties in summarizing texts and found that eighth graders with poor reading ability failed to identify information that should, by adult standards, be included in a summary; in addition, there were differences in the quality of the summaries written by these eighth graders, their more skillful peers (differentiated by scores on the Reading Comprehension subtest of the Stanford Achievement Test), and adults. That is, the quality of the summaries improved with proficiency. All of these studies report only on the task of summarizing a single piece of writing rather than using summaries from several sources in one's own work.

Synthesis of information from multiple sources by proficient and less proficient readers was the focus of two studies. Spivey (1983) asked college students to synthesize information from three different texts on the same topic into their own version and found significant differences in the organization, coherence, and quality of syntheses written by proficient and less proficient readers (as determined by scores on the Comprehension subtest of the Nelson-Denny Reading Test, Form E). Kennedy (1985) gave college students three related articles and instructed them to write an objective essay on the material in the articles. She found that the fluent readers (versus the less proficient readers, distinguished on the basis of scores on the Reading Comprehension test of the 1977 Descriptive Test of Language Skills) are active readers and notetakers (underlining, commenting on, and interacting with the text) who even revised their notes before incorporating them into their writing. On the other hand, the less proficient readers read passively, did not interact with the text much, and took notes, but simply reread their notes over and over rather than building them into their paper. The fluent readers received higher holistic scores on their papers than the less proficient readers. All of these studies demonstrate that reading ability affects the quality of summaries and syntheses.

Most of the studies cited here concern native speakers of English. Given the large nonnative college student population in North America, there is a practical need for more research on their academic English language skills, the results of which might lead to more relevant pedagogy (Johns 1985a). From a theoretical standpoint as well, more work should be done demonstrating the language use of both native and nonnative speakers performing the same tasks (Stotsky 1983), as well as the language use of speakers in both their native language and in ESL (Gaskill 1986; Carson et al. 1990). Some research on nonnative speakers of English has begun to address these issues in terms of transfer of high-level first language processes to second language writing (Edelsky 1982; Lay 1982; Jones 1983; Mohan and Lo 1985; Gaskill 1986), and the nature of the relationship between reading and writing skills (see Eisterhold, this volume). Several studies describe the processes followed by proficient and less proficient nonnative readers and writers (Zamel 1982, 1983; Jones 1983, 1985; Cooper 1984; Hosenfeld 1984; Raimes 1985; Gaskill 1986). Still other studies document differences between native and nonnative speakers carrying out the same reading and writing tasks (Carrell 1981; Jacobs 1982; Connor and McCagg 1983; Connor 1984; Scarcella 1984). None of these studies discuss the use of information from reading text in writing.

The purpose of this study is to document how, given the same task, native and nonnative speaker university students use information from a background reading text in their own academic writing. Their use of direct quotations, paraphrases, summaries, or other methods will be described as well as the function and location of textual information in the student papers. Students' attribution of information to the author of the background reading text will also be reported. Finally, instructor evaluations of the students' writing will be discussed.

Method

Subjects

The 30 subjects for this study were enrolled in various composition courses at UCLA. Ten subjects were chosen randomly from 15 students in two sections of a standard ESL composition course; 10 subjects were chosen randomly from 21 students in one section of a standard composition course for native speakers. The two standard courses satisfy the undergraduate composition requirement in UCLA's College of Letters and Sciences, and the low-level course is a prerequisite to the standard ESL composition course. The ESL composition students had completed the UCLA ESL multiskills language requirement, and all of the students, native and nonnative speakers alike, were placed in their composition section on the basis of essay examinations. Scholastic Aptitude Test (SAT)[1] scores for students enrolled in these three courses were as follows: The mean verbal SAT score was 241 for the low-level ESL composition students (or less proficient nonnative speakers), 291 for the standard-level ESL composition students (or more proficient nonnative speakers), and 467 for the standard-level native speaker students. The mean SAT English Composition Achievement Test score for each group was 298 for the less proficient nonnative speakers, 337 for the more proficient nonnative speakers, and 476 for the native speakers.

Materials and procedures

The instructors of the five composition classes gave the same reading/writing assignment to their classes. The students were given the first chapter of an undergraduate anthropology textbook by Harris (1983) to read for homework. Instructions attached to the chapter advised the students that this was background reading for an upcoming composition assignment and that it was not necessary to

---

1 Generally speaking, students seeking admission to colleges and universities in North America need a combined SAT score of 1,000 or above for verbal and mathematical performance; each component is scored on a 200–800 point scale. High mathematical scores for some students produce acceptable combined scores despite low verbal scores, such as those found in most of the subjects for this study.

learn everything presented in the chapter, but that demonstration of familiarity with anthropological terminology presented in the chapter was discussed with the class as a whole, focusing on such terms as *ethnography, enculturation, diffusion,* and *emic and etic points of view.* The students were then given a composition topic that involved the use and explanation of terminology from the anthropology text, which they were allowed to refer to during their composing. The topic required them to relate the anthropology terminology to fraternities and sororities as subcultures:

Composition Topic

Imagine that you are an anthropologist preparing to observe and report on a subculture. Write a composition in which you explain which anthropological concepts you plan to consider in your report. Make your explanations clear enough for a university student unfamiliar with anthropology to understand. The subculture you are preparing to observe is that of fraternities and/or sororities at UCLA. Make reference to the Harris chapter as you explain the concepts that you choose.

One class hour was given for the students to write a first draft, which was used in the data analysis.

Data analysis

In each of the 30 compositions analyzed for this study, excerpts were isolated where the writer had used information from the anthropology text. The excerpts – that is, the examples of use of information from the background text – were categorized by two raters as to type, function, location, and type of documentation. Percentage agreement ratings were calculated for the categorizations: intrarater agreement of .73 and interrater agreement of .75. Each student paper was also rated for holistic quality by two university writing instructors using an analytic scale, the ESL Composition Profile (Jacobs et al. 1981); the reliability of the ratings was determined by the Pearson product-moment correlation coefficient to be .82, a medium-high figure indicating an overlap of 67%.

In order to control for composition length, the following steps were taken. Each composition was divided into three sections (first paragraph, last paragraph, and body – i.e., those paragraphs between the first and last), and *t*-units were counted in each section. Hunt's (1965) definition was followed of a *t*-unit being a single independent clause including all modifying dependent clauses. Then each isolated example of use of information from the reading text was tabulated according to its number of *t*-units relative to the total *t*-units in its corresponding section of the composition. These percentages of *t*-units were used in conducting an analysis of variance.

t-unit

Results

Analysis, findings, and discussion

TYPE AND FUNCTION

Each of the 171 examples isolated from the 30 student compositions was categorized as one of the following types: Quotation, Exact Copy, Near Copy, Paraphrase, Summary, or Original Explanation. The *Quotation* category is self-explanatory. *Exact Copies* were direct quotations without the punctuating quotation marks. *Near Copies* were similar to Exact Copies with the addition that syntax was rearranged, or synonyms were used for one or two content words. For example, the quotation "Anthropology is the study of humankind, of ancient and modern people and their ways of living" (Harris 1983: 2) was incorporated by one student as the following Near Copy:

Anthropology, the study of people and their ways of living is a very broad topic.

Paraphrases involved more syntactic changes of the original anthropology text than Near Copies. For example, the quotation "Infrastructure consists of the etic and behavioral activities by which each society satisfies minimal requirements for subsistence" (Harris 1983: 16) was paraphrased as follows:

The infrastructure of this society consits [sic] of the activities that each sorority and fraternity take part in in order to survive.

(As presented here, the notions Exact Copy, Near Copy, and Paraphrase represented points along a continuum rather than clearly defined separate categories, making interpretation problematic, which is discussed at more length later.) *Summaries* represented the gist of information from the background reading. For the previous types, a single excerpt in the anthropology text directly corresponded to the excerpt from the student composition. With Summaries, however, the gist of information in the anthropology text was used in the student composition, rather than a single corresponding passage of text. The composition topic called for the students to explain the technical concepts that they would use in an anthropological study of sororities and/or fraternities. It was often found that information from the anthropology text was presented through the students' explanation of sororities/fraternities. These types constituted the category called *Original Explanation*, as represented by the following example from a student paper:

We will see that a subculture is prone to use the same processes a culture does in order to continue existing and it also shares other characteristics. We have the enculturation process for example. The "older" brothers" [sic] will teach the new members how the fraternity is run, what is done and what is not, maybe they will have a dress code and so. Enculturation is just the older generation (brothers) teach the new generation their ways...

As with Summaries, it was not possible to pinpoint a specific excerpt from the anthropology text that was used as the basis of these Original Explanations. Near Copies and Exact Copies are considered by academic writing conventions to be inappropriate use of information from the background text, whereas Quotations, Paraphrases, Summaries, and Original Explanations are considered appropriate.

As further explanation of the analysis of *type,* it should be noted that if these types of information from the background text were put on a scale of *degree* of integration, then Quotations would represent the least amount of integration in the student writing. Quotations would be least integrated since the exact wording of the source text is transferred to the student writing, signaled (ideally) by punctuation and reference to the author of the source text. Original Explanations would be most integrated, since an idea is taken from the source text and explained in terms of the composition topic regarding fraternities and sororities. The other types of information use would occur on the scale between these two extremes; from least to most integrated there would be Quotations, Exact Copies, Near Copies, Paraphrases, Summaries, and Original Explanations. The degree of integration of information from the background reading text in the student writing should not be confused with the quality of the integration. The quality of a Quotation may be excellent, just as the quality of an Original Explanation may be. Regardless of quality, a Quotation involves exact wording from the background text, and as such is the least integrated information in the student text, whereas an Original Explanation is the most integrated, since the background information is molded to fit the student text.

The categorization of the function of each example involved the notions of backgrounding and foregrounding (Hopper 1979). Hopper and Thompson (1980) define "that part of a discourse which does not immediately and crucially contribute to the speaker's goal, but which merely assists, amplifies, or comments on it.... as *background.* By contrast, the material which supplies the main points of the discourse is known as *foreground*" (p. 280). Using this distinction as a guideline, each example was categorized as either background or foreground.

Table 1 displays the use of information from the reading text as measured in *t*-units for each of the three student groups. A $3 \times 3 \times 6 \times 2$ repeated-measures analysis of variance was conducted to test differences in the students' use of information from the background text, as presented in descriptive statistics in Table 1, as well as the following factors: group (less proficient nonnative speakers, more proficient non-

TABLE I. MEAN PERCENTAGES OF USE OF INFORMATION FROM THE
READING TEXT

Section of composition[a]	Less proficient NN speakers		More proficient NN speakers		Native speakers	
	B[b]	F	B	F	B	F
Appropriate types						
Original Explanation						
First	.32	1.0	.44	1.0	.29	0
Body	.12	.22	.16	.15	.07	.20
Last	0	.10	0	.60	0	0
Summaries						
First	0	0	.07	0	.18	.14
Body	.11	.07	.09	.22	.08	.06
Last	0	0	.14	.58	0	0
Paraphrases						
First	0	0	.25	.25	.13	0
Body	0	.09	.14	.12	.05	.07
Last	.50	0	.14	0	0	.50
Quotations						
First	0	0	0	0	.24	0
Body	.05	.22	.12	.12	.10	.03
Last	.50	.33	0	0	0	0
Inappropriate types						
Near Copies						
First	.19	0	0	0	.12	.64
Body	0	.04	.05	0	.05	.12
Last	0	0	0	0	0	0
Exact Copies						
First	.20	0	0	0	.10	0
Body	0	.04	.12	.12	.08	0
Last	0	0	0	0	.25	0

[a]For each category, *First* indicates the mean percentage in *t*-units of information use relative to total *t*-units in the first paragraph of each student composition; *Body* indicates the mean percentage of information use relative to total *t*-units in the body paragraphs (those between the first and last paragraphs); and *Last* indicates the mean percentage of information use relative to total *t*-units in the last paragraph of each student composition. $N = 171$.
[b]B = background, F = foreground.

native speakers, native speakers), section of composition (first paragraph, body paragraphs, last paragraph), type (Original Explanations, Summaries, Paraphrases, Quotations, Near Copies, Exact Copies), and function (background, foreground). Significant pairs of means provided by the four-way analysis of variance were further tested by the Newman-Keuls studentized range statistic, $p < .05$.

Two significant interaction effects were found, the first regarding student group and section of composition, $F(3, 113) = 3.92, p < .05$. All three student groups used significantly more information from the background text in the final paragraph of their compositions than in the body paragraphs. However, regarding the first paragraph of the students' compositions, the two nonnative (NN) speaker groups used significantly more information from the background text than the native speakers. In other words, the nonnative speakers relied on the background text significantly more than the native speakers for getting started in their writing. In the body paragraphs, all of the students used some information from the background text as well as many of their own ideas. In the final paragraphs, all of the students returned to the background text, incorporating significantly more information from that source than they had in their body paragraphs.

The second significant effect indicated an interaction among three factors: type, function, and section of composition, $F(2, 113) = 5.08, p < .05$. Significantly more information from the background text was presented as Original Explanations and Near Copies, foregrounded, in the first paragraphs of the student compositions, than any other combination of factors. Figure 1 displays this significant difference.

Figure 1 also shows less use of information from the background text in the body paragraphs than in the first and last paragraphs, and little difference across types regarding backgrounding and foregrounding in body paragraphs. It can also be seen that for first and last paragraphs of the compositions, all of the types were foregrounded more than backgrounded (albeit not significantly), except for Quotations and Exact Copies. The latter two types behaved similarly to each other; in fact, Exact Copies might be considered faulty Quotations in that the punctuation is lacking. Quotations and Exact Copies were more often backgrounded than foregrounded since, within the student written discourse, they seemed to serve as background for an upcoming point, which was then foregrounded. *Original Explanations,* on the other hand, represent information from the reading text that is explained through the student's view of fraternities or sororities. Remember that on a theoretical scale of degree of integration, Original Explanations represent the most integration (as opposed to Quotations, the least integrated type, in which

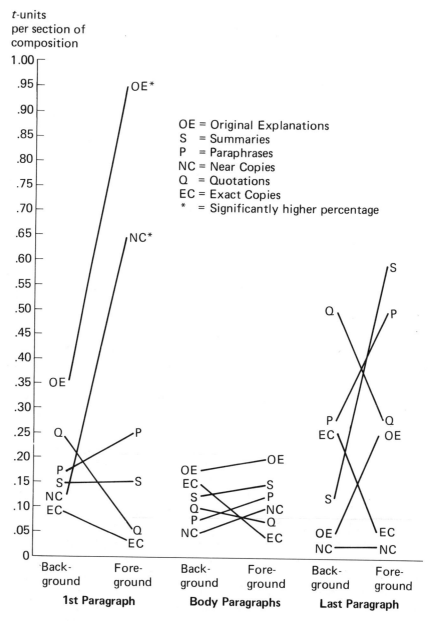

Figure 1   Types of use of information from the reading text by t-unit measure, function, and section of composition (N = 171)

the exact wording of the source text is transferred to the student writing). As the most highly integrated type found in the student papers, Original Explanations related directly to fraternities and sororities; this information was most often foregrounded in first paragraphs. Summaries, Paragraphs, and Near Copies were foregrounded more than backgrounded, as were Original Explanations.

Near Copies represent a borderline between word-for-word copying and paraphrasing; Figure 1 indicates that Near Copies behave more like Paraphrases than Exact Copies, in that the direction of the slope showing the distinction between backgrounding and foregrounding for Near Copies and Paraphrases runs in the opposite direction from the slope for Exact Copies. They might be considered faulty Paraphrases in that they exhibited inappropriately few syntactic or semantic changes from the original reading text. This study shows no indications of the students' meta-awareness of or attitudes toward copying or plagiarism. Granted, the copies may have been made by students without the knowledge that copied information and wording is generally unacceptable, or with disregard for this knowledge. However, in the absence of evidence to that effect, I prefer to assume that writing is such a complex process that attention cannot easily be given to everything at the same time. Given time constraints and the physical constraints of a full classroom, most writers find it difficult to produce quality writing. To include information from written sources without violating conventions of acceptability is even more difficult. The possibility exists that some of these students might have even intended to eliminate Near Copies in later revisions of their papers. As Pianko (1979) points out, in-class writing may control for time, place, and topic, but it fosters work that is done with less commitment and possibly with less effort than out-of-class writing. (Kroll, this volume, suggests the opposite is also possible, with students sometimes spending very little time on out-of-class writing.) In-class writing may be less of a measure of actual writing ability than of other factors, such as the student's ability to follow instructions. These students may have the ability to incorporate information from a background reading text without copying, but that ability may not emerge under the constraints of the classroom. When faced with the prospect of expressing information from the source text either by using "their own words," which may reflect a colloquial style, or by making slight syntactic or semantic changes in the wording of the background text (constituting Near Copies), thereby maintaining an academic style, the students may have opted for the latter for stylistic reasons. They have demonstrated their ability to adequately paraphrase, as well as summarize, and so forth; however, given the time constraints and classroom writing conditions, they may have lapsed occasionally, allowing Near Copies in favor of less colloquial, more academic style.

Related to this issue is the theory of Britton et al. (1975) that the elimination of copying is developmental. Perhaps university composition students are still completing the stage of being able to paraphrase, quote, summarize, and expand in academic style without copying, and with continued academic writing they will progress to a higher stage. In that case, those students who continue to write research reports and theses will also continue to pass through these theoretical stages, their own academic style will improve, and copying will be eliminated from their writing. For students who do not pursue studies involving writing, the issue is largely irrelevant. The pedagogical difficulty that this evolution poses is in helping student writers who, when faced with a term paper or other writing task involving the use of information from a background text, continue to copy, rather than develop skill in paraphrasing, summarizing, and incorporating information in other appropriate ways. (For a related discussion of university students' difficulties with approximating complex academic discourse, see Bartholomae 1985.)

DOCUMENTATION

Each example was categorized as showing either (1) no reference to the author, Harris, or to his text, or (2) reference by a prose phrase (e.g., "according to Harris," "in the book *Cultural Anthropology* it is stated that...," or "in the chapter 'Anthropology and the Study of Culture' I read that...."), or (3) reference by a footnote, or (4) reference by both a phrase and a footnote.

In general, very little reference was made to the author or text. If students made any such attribution at all, it was for Quotations, in a few cases for Paraphrases, and in isolated cases for other categories. The nonnative speaker groups provided more documentation in footnotes, and the native speakers in phrases acknowledging the author or reading text. In fact, the native speakers used no footnotes at all, and only two referencing phrases (vs. nine footnotes) were used by the nonnative writers. Together, the nonnative speaker groups acknowledged the anthropology author or text in some form for 42% of their combined quotations and paraphrases, while the native speakers provided such acknowledgement only 16% of the time.

These results, showing little student acknowledgment of the anthropology text or author, contrast distinctly with the language use of experienced academic writers who acknowledge the author or text for every quotation and most paraphrases in their revised work. The lack of acknowledgment may have occurred because the students were unfamiliar with the convention, they lacked experience with it, or they

TABLE 2. MEAN HOLISTIC SCORES OF WRITING QUALITY BY GROUP

	Less proficient NN speakers	More proficient NN speakers	Native speakers
M	74.1	76.65	87.15
SD	3.7	7.79	3.44

Note: Maximum score = 100. Measure = ESL Composition Profile (Jacobs et al. 1981). *N* = 30.

overlooked it. It seems more likely, however, that since the students relied on a single source and knew that their instructors were familiar with that source, it seemed to the students that referencing the source was unnecessary. Even though the students were instructed to write for a general university audience, they still knew that their composition instructor was the immediate audience. If these same students were given another writing task involving the use of a number of sources presenting conflicting views, they might have provided more documentation to clarify the sources of the various views.

In the few cases where native speakers referenced the author or text, they used a phrase within their composition rather than footnotes. The nonnative speakers referenced the author or text more often than the native speakers, but they did this by means of footnotes more often than phrases. The U.S. university community expects attribution of sources in any case, but generally considers footnotes unnecessary in in-class writing. Naturally, instructors expect citations in term papers, depending on the style and format of the academic field. The nonnative speakers may not realize this. They may use footnotes because footnotes are a more salient form of reference to another author than phrases within the text, especially the type of footnote used by the students in this study, which displayed a superscript within the text and a corresponding note at the bottom of the page. Apparently some of the nonnative speakers had learned to use formal footnotes following MLA (Modern Language Association) conventions (not widely used in the social sciences) and they have not mastered other ways to acknowledge another author, or did not understand the appropriateness of the various forms. In fact, none of the students in this study, native or nonnative, seem to have a mastery of the appropriate acknowledgment of another author.

INSTRUCTOR EVALUATIONS

The overall writing quality of the compositions as judged by instructors is represented in Table 2. The native speakers received a higher mean score (87.15) than the nonnative speakers (76.65 and 74.1). The standard deviation around the group mean of more proficient nonnative speaker scores (7.79) is rather high, indicating less homogeneity in this group than in the other two groups. Six of the ten students in the more proficient nonnative group mean (along with all 10 less proficient non-natives), and the remaining four had scores above the mean (as did all 10 native speakers). The native speaker holistic score proved to be significantly higher than the nonnative speaker scores, as seen by an analysis of variance, $F(2, 27) = 16.61$, $p < .01$, and a post-hoc Scheffé test demonstrating no significant difference between nonnative group scores. The native speaker compositions received significantly higher holistic scores than nonnative speaker compositions because the language, style, and tone were more consistent and more academic. Incorporation of the background reading text was smoother for the native speakers; there was a closer match between the level of sophistication of their language and that of the background text. The general style and tone of the nonnative speakers' compositions were less academic than those of the native speakers. The nonnative speakers' Paraphrases, Near Copies, Quotations, and Exact Copies produced momentary elaborative discourse within the context of their otherwise simpler language.

Further research

This study represents only a beginning in the investigation of use of information from a reading text in the academic writing of university students. Similar studies done with different writing tasks should eventually clarify the categorization of the function of information from background text and its effect on documentation. For example, as suggested earlier, students carrying out a writing task involving background reading presenting two or more authors with opposing views might document the source of their background information more often than in this study in order to distinguish among the various authors' opinions. Also, another way of examining the function of background information use might be through text analysis of academic writing in a number of disciplines.

From this study it is seen that language proficiency affects the use of information from background reading text in academic writing. The nonnative speakers referred to the background text significantly more than the native speakers in order to begin their compositions. Would nonnative speakers rely on background text, using more source text information than native speakers in their initial paragraphs of other writing tasks under other circumstances? More study of this issue would be worthwhile, with subjects carefully selected according to proficiency, in order to avoid the variability seen in this study's more proficient nonnative speaker group.

Exploring the effect of reading skills on the use of information from source texts in composition is another potential area for study. Correlating students' use of information from text with either their measured reading ability or comprehension tests of the specific reading text used in their compositions might prove significant, since such correlations were found in studies of synthesis and summarization (Spivey 1983; Winograd 1984; Kennedy 1985).

Cultural differences did not seem to explain the results in this study, but this warrants investigation, especially in the area of attitude. Attitudinal studies with native and nonnative speakers on the appropriateness or quality of use of information from reading texts would be worthwhile. Cross-cultural attitudes regarding plagiarism could be collected by having subjects evaluate the quality or stylistic appropriateness of discourse passages, including the types of use of information from text found in this study (Quotations, Exact Copies, Near Copies, Paraphrases, etc.), both with and without reference made to the author or text.

Some of these areas might better be investigated by means of process studies. An interesting issue to consider would be the decision making that occurs during the reading and writing processes of students completing a writing task involving the use of information from a text. This could be compared to the decision making that has been documented involving other writing tasks, such as those with L1 speakers reported by Emig (1971), Stallard (1974), Flower and Hayes (1977), Perl (1979), Pianko (1979), and Peitzman (1981), and with L2 speakers reported by Arthur (1979), Zamel (1982), Jones (1983), Scarcella (1984), Gaskill (1986), and Friedlander (this volume).

Teaching implications

The results of this study show that when these university students integrated information from the anthropology text into their in-class compositions, they relied on copying as their primary method of text integration and they referenced the anthropology author or text too little. These students have the ability to paraphrase, summarize, quote, and integrate information from a source text into their original examples and explanations; however, they need to be given ample opportunity to practice this type of writing in order to train themselves to edit out instances of copying. They also need to be trained in the various methods of documenting sources, from a simple phrasal reference (e.g., "according to the author"), which is likely sufficient for in-class essay writing, to brief parenthetical attributions within a text – for example, (Harris, 1983) – which would be more appropriate for formal term papers. It is most likely that the students in this study did not realize how simple it would have been for them to reference their background source. Writing handbooks are rarely helpful in this matter, for they usually either avoid the issue of documentation altogether, or they present an anxiety-producing harangue about plagiarism, followed by confusing rules about the punctuation of footnotes and bibliographical citations. For an exception, see Spatt (1987).

Writing instructors working with nonnative speakers need to emphasize that source material is most often used as background and support for their own written ideas. Nonnative composition students require the inspiration of confidence in their own language and ideas to help them avoid an overreliance on background sources. Nonnative speakers also need to develop academic style and tone in their writing. Although the language, style, and tone of the nonnative speakers' work was considered inconsistent and inferior to that of the native speakers in this study, informal observations by the instructors of the nonnative students suggest that their writing sounded more academic than in previous assignments that did not involve background text. More assignments of this sort would encourage the development of academic language by non-native speakers. Spack (1988) discusses writing from sources as a useful way to help students write academic papers.

All compositions instructors at the university level, and even those at the college-bound secondary level, should provide their students with more assignments to develop better awareness and skill in using information from background reading texts and acknowledging that text's author. Initial assignments might involve structured practice in the use of quotations, paraphrases, summaries and references to authors and texts (Edge 1983). Other assignments might be open-ended writing tasks such as the one used in this study, which require the students to read and incorporate information from reading texts in their writing. Johns (1985b) presents a useful top-down approach to working with students on a research paper, and Hill, Soppelsa, and West (1982) offer suggestions for helping students read and write research papers. Spack (1985) discusses literary criticism as a focus in the curriculum of writing classes. Regarding the teaching of English for specific purposes (ESP) reading, Johns and Davies (1983) discuss using text as a vehicle for information rather than as a linguistic object, thus emphasizing practice in the process of purposeful reading. Some current freshman composition textbooks that address the use of information in academic papers directly include Kennedy and Smith (1986) and Spatt (1987).

Along with more writing assignments that use information from background reading texts, composition students could also benefit from reading and analyzing academic pieces that involve reference to other academic works (see, e.g., Kantz 1990). Smith (1983), Bereiter and Scardamalia (1984), McGinley and Tierney (1989), and others suggest that students can learn much about writing from reading. University students do a great deal of reading for their content courses, but that reading primarily involves learning content rather than the style of the material. Undergraduates may not take sufficient notice of how their course textbook authors incorporate information from sources. Composition instructors need to direct students' attention to how academicians reference their sources, when they provide quotations rather than paraphrases or summaries of information, and, probably most importantly, how these references support rather than govern the writer's content.

A process-oriented writing class is the most promising means of developing this aspect of student writing. This type of class abandons notions that writing is a separate language skill unto itself and that writing can be dissected and practiced through smaller separate skills. Instead, the class works seriously with authentic text. The class reads a great deal, analyzes academic writing, and writes – both to respond to content and to incorporate readings and other data into academic papers. (See Reid 1989 for specific suggestions in this area.) The class writes for audiences that may not be familiar with the background material (i.e., for audiences other than simply the teacher) and revises and edits according to audience response. In this way students develop an awareness of and respect for other authors and academic texts which enables them to use information from background text appropriately in their own writing.

References

Arthur, B. (1979). Short-term changes in EFL composition skills. In C. A. Yorio, K. Perkins, and J. Schachter (Eds.), *On TESOL '79: The learner in focus* (pp. 330–342). Washington, D.C.: TESOL.

Bartholomae, D. (1985). Inventing the university. In M. Rose (Ed.), *When a writer can't write: Studies in writer's block and other composing-process problems* (pp. 134–165). New York: Guilford Press.

Bereiter, C., and Scardamalia, M. (1984). Learning about writing from reading. *Written Communication, 1,* 163–188.

Britton, J.; Burgess, T.; Martin, N.; McLeod, A.; and Rosen, H. (1975). *The development of writing abilities (11–18).* London: Macmillan.

Brown, A. L.; Campione, J. C.; and Day, J. D. (1981). Learning to learn: On training students to learn from texts. *Educational Researcher, 10,* 14–21.

Brown, A. L., and Day, J. D. (1983). *Macrorules for summarizing texts: The development of expertise.* Technical Report No. 270. Urbana, Ill.: Center for the Study of Reading.

Brown, A. L.; Day, J. D.; and Jones, R. S. (1983). *The development of plans for summarizing texts.* Technical Report No. 268. Urbana, Ill.: Center for the Study of Reading.

Campbell, C. C. (1987). Writing with others' words: The use of information from a background reading text in the writing of native and nonnative university composition students. Unpublished doctoral dissertation, Program in Applied Linguistics, University of California, Los Angeles.

Carrell, P. L. (1981). Culture-specific schemata in second-language comprehension. In R. Orem and J. Haskell (Eds.), *Selected papers from the ninth Illinois TESOL/BE Annual Convention and the first Midwest TESOL Conference* (pp. 123–132). Champaign, Ill.: Illinois TESOL/BE.

Carson, J. E.; Carrell, P. L.; Silberstein, S.; Kroll, B.; and Kuehn, P. A. (1990). Reading-writing relationships in first and second language. *TESOL Quarterly, 24.*

Connor, U. (1984). Recall of text: Differences between first and second language readers. *TESOL Quarterly, 18,* 239–256.

Connor, U., and McCagg, P. (1983). Cross-cultural differences and perceived quality in written paraphrases of English expository prose. *Applied Linguistics, 4,* 259–268.

Cooper, M. (1984). Linguistics competence of practiced and unpracticed nonnative readers of English. In J. C. Alderson and A. H. Urquhart (Eds.), *Reading in a foreign language* (pp. 122–135). New York: Longman.

Edelsky, C. (1982). Writing in a bilingual program: The relation of L1 and L2 texts. *TESOL Quarterly, 16,* 211–228.

Edge, J. (1983). Reading to take notes and to summarize: A classroom procedure. *Reading in a Foreign Language, 1,* 93–98.

Emig, J. (1971). *The composing processes of twelfth graders.* Research Report No. 13. Urbana, Ill.: National Council of Teachers of English.

Flower, L., and Hayes, J. R. (1977). Problem-solving strategies and the writing process. *College English, 39,* 449–461.

Gaskill, W. H. (1986). Revising in Spanish and English as a second language: A process-oriented study of composition. Unpublished doctoral dissertation, University of California, Los Angeles.

Harris, M. (1983). *Cultural anthropology.* New York: Harper & Row.

Hill, S. S.; Soppelsa, B. F.; and West, G. K. (1982). Teaching ESL students to read and write experimental-research papers. *TESOL Quarterly, 16,* 333–347.

Hopper, P. J. (1979). Observations on the typology of focus and aspect in narrative language. *Studies in Language, 3,* 37–64.

Hopper, P. J., and Thompson, S. A. (1980). Transitivity in grammar and discourse. *Language, 56,* 251–299.

Hosenfeld, C. (1984). Case studies of ninth grade readers. In J. C. Alderson and A. H. Urquhart (Eds.), *Reading in a foreign language* (pp. 231–249). New York: Longman.

Hunt, K. W. (1965). *Grammatical structures written at three grade levels.* Champaign, Ill.: National Council of Teachers of English.

Jacobs, H. L.; Zinkgraf, S. A.; Wormuth, D. R.; Hartfiel, V. F.; and Hughey, J. B. (1981). *Testing ESL composition: A practical approach.* Rowley, Mass.: Newbury House.

Jacobs, S. E. (1982). *Composing and coherence: The writing of eleven premedical students.* Washington, D.C.: Center for Applied Linguistics.

Johns, A. M. (1985a). Genre and evaluation in general education classes. Unpublished manuscript, San Diego State University.

(1985b). Coherence and information load: Some considerations for the academic classroom. Unpublished manuscript, San Diego State University.

Johns, T., and Davies, F. (1983). Text as a vehicle for information: The classroom use of written texts in teaching reading in a foreign language. *Reading in a Foreign Language, 1,* 1–19.

Jones, S. (1983). Attention to rhetorical information while composing in a second language. In C. Campbell, V. Flashner, T. Hudson, and J. Lubin (Eds.), *Proceedings of the Los Angles Second Language Research Forum,* Vol. 2 (pp. 130–143). Los Angeles: Department of English, ESL Section, UCLA.

(1985). Problems with monitor use in second language composing. In M. Rose (Ed.), *When a writer can't write: Studies in writer's block and other composing-process problems* (pp. 96–118). New York: Guilford Press.

Kantz, M. (1990). Helping students use textual sources persuasively. *College English, 52,* 74–91.

Kennedy, M. L. (1985). The composing process of college students writing from sources. *Written Communication, 2,* 434–456.

Kennedy, M. L., and Smith, H. M. (1986). *Academic writing: Working with sources across the curriculum.* Englewood Cliffs, N.J.: Prentice-Hall.

Kintsch, W., and van Dijk, T. (1978). Toward a model of text comprehension and production. *Psychological Review, 85,* 363–394.

Lay, N.D.S. (1982). Composing processes of adult ESL learners: A case study. *TESOL Quarterly, 16,* 406.

McGinley, W., and Tierney, R. J. (1989). Traversing the topical landscape: Reading and writing as ways of knowing. *Written Communication, 6,* 243–269.

Mohan, B. A., and Lo, W. A. (1985). Academic writing and Chinese students: Transfer and developmental factors. *TESOL Quarterly, 19,* 515–534.

Peitzman, F. (1981). The composing processes of three college freshmen: Focus on revision. Unpublished doctoral dissertation, New York University.

Perl, S. (1979). The composing processes of unskilled college writers. *Research in the Teaching of English, 13,* 317–336.

Pianko, S. (1979). A description of the composing process of college freshmen writers. *Research in the Teaching of English, 13,* 5–22.

Raimes, A. (1985). What unskilled ESL students do as they write: A classroom study of composing. *TESOL Quarterly, 19,* 229–258.

Reid, J. (1989). English as a second language composition in higher education: The expectations of the academic audience. In D. M. Johnson and D. H. Roen (Eds.), *Richness in writing: Empowering ESL students* (pp. 220–234). New York: Longman.

Rose, M. (1984). *Writer's block: The cognitive dimension.* Carbondale, Ill: Southern Illinois University Press.

Rumelhart, D. E. (1977). Understanding and summarizing brief stories. In D. LaBerge and S. J. Samuels (Eds.), *Basic processes in reading: Perception and comprehension* (pp. 265–303). Hillsdale, N.J.: Erlbaum.

Scarcella, R. (1984). How writers orient their readers in expository essays: A comparative study of native and nonnative English writers. *TESOL Quarterly, 18,* 671–688.

Smith, F. (1983). Reading like a writer. *Language Arts, 60,* 558–567.

Spack, R. (1985). Literature, reading, writing, and ESL: Bridging the gaps. *TESOL Quarterly, 19,* 703–725.

  (1988). Initiating ESL students into the academic discourse community: How far should we go? *TESOL Quarterly, 22,* 29–51.

Spatt, B. (1987). *Writing from sources,* 2nd ed. New York: St. Martin's Press.

Spivey, N. N. (1983). Discourse synthesis: Constructing texts in reading and writing. Unpublished doctoral dissertation, University of Texas, Austin.

Stallard, C. K. (1974). An analysis of the writing behavior of good student writers. *Research in the Teaching of English, 8,* 206–218.

Stotsky, S. (1983). Research on reading/writing relationships: A synthesis and suggested directions. *Language Arts, 60,* 627–642.

Taylor, B. N., and Beach, R. W. (1984). The effects of text structure on middle-grade students' comprehension and production of expository text. *Reading Research Quarterly, 19,* 134–146.

Taylor, K. K. (1984). The different summary skills of inexperienced and professional writers. *Journal of Reading, 17,* 691–699.

Winograd, P. N. (1984). Strategic difficulties in summarizing texts. *Reading Research Quarterly, 19,* 404–425.

Zamel, V. (1982). Writing: The process of discovering meaning. *TESOL Quarterly, 16,* 195–209.

  (1983). The composing processes of advanced ESL students: Six case studies. *TESOL Quarterly, 17,* 165–187.

Index

The following abbreviations are used in the index: *n*, footnote on page; *t*, table; *f*, figure.

and validity in direct test of writing, 73, 76, 81–2
reader expectations, culturally based,
94 *n*2
reader training, 81–2
reading, 211, 212
incorporation of, into academic assignments, 106–7
as information source, 93
learning writing from, 226–7
narrow, 64
purposeful, 226
strategies for, 96
see also background information
reading ability, 100
and summaries/syntheses, 213
reading comprehension, 205
reading literature, ESL, 30
reading skills
effect on use of background information, 225
and writing skills, 213
reading-to-writing model, 89–90,
92–3
reading-writing relationship (connection), 10, 88–101, 106
first language, 89–93
second language, 93–4, 99–100
reality/truth
in expressivism, 31
in interactive approaches, 31–2
in first language composition theory, 24–5, 31–2
in social constructivism, 32
recursiveness, 15, 26, 41, 212
Reid, J., 9, 16, 74, 106, 227
reinforcement, positive, 174
see also praise
reliability (assessment), 72–3, 76, 80
interrater, 128*n*, 144
see also scoring procedures,
reliability
research
comparability of, 51
empirical, 19, 20
future, 3, 11, 51–3, 205–6, 224–5
interpretation of, 50
logistics of, 51–2
second language writing, 2, 37–56,
179–80

subjects of, 48
substance of, 52–3
themes in, 39
valid, reliable, 19, 20
see also case study approach
(research)
research design, 51
and contradictory results, 52
feedback on compositions, 156–9,
173
home vs. class composition, 142–4
second language writing process,
48–9
teacher response to student writing, 181–2
writing process research, 38–9
research methodology, 51–2, 206
background reading text, 214–15
home vs. class composition, 142–4
researchers, 3–4
response expectations, 75, 76
response to writing, 9
different topic types, 191–210
see also comments (teacher); feedback; written response
restructuring, 97, 98, 99–100
revision, 8, 15, 26, 44, 143, 158 *n*5,
174, 212
and academic writing, 211
at discourse level, 41
effect on meaning, 38
feedback and, 105–6, 155–6, 185,
186
by good writers, 179
in process approach, 15, 126, 143,
175*n*
situational and contextual causes
of, 126
in Spanish and English, 46
stage of, 187
text analysis in, 104
see also rewriting
revision strategies, 156
topical structure analysis as, 126–
39
rewriting, 158 *n*5, 161
feedback and, 181, 182, 183–7,
184*t*
incorporating teacher comments,
170, 171, 175